WITHDRAWN

Montagu, Ashley
Man and aggression

DATE DUE

NOV 9 '89			
MAY 8 '90			
NOV 13 '90			
NOV 22 '94			
NOV 2 9 1999			
NOV 0 9 2000			

Contributors

S. A. Barnett, *Australian National University*

Leonard Berkowitz, *University of Wisconsin*

Kenneth E. Boulding, *University of Colorado*

Sally Carrighar, *Guernsey, Channel Islands*

John Hurrell Crook, *University of Bristol*

René Dubos, *The Rockefeller University*

Leon Eisenberg, *Harvard University*

Geoffrey Gorer, *Haywards Heath, Sussex*

Hermann Helmuth, *Trent University*

Ralph Holloway, *Columbia University*

Morton Hunt, *New York*

Peter H. Klopfer, *Duke University*

Edmund Leach, *King's College, Cambridge*

Ashley Montagu, *Columbia University*

David Pilbeam, *Yale University*

Marshall D. Sahlins, *University of Michigan*

T. C. Schneirla, *The American Museum of Natural History*

J. P. Scott, *Bowling Green State University, Ohio*

Omer C. Stewart, *University of Colorado*

Man and Aggression

Second Edition

Edited by
ASHLEY MONTAGU

New York
OXFORD UNIVERSITY PRESS
1973

To Morris Ginsberg

Preface to the Second Edition

When *Man and Aggression* was published in 1968 it was hoped that it would fill the need for a critical examination of the popular writings of Konrad Lorenz and Robert Ardrey. The critiques available at that time were relatively few. Now there are many. With more to draw on eight new essays have been added to the present edition, and to keep the book within reasonable dimensions, three essays have been reluctantly omitted.

Since cannibalism has been cited as evidence of man's innate aggressiveness, we are fortunate to be able to include Professor Hermann Helmuth's essay, "Cannibalism in Paleoanthropology and Ethnology," an essay which has been specially translated by the author from the German for inclusion in the present volume.

A.M.

16 November 1972
Princeton, N.J.

Contents

Introduction

The purpose of this book is to inquire into the validity of the views on human nature expressed in the widely read and influential books of Robert Ardrey and Konrad Lorenz. Ardrey's books are *African Genesis* (Atheneum, 1961), and *The Territorial Imperative* (Atheneum, 1966). Lorenz's book is *On Aggression* (Harcourt, Brace & World, 1966). In these books the authors argue that man is by instinct an aggressive creature, and it is this innate propensity to violence that accounts for individual and group aggression in man. This Hobbesian view of human nature is not new; it is possibly older than the doctrine of Original Sin, and was widely prevalent during the reign of muscular Darwinism and its subsequent offspring Social Darwinism.[1] It was a view that was embraced by Freud who, writing at the end of World War I, concluded that "a powerful measure of desire for aggression has to be reckoned as part of man's instinctual endowment. . . . *Homo homini lupus;* who has the courage to dispute it in the face of all the evidence in his own life and in history?"[2] Freud's postulation of a drive toward death, *thanatos,* as an intrinsic part of human nature is well

---

[1] Ashley Montagu, *Darwin, Competition, and Cooperation.* New York: Schuman, 1952; Richard Hofstadter, *Social Darwinism in American Thought, 1860–1915.* Boston: Beacon Press, 1961.
[2] Sigmund Freud, *Civilization and Its Discontents.* London: Hogarth Press, 1930.

known.[3] The death instinct, as it came to be known, has been largely repudiated by psychoanalysts, but the conception of such an instinct or drive toward destruction has lost none of its force in the minds of many people. Its revival, in the new garb given it in the writings of Ardrey and Lorenz, comes at a period in the history of man which renders the views expressed by such writers most acceptable to their lay readers.

The layman is bewildered. Two World Wars, the breakdown in political, public, and private morality, the ever-increasing crime rates, the development of a climate and a culture of violence, together with the consciousness of an apocalyptic realization of irreversible disaster, are quandaries enough to cause men to look desperately about them for some sort of answer, for some explanation of the meaning, of the causes which seem to be leading man to destruction.

It is understandable that under such circumstances men will readily embrace an explanation having the appearance of plausibility, especially when that explanation is offered pretentiously, with at least the appearance of support from the apparatus of scientific learning, observation, discoveries, experiments, facts, and authorities. In addition to this, when the proponents of that explanation are able and eloquent writers, it is all the more easy for those who are not themselves authorities to be carried away by the arguments. What is almost certain to escape many readers, including some scientists, is that the apparatus of scientific learning, observations, experiments, and facts, however authoritative, do not speak for themselves but are always at the mercy of their interpreters. However thoroughly established the facts, their interpretation is always subject to human error, tendentiousness, scientism, and prejudice.[4] Hence, the checks and controls that scientists from the relevant fields bring to bear upon the interpretation of the facts concerning which they are experts, constitute the means and the measure by which such interpretations are judged. This is what has been done

[3] Sigmund Freud, *Beyond the Pleasure Principle*. London: Hogarth Press, 1922. For a critical examination of Freud's instinctivist views of man's aggressive nature see Ashley Montagu, "Man—And Human Nature," *American Journal of Psychiatry*, vol. 112, 1955, pp. 401–10.

[4] See Malachi Martin, "The Scientist as Shaman," *Harper's Magazine*, March 1972, pp. 54–61.

in the present volume with respect to the writings of Ardrey and Lorenz.

As the reader will be able to judged for himself, the experts have found the theories of Ardrey and Lorenz unsound. What is most serious is that Ardrey and Lorenz show themselves to be so enamored of their own theories that they overlook or evade bodies of fact that do not support their views. It is therefore not surprising that they often get the pieces of fact they choose to offer, as demonstrating their theories, twisted, or even wrong. It is to be hoped that the present volume will serve to put the record straight, to correct what threatens to become an epidemic error concerning the causes of man's aggression, and to redirect attention to a consideration of the real causes of such behavior, whatever they may be.

It is very easy to accept the idea of an instinctive cause for man's aggression, for it is a simple idea and it explains everything. But what explains everything in fact explains nothing. There is an old English proverb, at least as old as the seventeenth century, which says, "Let him make use of instinct, who cannot make use of reason." I am not sure that it has quite the meaning intended here, but it will serve to make the point in much the same sense that John Stuart Mill intended when he observed, in 1848, that "Of all the vulgar modes of escaping from the consideration of the effect of social and moral influence on the human mind, the most vulgar is that of attributing the diversities of conduct and character to inherent natural differences." [5] If no other rational explanation appeals, or even when it does, instinct is likely to trump every other card in the pack because it appears to be so fundamental, so recondite, so all-embracing, and so simple. For these reasons, among others, the notion of "instinct" as an explanation of human aggression has so much greater an appeal than any other exegesis. To those who find such an explanation acceptable it makes little difference that for many years scientists have entertained such grave doubts concerning the existence of instincts in man, that for almost half a century fewer and fewer scientists have used the term in connection with man. The attack on the concept of instinct in man began in 1919

[5] John Stuart Mill, *Principles of Political Economy.*

with the appearance of Knight Dunlap's article, "Are There Any Instincts?" [6] and was thoroughly discredited with the publication in 1924 of L. L. Bernard's fine work, *Instinct: A Study of Social Psychology*.[7] In spite of periodic attempts to revive the idea of the existence of instincts in man [8] the notion has no scientific validity whatever. Attempts to smuggle the idea, by fudging, simply will not do.

The best known and most widely quoted definition of an instinct was that given by William McDougall in *An Introduction to Social Psychology,* first published in 1908. In this widely influential book an instinct was defined as "an inherited or innate psycho-physical disposition which determines its possessor to perceive, and to pay attention to, objects of a certain class, to experience an emotional excitement of a particular quality upon perceiving such an object, and to act in regard to it in a particular manner, or, at least, to experience an impulse to such action." [9] Definitions of instinct, whatever form they may have taken—and they have seemed almost infinitely varied—have widely tended to follow the essentials of McDougall's model. Tinbergen's rather elaborate ethological definition, for example, constitutes only one of many variations on the McDougallian theme. An instinct, according to Tinbergen, is "a hierarchically organized nervous mechanism which is susceptible to certain priming, releasing and directing impulses of internal as well as of external origin, and which responds to these impulses by coordinated movements that contribute to the maintenance of the individual and the species." [10]

Essentially, we find that most definitions of *instinct* embody the same assumptions. The most common of these appear to be: (1) *innate* determiners of some kind which, (2), when affected by

[6] Knight Dunlap, "Are There Any Instincts?" *Journal of Abnormal and Social Psychology, 14*:307–11, 1919–20. See also L. L. Bernard, "The Misuse of Instinct in the Social Sciences," *Psychological Review*, 28:96–118, 1921; Ellsworth Faris, "Are Instincts Data or Hyotheses?" *American Journal of Sociology*, 27:184–96, 1921–22; Zing Yang Kuo, "Giving Up Instincts in Psychology," *Journal of Philosophy, 18*:645–64, 1921.

[7] L. L. Bernard, *Instinct: A Study in Social Psychology.* New York: Holt, 1924.

[8] Ronald Fletcher, *Instinct in Man.* New York: International Universities Press, 1957.

[9] William McDougall, *An Introduction to Social Psychology,* 14th ed., New York: Barnes & Noble, 1960, p. 25.

[10] N. Tinbergen, *The Study of Instinct.* Oxford: Clarendon Press, 1951, p. 112.

particular stimuli, (3), call into function certain neural, glandular, and muscular mechanisms, (4), that underlie particular patterns of behavior or even "psychological states." Such definitions of instinct are invariably based upon the study of behavior in "lower" animals, and not the behavior of man. Tinbergen, for example, is properly cautious when he comes to touch upon the possibility of instincts in man. What has been proved in other animals, he writes, has not been proved in man. "Further, different species have different instincts. For instance, while many species have a parental instinct, others never take care of their offspring and hence probably do not have the corresponding neurophysiological mechanisms. . . ." Furthermore, "a species might lack a certain instinct because, having lost it relatively recently, it retained the nervous mechanism but not the required motivational mechanism. So long as we know nothing about such things, it would be as well to refrain from generalizations." [11]

That sounds a proper note of caution. But even Tinbergen's assumption that his interpretation of "instinct" holds for lower animals, calls for the most careful, skeptical examination. The truth is that the concept of "instinct" has assumed the form of a doctrine, and perhaps represents the outstanding example of reification in the whole realm of science, the employment of an abstraction as if it had a real existence. The revival of the abstraction "instinct" by Lorenz and Tinbergen in their studies of animal behavior has been thoroughly examined and their interpretation of the term rejected on strong grounds of evidence and theory.[12]

Rationalizing on the basis of insufficiently analyzed evidence (or both, together with procedures which distort the evidence) is a practice which is probably as old as man himself. This is a dangerous practice which is liable to produce pseudological arguments.

[11] Ibid.
[12] See especially D. S. Lehrman, "A Critique of Konrad Lorenz's Theory of Instinctive Behavior," *Quart. Rev. Biol.*, 28:337–63, 1953. L. R. Aronson *et al.*, (eds.), *Development and Evolution of Behavior*. San Francisco: W. H. Freeman & Co., 1970. J. H. Crook (ed.), *Social Behaviour in Birds and Mammals*. London & New York: Academic Press, 1970. E. Tobach, L. Aronson, & E. Shaw (eds.), *The Biopsychology of Development*. London & New York: Academic Press, 1971. D. C. Glass (ed.), *Environmental Influences*. New York: Rockefeller University Press, 1968.

Even scientists are not immune to it, especially when they become enamored of theories which tend to make them insensible to alternative interpretations of the facts.

The trouble is that many people confuse fact with theory. *Facts* are evidence; *theory* is interpretation of that evidence. Facts are reliable if they hold up in repetitions of investigations of their reality; a theory is valid if it offers the best possible interpretation of the facts—that is, the soundest and most logical.

For example, with respect to the problem of aggression we face two major questions. Question One concerns Lorenz's evidence for an "instinct" of aggression in lower animals. We ask: Is this evidence he offers reliable; does it include all of the important facts now available and relevant to behavior in lower animals; and how validly does he interpret this evidence—for example, without appealing to authority or to personal prejudices, and so on? This is one question.

Question Two is: How well do the evidence and the argument that Lorenz offers for lower animals apply to man? Readers must accept the possibility that Lorenz's proffered answer to Question One is not valid; for example, that it is so misleading that his theory of aggression as innate is not really supported even for lower animals. If this is the case, and we think it is the case, anyone (e.g. Ardrey) who relies on Lorenz for an answer to Question One had better reconsider any arguments he bases on Lorenz.

Lorenz himself takes for granted (and abundantly rationalizes) his conclusion that he has answered Question One correctly. That is, he thinks he has demonstrated the soundness of his belief that "instinctive aggression" exists in lower animals. We doubt that he has done so, for reasons made clear in this book. Moreover, we hold that Lorenz has not demonstrated how any answer to Question One may bear on Question Two. This is not to say that a really valid answer to Question One could have some important bearing on Question Two. We agree with those critics who have stated that Lorenz's procedure of applying his doctrine of innate aggression in lower animals directly to man is naïve.

It seems rather hard on other animals to project the failings of mankind upon them, and then blame them for having bequeathed those failings to us. Yet this kind of protective anthropomorphism (like Mr. Laird's "protective reaction" bombing of Vietnam), constitutes an only too common rationalization for the deplorabilities of human behavior.

In the case of man it is possible to say that in spite of all attempts to saddle him with instincts, all such attempts have thus far failed.

The notable thing about *human* behavior is that it is learned. It is nonsense to talk about the genetic determinance of human behavior. Allowing for whatever idiosyncratic contribution the genes may make, everything a human being does as such he has to learn from other human beings. From any dominance of biologically or inherited predetermined reactions that may prevail in the behavior of other animals, man has moved into a zone of adaptation in which his behavior is dominated by learned responses. It is within the dimension of culture, the learned, the man-made part of the environment, that man grows, develops, and has his being as a behaving organism. Whatever other recondite elements may be involved in his behavior, and whatever the limits that his genetic constitution may set upon his learning capacities, this is the conclusion of the behavioral sciences—the sciences concerned with the study of the origins and causes of man's behavior. If anyone has any evidence to the contrary, let him bring it forth. That heredity plays a part in all human behavior is patently false,[13] but that heredity plays a role in some human behavior can scarcely be doubted; but this is a very different thing from saying that every form of human behavior is determined by heredity.[14]

I have already discussed some of the probable reasons for the popularity of Ardrey's and Lorenz's explanations of the supposed causes of human aggression. There is yet another, perhaps the principal, reason for the popularity of works of this kind, including novels such as William Golding's *Lord of the Flies*[15] and Desmond Morris's zoomorphic studies[16] *The Naked Ape,* and *The Human Zoo,*[17] which all serve to underscore that putative trait of human

13 For example, the fact that many readers of this book were born in the English-speaking world, and therefore learned to speak English rather than Swahili, is a behavior that was in no way influenced by heredity, but wholly by environment.
14 See, for example, the studies in Jerry Hirsch (ed.), *Behavior-Genetic Analysis.* New York: McGraw-Hill, 1967.
15 William Golding, *Lord of the Flies.* New York: Harcourt, Brace, 1954.
16 Desmond Morris, *The Naked Ape.* New York: McGraw-Hill, 1968.
17 Desmond Morris, *The Human Zoo.* New York: McGraw-Hill, 1969.

nature which our Victorian ancestors so engagingly called "innate depravity." In a world in which hostility and aggression seem to be a part of every man's nature, in which individual and group violence appear to constitute the incontrovertible evidence of the mark of Cain that every man carries upon him, it is very gratifying to be told that this is indeed so; for those who are ready to grasp at such an explanation of human aggression it provides relief for that heavy burden of guilt most individuals carry about with them for being as they are. If one is born innately aggressive, then one cannot be blamed for being so. One can try not to be nasty, and even though nastiness does keep breaking out one cannot be held responsible, for who can successfully resist the pressure of so powerful and so "spontaneous" an "instinct" as aggression? Hence when books like those of Ardrey and Lorenz appear they are welcomed with all the fervor of a sinner seeking absolution for his sins. Ardrey and Lorenz stand in a sort of apostolic succession to those who with millennial ardor have sought to restore the wicked and the unregenerate to the true faith. For is it not written in Romans 7:18–24:

> For I know that in me (that is, in my flesh,) dwelleth no good thing: for to will is present with me; but how to perform that which is good I find not.
> For the good that I would I do not: but the evil that I would not, that I do.
> Now if I do that I would not, it is no more I that do it, but sin that dwelleth in me.
> I find then a law, that, when I would do good, evil is present with me.
> For I delight in the law of God after the inward man:
> But I see another law in my members, warring against the law of my mind, and bringing me into captivity to the law of sin which is in my members.
> O wretched man that I am! who shall deliver me from the body of this death?

Never was the question more eloquently and poignantly put. But most people, like Pontius Pilate in a similar situation, would not stay for an answer, but continued to seek a response that was more congenial to them, one that promised absolution from the sin that held them captive. But for emancipation from that sin they would not look, for is it not written into the very flesh of man that that can never be?

It is this sort of thinking, so damaging, so pessimistic, so fettering of the human spirit, that is so dangerous because it diverts the focus of attention from the real causes of "sin," of aggression, and encourages a Jansenist view of the nature of the human condition. The evidence of scientific inquiry does not support this dismal view of human nature, still less does it provide any support for the idea of "innate depravity," whatever form that doctrine may take. Certainly the views of Ardrey and Lorenz and others like them concerning man's nature have no scientific validity whatever. It is our hope that the critique of those views presented in the pages which follow will serve to show why.

A.M.

8 June 1968
Princeton, N.J.

Revised
16 November 1972

Man and Aggression

ASHLEY MONTAGU

The New Litany of "Innate Depravity," or Original Sin Revisited

It is reported that when the Bishop of Worcester returned from the Oxford meeting of the British Association in 1860, he informed his wife, at tea, that the horrid Professor Huxley had declared that man was descended from the apes. Whereupon the gentle lady is said to have exclaimed, "My dear, descended from the apes! Let us hope it is not true, but if it is, let us pray that it will not become generally known."

It would seem that the last forty years of anthropological research and discovery in the field and in the laboratory, taken together with the findings of the behavioral sciences, place us in much the same position as the Bishop's lady, for while the findings of these disciplines are wholly opposed to the deeply entrenched view that man is an innately aggressive creature, most people tend to dismiss these findings out of hand or ridicule them as a rather eccentric idealistic heterodoxy, which do not deserve to become generally known. In preference to examining the scientific findings they choose to cast their lot with such "authorities" as William Golding who, in his novel *Lord of the Flies*,[1] offers a colorful account of the allegedly innate nastiness of human nature, and Robert Ardrey who, in *African Genesis*[2] and in a second volume *The Territorial Imperative*,[3] similarly seeks to show that man is an innately aggressive creature.

From *The Human Revolution*, Bantam Books, 1967. Reprinted by permission. New material added by author, 1968.

The first part of *African Genesis* is devoted to a demonstration, which the author brings off quite convincingly and with éclat, of the validity of Professor Raymond Dart's claims for an osteodontokeratic culture among the australopithecines. It is in the second part that Mr. Ardrey makes one of the most remarkable extrapolations from the first part I have ever encountered in any work. Mr. Ardrey argues that since the australopithecines made use of tools, and employed some of them as implements with which to bash in the skulls of baboons, the australopithecines were therefore "killers," and that *therefore* human beings are "killers" by nature! Mr. Ardrey's book constitutes, perhaps, the most illuminating example of the manner in which a man's prejudices may get in the way of his reason and distort his view of the evidence. Mr. Ardrey refers to some of his early personal experiences of violence which convinced him of the murderousness of human nature. Hence, when through the distorting glass of his prejudgments he looks at a tool it becomes not simply a scraper but a weapon, a knife becomes a dagger, and even a large canine tooth becomes "the natural dagger that is the hallmark of all hunting mammals," while in "the armed hunting primate" it becomes "a redundant instrument." "With the advent of the lethal weapon natural selection turned from the armament of the jaw to the armament of the hand."

But the teeth are no more an armament than is the hand, and it is entirely to beg the question to call them so. Virtually all the members of the order of primates, other than man, have large canine teeth, and these animals, with the exception of the baboons, are predominantly vegetarians, and it is because they are vegetarians that they require large canine teeth; that such teeth may, on occasion, serve a protective purpose is entirely secondary to their main function, which is to rip and shred the hard outer coverings of plant foods. Primates are not usually belligerent unless provoked, and the more carefully they are observed the more remarkably revealing do their unquarrelsomeness and cooperativeness become. The myth of the ferocity * of "wild animals" constitutes one of Western man's supreme rationalizations, for it not only has served to "explain" to

* For an admirable discussion of the meaning of "ferocity" in animals, see J. L. Cloudsley-Thompson, *Animal Conflict and Adaptation*. London: G. T. Foulis & Co., 1965.

him the origins of his own aggressiveness, but also to relieve him of the responsibility for it—for since it is "innate," derived from his early apelike ancestors, he can hardly, so he rationalizes, be blamed for it! And some have gone so far as to add that nothing can be done about it, and that therefore wars and juvenile delinquents, as Mr. Ardrey among others tells us, will always be with us! From one not-so-minor error to another Mr. Ardrey sweeps on to the grand fallacy.

At this point it needs to be said that Mr. Ardrey's views are firmly based on and derived from those of Professor Raymond Dart, who in an article entitled, "The Predatory Transition from Ape to Man," [4] published in 1953, argued that man's animal ancestry was carnivorous, predatory, and cannibalistic in origin, and went on to add that "The blood-bespattered, slaughter-gutted archives of human history from the earliest Egyptian and Sumerian records to the most recent atrocities of the Second World War accord with early universal cannibalism, with animal and human sacrificial practices or their substitutes in formalized religions and with the world-wide scalping, head-hunting, body-mutilating and necrophiliac practices of mankind in proclaiming this common bloodlust differentiator, this predaceous habit, this mark of Cain that separates man dietetically from his anthropoidal relatives and allies him rather with the deadliest of Carnivora." [5]

Mr. Ardrey puts this in the following words: "The human being in the most fundamental aspects of his soul and body is nature's last if temporary word on the subject of the armed predator. And human history must be read in these terms."

In furtherance of this argument "tools" for Mr. Ardrey are not only identified as "weapons," but, he goes on to imply, nay, indeed, he states, "that when any scientist writes the word, 'tool,' as a rule he refers to weapons. This is a euphemism" (p. 306).

Perhaps this opportunity should be taken to assure Mr. Ardrey that when scientists write the word "tool" they mean exactly what they say, and that euphemisms are not, as Mr. Ardrey says, "normal to all natural science" (p. 306). Some tools may be used as weapons and even manufactured as such, but most tools of prehistoric man, from his earliest days, were most certainly not designed primarily to serve as weapons. Knives were designed to cut, scrapers to scrape, choppers to chop, and hammers to hammer. That such tools could be used as weapons is true, but to serve as weapons was not their primary purpose nor the reason for which they were devised.

"Man," Mr. Ardrey tells us, "is a predator whose natural instinct is to kill with a weapon" (p. 316). But man has no instincts, and if he had, they could hardly include the use of weapons in their psychophysical structure.

Early man's hunting, according to Mr. Ardrey, was due to instinctive belligerence, not to the hunger for food. "When the necessities of the hunting life encountered the basic primate instincts, then all were intensified. Conflicts became lethal, territorial arguments minor wars. . . . The creature who had once killed only through circumstance now killed for a living" (p. 317). This was "the aggressive imperative."

The evidence does not support Mr. Ardrey's theories. Whatever "the basic primate instincts" may be, they are not what Mr. Ardrey implies. Indeed, when he forgets himself, he writes of "the non-aggressive, vegetarian primate," which is precisely what all primates tend to be. But Mr. Ardrey would have us believe the contrary: the basic primate instincts according to him are aggressive. And, of course, with the assumption of hunting as a way of life, these, according to him, would become intensified. But in previous pages, and at greater length elsewhere, I have given the evidence for the contrary view. This evidence renders Mr. Ardrey's interpretations quite unacceptable. Everything points to the non-violence of the greater part of early man's life, to the contribution made by the increasing development of cooperative activities, the very social process of hunting itself, the invention of speech, the development of food-getting and food-preparing tools, and the like. These facts are never once mentioned by Mr. Ardrey, except perhaps obliquely as a doctrine which scheming scientists have foisted upon an unsuspecting world. The truth is that Mr. Ardrey is arguing a thesis. It is the thesis of "innate depravity." It is an unsound thesis, and it is a dangerous one, because it perpetuates unsound views which justify, and even tend to sanction, the violence which man is capable of learning, but which Mr. Ardrey erroneously believes to be inherited from man's australopithecine ancestors.

When man hunts he is the predator and the hunted animal is the prey. But prehistoric man did not hunt for pleasure, in order to satisfy his "predatory instincts." He hunted for food, to satisfy his hunger, and the hunger of those who were dependent upon him. He did not hunt because he was a "killer," any more than contemporary men are "killers" who kill animals in abattoirs so that others may eat them. Prehistoric man was no more a "killer" than we are "killers" when we sit down at table to consume a chicken or a steak which, by proxy, someone else has "killed" for us. It would be interesting to know who are the "murderers," the men who are paid to slaughter the animals we eat, or we who pay the cashier at the supermarket? Or perhaps it is really the owner of the store in which we buy meat who is the "murderer," the "killer"? Prehistoric man hunted because he desired to live—*that* hardly makes him a killer, any more than our continuing in the habit of eating meat makes us killers.

When Mr. Ardrey admiringly presents us with *West Side Story* as a "vivid portrait of natural man," in which "we watch our animal legacy unfold its awful power," in the form of juvenile delinquents in their "timeless struggle over territory, as lunatic in the New York streets as it is logical in our animal heritage," we can only say, "in police parlance," that it is worthy of William Golding's *Lord of the Flies*, in which a similar view of the depravity of human nature is unfolded. In Golding's novel two groups of children, abandoned on an island, take to hunting each other to the death. This novel has enjoyed a wide readership on American college campuses, and it has been made into a film. Its appeal to young people is not strange, for in the world of violence in which they live Golding's novel supplies them with an easy "explanation." I understand that the novel is used in some sociology courses as a good exemplification of "innate depravity," of the alleged natural nastiness of man. It could hardly be expected to be otherwise.[6]

Mr. Ardrey has further elaborated his views in his book entitled *The Territorial Imperative*,[7] published in August 1966. In this work Mr. Ardrey endeavors to show that man's aggressiveness is based on his allegedly innate territorial nature. Man, he argues, has an innate compulsion to gain and defend exclusive territory, preserve or property. The territorial nature of man, he says, is genetic and ineradicable.

Mr. Ardrey devotes the greater part of his book to a discussion of territoriality in many different kinds of animals. He attempts to show that territoriality in animals is innately determined. The informed student of these matters would be interested in knowing why the evidence has not been considered which leads to the opposite conclusion. Mr. Ardrey writes that "The disposition to possess a territory is innate. . . . But its position and borders will be learned" (p. 25). Certainly it is biologically and socially valuable for many animals to possess their own special territory, and certainly there are strong drives in most animals to defend their territory against trespassers, but such drives are not necessarily innate. They may be learned in just the same way in which animals learn the position and borders of their territory. Territory is defined as an area defended by its occupant against competing members of the same species. But there are many animals that do not exhibit such behavior. The California ground squirrel, adult male long-tailed field mice, she-wolves, the red fox, the Iowan prairie spotted skunk, the northern plains red fox, and in the superfamily to which man belongs, the Hominoidea, the orang-utan, the chimpanzee, and the gorilla, as well as many other animals. As Bourlière has observed in his admirable book, *The Natural History of Animals,* "It would seem that territorial behavior is far from being as important in mammals as in birds." [8] Somehow, Ardrey manages to neglect to consider the significance of these many exceptional cases. And while he does mention the chimpanzee, he omits any reference to the orang-utan [9] and the gorilla. [10] On the naturally amiable chimpanzee's non-territoriality he comments, "The chimpanzee has demonstrated, I presume, that we must reckon on some degree of innate amity in the primate potential; but as I have indicated, it is a very small candle on a very dark night" (p. 222).

On the contrary, the non-territoriality of great apes constitutes, one would have thought, a very bright lodestar in a cloudless sky, for if, as is evident, man's nearest collateral relatives are wanting in anything resembling an inborn territorial drive, it is highly improbable that any form of man was ever characterized by such a drive. Arguments based on fish, birds, and other animals are strictly for them. They have no relevance for man. "The otherwise admirable animal," the chimpanzee, is for Mr. Ardrey, "an evolutionary failure" (p. 223), while the aggressive baboon is "an outrageous evolutionary success" (p. 222).

Apparently evolutionary failure or success is to be measured by the yardstick of population number. The baboons are many, the great apes are few and are threatened with extinction. There is little evidence that the great apes were ever numerous, but that they are today few in number and threatened with extinction is all too tragically true. The diminishing numbers of these animals is due not to their lack of territoriality, but to the encroachments upon both their habitats and their lives by men with weapons against which they are utterly defenseless. No matter how highly developed their territorial sense might have been, they could never have withstood these onslaughts.

What we are witnessing in Mr. Ardrey's "territorial imperative" is a revival in modern dress of the good old "Instinct of Property" which, together with such oddities as the "Instinct of Philoprogenitiveness" and other such curiosities were repudiated by scientists half a century ago.[11]

Mr. Ardrey deplores the rejection of "instinct" in man, and actually goes so far as to suggest that "a party line" has appeared in American science designed to perpetuate the "falsehood" that instincts do not exist in man. Mr. Ardrey needs the concept of "open instincts," of innate factors, to support his theorizing. But that requirement constitutes the fatal flaw in his theory, the rift in the playwright's lute, for man is man because he has no instincts, because everything he is and has become he has learned, acquired, from his culture, from the man-made part of the environment, from other human beings.* Mr. Ardrey declines to accept that fact, being more enamored of his theories than he is of facts. This is rather a pity because he would serve himself and us all a great deal more worthily if he would only realize that a scientist is not interested in proving or in disproving theories, in believing or in disbelieving, but in discovering what *is*. Thomas Henry Huxley once remarked of Herbert Spencer that his idea of a tragedy was a beautiful theory killed by an ugly fact. In Mr. Ardrey's case the beautiful facts render his ugly theories otiose.

---

* For his comments on this see Robert Ardrey, "Four-Dimensional Man," *Encounter*, vol. 38, 1972, pp. 9–21.

What is the explanation of the appeal such books have for so many people? Golding's novel is a rattling good story. Ardrey's books are excitingly written and hold the reader spellbound. But these qualities are not the secret of their appeal. What, then, is?

Such books are both congenial to the temper of the times and comforting to the reader who is seeking some sort of absolution for his sins. It is gratifying to find father confessors who will relieve one of the burdensome load of guilt we bear by shifting the responsibility for it to our "natural inheritance," our "innate aggressiveness."

If it is our "nature" to be what we are, if we are the lineal descendants of our "murderous" ancestors, we can hardly be blamed or blame ourselves for the sin of being little more than made-over apes. Our orneriness is explained, and so is the peccant behavior of children, juvenile delinquency, crime, rape, murder, arson, and war, not to mention every other form of violence. It is all simply explained: it is due to man's innate aggressiveness.

There is nothing new in all this. We have heard it before. During the latter half of the 19th century, and during the early part of the 20th century, this viewpoint formed the foundation for the doctrine of "Social Darwinism." It was implied in such ideas as "The Survival of the Fittest" and "The Struggle for Existence," and in such phrases as "The weakest go to the wall," "Competition is the lifeblood of a nation," and the like.

Such ideas were not merely taken to explain, but were actually used to justify, violence and war. As General von Bernhardi put it in 1912, "War is a biological necessity . . . it is as necessary as the struggle of the elements in Nature . . . it gives a biologically just decision, since its decisions rest on the very nature of things." [12] One wonders what von Bernhardi would have said after the "biologically just" defeat of Germany in two World Wars? No doubt, the general would have had little difficulty in finding an "explanation."

The new liturgy of "innate aggression," as an explanation of man's proclivities to violent behavior, does not seek to justify that behavior, but by thus "explaining" it to point the direction in which we must proceed if we are to exercise some measure of control over it. Toward this end, Dr. Konrad Lorenz, one of the founders of the modern science of ethology—the study of behavior under natural conditions of life—has dedicated himself in his book, *On Aggression,* published in April 1966.[13]

In *On Aggression* Lorenz has set out his views at length. In many respects they parallel those of Ardrey.

Ardrey's and Lorenz's views suffer from the same fatal defect, namely, extrapolation from other animals to man.

Why do reasonable beings behave so unreasonably, asks Lorenz. And he answers, "Undeniably, there must be superlatively strong factors which are able to overcome the commands of individual reason so completely and which are so obviously impervious to experience and learning" (p. 237). "All these amazing paradoxes, however, find an unconstrained explanation, falling into place like the pieces of a jigsaw puzzle, if one assumes that human behavior, far from being determined by reason and cultural tradition alone, is still subject to all the laws prevailing in all phylogenetically adapted instinctive behavior. Of these laws we possess a fair amount of knowledge from studying the instincts of animals" (p. 237).

It is in these sentences that the flaws in Lorenz's argument are exhibited. First he assumes that man's frequent irrational behavior is phylogenetically based. Second, this enables him to conclude that the "laws" derived from the "study of the instincts of animals" are applicable to man.

There is, in fact, not the slightest evidence or ground for assuming that the alleged "phylogenetically adapted instinctive" behavior of other animals is in any way relevant to the discussion of the motive-forces of human behavior. The fact is, that with the exception of the instinctoid reactions in infants to sudden withdrawals of support and to sudden loud noises, the human being is entirely instinctless.

Those who speak of "innate aggression" in man appear to be lacking in any understanding of the uniqueness of man's evolutionary history. Unacquainted with the facts or else undeterred by them they insist on fitting whatever facts they are acquainted with into their theories. In so doing they commit the most awful excesses. But, as is well known, nothing succeeds like excess. Lorenz's assumptions and interpretations are typical.

"There is evidence" he writes, "that the first inventors of pebble tools—the African Australopithecines—promptly used their new weapon to kill not only game, but fellow members of their species as well" (p. 239). In fact there is not the slightest evidence for such a statement.

Lorenz continues, "Peking Man, the Prometheus who learned to preserve fire, used it to roast his brothers: beside the first traces of the regular use of fire lie the mutilated and roasted bones of Sinanthropus pekinesis himself" (p. 239).

Lorenz's interpretation of the "evidence" is one he shares with many others, but it is gravely doubted whether it is sound. The cracked bones of Peking man may represent the remains of individuals who died during a famine and who may well have been eaten by their surviving associates. This sort of thing has been known to occur among most peoples of whom we have any knowledge. There is, however, no record of any people, prehistoric, nonliterate, or anywhere in the annals of human history, who made a habit of killing their fellow men in order to dine off them.* It is absurd to suggest that Peking man used fire "to roast his brothers." Does Lorenz seriously believe that Peking man made a practice of "roast brother"? As another possibility it does not appear to have occurred to Lorenz that, like some contemporary peoples, burning the corpse may have been Peking man's way of disposing of the dead.

Lorenz writes, "One shudders at the thought of a creature as irascible as all pre-human primates are, swinging a well-sharpened hand-ax" (pp. 241–42). For a serious student of animal behavior Dr. Lorenz appears to be singularly ill-informed on the temperaments of prehuman primates. It is not "irascibility" which is the term most frequently used to describe the temperaments of "prehuman primates" by those who know them best, but "amiability." The field studies of Schaller on the gorilla, of Goodall on the chimpanzee, of Harrisson on the orang-utan, as well as those of others,[14] show these creatures to be anything but irascible. All the field observers agree that these creatures are amiable and quite unaggressive, and there is not the least reason to suppose that man's prehuman primate ancestors were in any way different. Captured monkeys and apes in zoos and circuses are not the best examples from which to deduce the behavior of such creatures under natural conditions.

* See Helmuth's discussion, pp. 229–53 of the present volume.

Lorenz writes of early man faced with "the counter-pressures of hostile and neighboring hordes" (p. 243). Again, there exists not the slightest evidence of hostility between neighboring hordes of early man. The populations of early man were very small, a few score or a few hundred individuals at most. "Neighboring hordes" would have been few and far between, and when they met it is extremely unlikely that they would have been any less friendly than food-gathering hunting peoples are today.

The hostile neighboring tribe," writes Lorenz, "once the target at which to discharge phylogenetically programmed aggression, has now withdrawn to an ideal distance, hidden behind a curtain, if possible of iron. Among the many phylogenetically adopted norms of human social behavior, there is hardly one that does not need to be controlled and kept on a leash by responsible morality" (p. 253).

And there we have it: man's aggressiveness is "phylogenetically programmed," and can be kept on a leash by "responsible morality." The reference to an "iron" curtain is presumably not undeliberate; the whole passage has an ominous political overtone. One wonders whether it is the State or the individual who is to hold the leash.*

Lorenz knows a great deal about the behavior of animals, but with respect to man he apparently knows very little else that is not in the realm of nineteenth-century desk anthropology. Like Ardrey, he extrapolates his dubious interpretations of animal behavior to still more dubious conclusions concerning man.

Since all instincts, according to Lorenz, are characterized by "spontaneity," and it is this spontaneity which makes "the aggression drive" so dangerous, one would have thought that he would have provided the reader with some convincing examples of such spontaneous aggression in man. But all that Lorenz can do is to cite the "very exact psychoanalytical and psycho-sociological studies on Prairie Indians, particularly the Utes" of Sydney Margolin (p. 244). According to these "very exact" studies the Prairie Indians "led a wild life consisting almost entirely of war and raids," and that therefore, "there must have been an extreme selection pressure at work, breeding extreme aggressiveness." Since Dr. Omer Stewart has shown how utterly erroneous this account is of the Prairie

* See the article by Eisenberg in the present volume, pp. 53–69.

Indians in general and of the Utes in particular,† it only needs to be remarked that Lorenz's example of spontaneous aggression in man has not a leg to stand upon, and that the alleged "excess of aggression drive" "may have produced changes in the hereditary pattern" (p. 244) of the Utes are statements which derive no support whatever from the facts.

But Lorenz chooses to see aggression his way. Nowhere, for example, does he deign to consider how other scientists have looked at aggression. He neglects, for example, to discuss the possibility that a considerable proportion of aggressive behavior represents a reaction to frustration.[15] Nor does he pay the least attention to the view that in many instances aggressive behavior is situational, provoked by situations and conditions which have nothing whatever to do with anything "phylogenetically" or otherwise "programmed" in the individual. As a general and outstanding example of the spontaneity of instinctive aggression in man Lorenz cites "militant enthusiasm" which can be "elicited with the predictability of a reflex" when the proper environmental stimuli are available (p. 272). The possibility that "militant enthusiasm" may be learned behavior is not even considered by Lorenz. Lorenz's declarative statements are no substitute for the hard evidence that militant enthusiasm, like every other kind of enthusiasm, is learned.

The roles of learning and experience in influencing the development and expression of aggression are largely ignored by Lorenz. Yet the evidence is abundant and clear, both for animals and man, that learning and experience play substantive roles in the history of the individual or of the group in relation to the development of aggression. Where aggressive behavior is unrewarded and unrewarding, as among the Hopi and Zuñi Indians, it is minimally if at all evident.

"Let dogs delight to bark and bite, it is their nature to." Lorenz, who has written a charming book on dogs,[16] feels it is the nature, too, of men. Is it? What is human nature?

What is most important to understand in relation to that question is man's unique evolutionary history, the manner in which an ape was gradually transformed into a man as he moved from a dimension of limited capacity for learning into an increasingly enlarging zone of adaptation in which he became entirely dependent upon

† See pages 221–28 of the present volume.

learning from the man-made part of the environment, *culture,* for his development as a functioning human being; that his brain, far from containing any "phylogenetically programmed" determinants for behavior, is characterized by a supremely highly developed generalized capacity for learning; that this principally constitutes his innate *hominid* nature, and that he has to learn his *human* nature from the human environment, from the culture that humanizes him, and that therefore, given man's unique educability, human nature is what man learns to become as a human being.

This is not to say that man is born a *tabula rasa.* Clearly the reason why man is not an ape is that he possesses certain genetic capacities, the result of a long and unique evolutionary history, which, under the appropriate environmental stimulation enable him to function as a human being. The most important of these genetic capacities is that for learning, educability, literally the species trait of *Homo sapiens.* Man is capable of learning virtually anything.

As we trace the details of man's evolutionary history we see that it is with the development of culture that man's brain began to grow and develop in a simultaneous feedback interaction with culture as an organ of learning, retrieval, and intelligence. Under the selection pressures exerted by the necessity to function in the dimension of culture, instinctive behavior would have been worse than useless, and hence would have been negatively selected, assuming that any remnant of it remained in man's progenitors. In fact, I also think it very doubtful that any of the great apes have any instincts. On the contrary, it seems that as social animals they must learn from others everything they come to know and do. Their capacities for learning are simply more limited than those of *Homo sapiens.*

As Clifford Geertz has put it,

> "Recent research in anthropology suggests that the prevailing view that the mental dispositions of man are genetically prior to culture and that his actual capabilities represent the amplification or extension of these pre-existent dispositions by cultural means is incorrect. The apparent fact that the final stages of the biological evolution of man occurred after the initial stages of the growth of culture implies that "basic," "pure," or "unconditioned," human nature, in the sense of the innate constitution of man, is so functionally incomplete as to be unworkable. Tools, hunting, family organization, and, later, art, religion, and "science" molded man

somatically; and they are, therefore, necessary not merely to his survival but to his existential realization. It is true that without men there would be no cultural forms; but it is also true that without cultural forms there would be no men.[17]

Given the limits set by his genetic constitution, whatever man is he learns to be.

Throughout the five million or so years of man's evolution the highest premium has been placed on cooperation, not merely *intra*group cooperation, but also upon *inter*group cooperation, or else there would be no human beings today.[18] Intra- or intergroup hostilities, in small populations, would have endangered the very existence of such populations, for any serious reduction in numbers would have made the maintenance of such populations impossible. There is not the slightest evidence nor is there the least reason to suppose that such conflicts ever occurred in human populations before the development of agricultural-pastoral communities, not much more than 12,000 years ago.

The myth of early man's aggressiveness belongs in the same class as the myth of "the beast," that is, the belief that most if not all "wild" animals are ferocious killers. In the same class belongs the myth of "the jungle," "the wild," "the warfare of Nature," and, of course, the myth of "innate depravity" or "original sin." These myths represent the projection of our *acquired* deplorabilities upon the screen of "Nature." What we are unwilling to acknowledge as essentially of our own making, the consequence of our own disordering in the man-made environment, we saddle upon "Nature," upon "phylogenetically programmed" or "innate" factors. It is very comforting, and if, somehow, one can connect it all with findings on greylag goslings, studied for their "releaser mechanisms," and relate the findings on fish, birds, and other animals to man, it makes everything all the easier to understand and to accept.

What, in fact, such writers do, in addition to perpetrating their wholly erroneous interpretation of human nature, is to divert attention from the real sources of man's aggression and destructiveness, namely, the many false and contradictory values by which, in an overcrowded, highly competitive, dehumanized, threatening world, he so disoperatively attempts to live. It is not man's nature, but his nurture, in such a world, that requires our attention.

REFERENCES

1. William Golding, *Lord of the Flies*, New York: Harcourt, Brace & Co., 1954.
2. Robert Ardrey, *African Genesis*, New York: Atheneum, 1961.
3. Robert Ardrey, *The Territorial Imperative*, New York, Atheneum, 1966.
4. Raymond A. Dart, "The Predatory Transition from Ape to Man," *International Anthropological and Linguistic Review*, vol. 1, 1953, pp. 201–8.
5. Ibid. pp. 207–8.
6. For a critical examination by various authors of Golding's thesis, see William Nelson (ed.), *William Golding's Lord of the Flies: A Source Book*, New York: Odyssey, 1963.
7. Robert Ardrey, *The Territorial Imperative*.
8. François Bourlière, *The Natural History of Animals*, New York: A. A. Knopf, 1954, pp. 99–100.
9. Barbara Harrisson, *Orang-Utan*, New York: Doubleday, 1963.
10. George Schaller, *The Mountain Gorilla: Ecology and Behavior*, Chicago: University of Chicago Press, 1963, and the same author's *The Year of the Gorilla*, Chicago: University of Chicago Press, 1964.
11. L. L. Bernard, *Instinct*, New York: Holt, 1924; Otto Klineberg, *Social Psychology*, New York: Holt, 1954, pp. 63–75; David Krech and Richard S. Crutchfield, *Theory and Problems of Social Psychology*, New York: McGraw-Hill, 1948.
12. Friedrich von Bernhardi, *Germany and the Next War*, New York: Longmans, 1912.
13. Konrad Lorenz, *On Aggression*, New York: Harcourt, Brace & World, 1966.
14. Jane Goodall, "My Life among Wild Chimpanzees," *National Geographic*, vol. 124, 1963, pp. 272–308; George B. Schaller, *The Mountain Gorilla*; Barbara Harrisson, *Orang-Utan*; Charles H. Southwick (ed.), *Primate Social Behavior*, Princeton, N.J.: Van Nostrand, 1963; Irven DeVore (ed.), *Primate Behavior*, New York: Holt, Rinehart & Winston, 1965; Allan M. Schrier, Harry F. Harlow & Fred Stollnitz (eds.), *Behavior of Nonhuman Primates*, 2 vols., New York: Academic Press, 1965.
15. John Dollard *et al.*, *Frustration and Aggression*, New Haven, Yale University Press, 1935.

16. Konrad Lorenz, *Man Meets Dog*, Boston: Houghton Mifflin, 1955.
17. Clifford Geertz, "The Growth of Culture and the Evolution of Mind," in Jordan Scher (ed.), *Theories of the Mind*, New York: Free Press, 1962, p. 736.
18. Ashley Montagu, *Darwin, Competition and Cooperation*, New York: Schuman, 1952; Ashley Montagu, *The Human Revolution*, New York: Bantam Books, 1967.

MORTON HUNT

Man and Beast

It would hardly seem likely that a man who spends every day
watching ringdoves building their nests or bees gathering honey or
mother rats nursing their newborn pups would be particularly well
qualified to analyze the human psyche, prescribe ways to better
mental health or advise mankind how to minimize the likelihood of
nuclear war. Such, however, is apparently the case. In the past few
years, the scientific study of animal behavior has emerged from relative obscurity into the glare of world-wide attention, and its practitioners, once viewed as harmless bird watchers, are now regarded
as scientist prophets at whose feet modern man sits all atremble,
waiting for the word. The reason is that in studying doves, bees and
rats, along with hundreds of other species, zoologists and animal
psychologists have recently made a number of discoveries that seem
filled with profound implications for mankind. And since today we
are in all sorts of trouble—personal, social and international—we
are pathetically eager for any new understandings about ourselves
that may hold the key to salvation. If those who study man—
psychologists and sociologists—have not been able to tell us what we
need to know, perhaps we can find it out from those who study
animals.

But what they have been telling us is scarcely comforting. The school of animal-behavior studies that has suddenly had great impact on our thinking is known as ethology. The immensely popular books of Konrad Lorenz, Robert Ardrey and Desmond Morris are based mainly on ethological research, which holds that man is the most brutal and uninhibitedly aggressive of all animals and that those traits are genetically built into him. Ethologists believe that animal behavior is, to a great degree, chemically encoded in those long twisted chains of thousands of molecules that we call genes and that are the determiners of the biochemical processes in every cell of the body, and, therefore, of the physical traits of the whole creature. Everyone agrees that it is the genes that make the fertilized ovum of, say, the mosquito grow up to be another mosquito, rather than a butterfly, swallow or rhinoceros. The ethologists, however go much further, maintaining that the genes prescribe not just physical traits and behavioral tendencies but behavior itself, down to its finest details. The exact way a dog scratches its ear, the particular melody sung by the nightingale, the distinctive sequences of head bobbing, tails wiggling and other movements used by each species of duck during courting and the fierce but usually bloodless fights of rival male elk are all programed in advance within the genes.

So far, so good. But the ethologists argue that man, too, though he is born more helpless than any other animal and has to spend nearly the first quarter of his life acquiring the skills he needs to live the rest of it, behaves largely in accordance with genetic commands. In other words, he is largely governed by inborn instincts and, even if they don't prescribe the precise songs he sings or the exact ways he goes about courting, they do make him innately and inescapably selfish, suspicious, acquisitive—and murderous. Where other predators kill their prey but rarely their own kind, man is said to be an instinctive killer who is particularly savage toward his own species. He is not just a beast but the beastliest of all; he is, in the words of one ethological writer, "the cruelest and most ruthless species that has ever walked the earth."

Oddly enough, we seem to be fascinated by and receptive to this depressing news about ourselves. A century ago, one good Victorian lady, upon hearing the new theory that man was descended from the apes, cried out, "Let us hope it is not true—but if it is, let us pray it will not become generally known." In contrast, not only have we accepted the theory that we are the worst of beasts, we enjoy seeing it presumably verified.

When Konrad Lorenz tells us, in *On Aggression,* that a hereditary "hypertrophy of aggression," coupled with an evolutionary lack of inhibition against killing our fellow man, makes us far more savage to our own kind than the wolf is to other wolves, we devour his every word and his book becomes a runaway best seller. When Robert Ardrey says, in *The Territorial Imperative,* that we are innate enemies of our own species and that, far from hating war, we really find it "outrageously satisfying," we all but cry amen and make his book a household word. When Desmond Morris writes of man as *The Naked Ape,* whose intelligence will never be able to rule his "raw animal nature" nor control his biological urge to aggression, we make his charges the stuff of cocktail conversation, smiling bitterly and dolefully, as if to say, "How true."

But a large number of those engaged in animal-behavior research disagree with the hard-line ethological view. Many zoologists, biochemists and animal psychologists reject the theory that most behavior is preprogramed and stored in the genes. They agree that, for biochemical reasons, animals have built-in "tendencies" to behave in certain ways but that these are specific and automatic only in lower animals; the higher the animal on the evolutionary scale, the more its tendencies are shaped, developed and organized into behavior by its interactions with its environment. A cricket will chirp, given the right conditions, without ever having heard it done; a human being, despite his tendency to use language, has to learn every word of the language he speaks. The most vigorous opponents of the ethological view of man—including anthropologists Ashley Montagu and Margaret Mead, philosopher Susanne Langer and a number of distinguished zoologists and animal psychologists—insist that even if insects and lower animals are largely guided by instincts, man himself is almost instinctless and, in any case, has no instinct to kill his own kind.

Each side in this quarrel accuses the other of spouting scientific humbug; each asserts that the other's views are dangerous to the human race; and each accuses the other of political bias in its science. Some ethologists charge their opponents with rigid adherence to a liberal and egalitarian ideology that makes them refuse to admit man's nastiness and the inherent differences among races. And some anti-ethologists see their opponents as Neo-Calvinists and social reactionaries whose views on man lend support to racist and fascist ideologies.

Great issues are thus at stake. If man is largely controlled by his instincts and if his behavior is encoded in his genes, man and his future can only be regarded with pessimism; man must then be viewed as innately dangerous and brutal and dealt with accordingly. If the poor, the indolent, the criminal, the greedy and the sadistic are acting according to their hereditary inclinations, there is little point in trying to change them: We might as well forget about compensatory education, welfare, equal job opportunities, rehabilitation of convicts and preventive mental-health programs. And if mankind is innately aggressive and warlike, it is absurd to suppose that he can ever become peaceful and loving toward his fellow man—or even that he would like to be.

But if man is not instinct-controlled, or if his instincts are amorphous and do not result in specific behavior patterns—if, in other words, he has a highly educable and modifiable nature—then it is possible to be hopeful about him and his future, despite his wretched history. One can believe that poverty is rarely the fault of the poor and that with better opportunities, they might become productive and useful; that crime is largely a product of social and psychological conditions that can be modified and perhaps eliminated; that sadism, greed, ignorance and psychosis are not inevitable expressions of our nature but forms into which the nature has been forced by circumstances. And, finally, one can even believe that it is still possible, if unlikely, that man may find ways to live in peace and to realize his ancient dream of loving and being loved by his fellow man.

Great issues, indeed. But neither the ethologists nor the other students of animal behavior seem, in their daily work, to be dealing with such matters. Their research generally looks scientifically pure, aloof and sometimes even pastoral. Some researchers, for instance, are basically naturalists, albeit with a modern touch. They observe animals under field conditions, recording and analyzing their sounds, tabulating their actions, their behavior in groups and as individuals, and making computer analyses of the data to discover meaningful patterns. One dedicated young zoologist lives alone for months at a time in the savannas of south-central Kenya, watching various members of a troop of vervet monkeys and noting their every act of eating, defecating, grooming, fighting and copulating, until he begins to perceive the social structure of the troop. Other scientists observe and virtually live with particular species of insect, fish, bird or mammal, until they recognize every gesture, every nuance of sound and behavior—until, indeed, they could advise the young stickleback, pigeon, gorilla or gerbil how best to fight off its rival and woo its mate.

While observing animals in their native habitat, some researchers tinker with one or more of the natural conditions, hoping to find a cause-and-effect relationship to behavior. A team in Antarctica captured penguins at Cape Crozier, took them 180 miles away to the middle of the perfectly flat, featureless Ross Shelf Ice and released them, to see if the birds could find their way home and, if so, how. They could and did, apparently by using the sun; under cloudy skies, they blundered around, but under clear skies, they would look up, seem to think a bit and then waddle off toward Cape Crozier. One mystery was thus solved, but another and larger one appeared: How do the penguins know about the use of solar guidance? Two contrasting theories exist: (1) Something in their genes makes them automatically use the sun as a directional guide; and (2) Some conditioning that occurs during their growing up has made them associate the sunward direction with water and food. Thus, penguin navigation, itself a trivial matter, touches upon the central issue in animal psychology—the meaning of instinct and the mechanisms through which instinctive behavior is manifested.

Some researchers have removed animals from the field and studied them in the laboratory, introducing unnatural conditions to try out the hypothesized mechanisms underlying behavior. Among ducks and many other birds, the young follow the mother faithfully about within a few hours after hatching. Lorenz was curious as to why this happens; he therefore divided the eggs laid by a goose into two batches and had one batch hatched by the mother and the other by an incubator. The goslings hatched by the mother saw her first and followed her wherever she went; the others saw Lorenz first and followed him, even when they saw their mother nearby. In popular terms, they "thought" Lorenz was their mother; in scientific terms, they had been "imprinted" with his image. (Ducklings have been imprinted to follow wooden decoys, a football and a green box containing an alarm clock, any of which looks good to them if it is the first thing they see.) Imprinting in animals seems to be the fixing in the memory of an image at a time when the nervous system is undergoing a special stage of maturation. By studying it, ethologists learn something about nature's invention of devices for survival: If ducklings don't follow the mother shortly after birth, they will be abandoned and die. More importantly, ethologists learn something about the critical periods of maturation in the nervous system—a subject that has meaning for human parents as well.

In another experiment, an American animal psychologist built a community for Norway rats, complete with unlimited supplies of food, water and nesting materials, and allowed the rat population to grow until it was far denser than ever occurs in normal circumstances. The results were startling: Some of the males became bullies, others became homosexuals and cannibals and yet others became withdrawn neurotics; the females began to abort or take poor care of their young; and infant mortality rose as high as 96 percent. Since all the physical wants of the rats were satisfied, this pathology could only mean that excessive social interaction was to blame. Rats are not men and from this study one cannot lean to conclusions about our own urban life, but at least it suggests that the interaction needed by social animals has its limits and that beyond those limits it produces a variety of behavioral disorders.

Some researchers have castrated cocks to see what becomes of their sex drive and their aggressiveness (not surprisingly, both markedly diminish); some have transfused the blood of a mother rat into the veins of a virgin rat to see if the hormones and other substances in it would stimulate the virgin's responses to young rat pups and make her behave like a mother (they did); some have raised monkeys in isolation, apart from their mothers and friends, and later introduced them, as adults, to normal monkey society to see how they fared (very badly; they were fearful, hostile, unable to mate—and never got better).

Such studies are, for the first time, yielding down-to-earth explanations of some of life's great, enduring mysteries—mother love, sexual attraction, the homemaking urge, competition and cooperation, intelligence, kindness, aggression, et al. These are obviously matters of immense intellectual interest—and of self-interest, as well, for if we understood them thoroughly in lower animals, we might understand them somewhat better in man. We are faced with self-extinction from many sources, all of our own making: overpopulation, the selfish despoiling of our air and water, the potential incineration of man in a nuclear war. It might be—and any hope is worth pursuing —that we could learn something from animals that would enable us to save us from ourselves.

In fact, however, most of the animal-behavior researchers are not seeking insights into the larger mysteries of human nature. Most of them, like other scientists, are so fascinated by some small mystifying phenomenon they've noticed that they are willing to spend years exploring it just for the pleasure of discovering what makes it so.

"I got into ethology because it was intellecually intriguing," says Dr. William Dilger of Cornell University. "I've spent ten years studying nest building in one species of bird because I was fascinated by the fact that all females of that species prepare and carry their nesting materials in the same peculiar way, even if they've never seen it done by others. I wanted to find out how that works and I think I have. But today people want ethologists to come up with answers to the big questions troubling mankind; they think we have the answers up our sleeves. I'm not at all sure we do. And I rather resent it—it's disturbing to have such responsibility thrust on one. Ethology used to be fun but not very important; now it's become important but not nearly so much fun." For better or for worse, that's the way it's going to be. The study of animal behavior will never again be a quiet backwater of zoology. Men now fervently hope, and almost demand, that animal-behavior researchers help them understand themselves and one another; and, given the present human condition, who can blame them?

Before drawing any conclusions about man, however, the first order of business is to find out how things really work among other animals, resolutely avoiding the tendency to read human feelings and motives into what they do. Anthropomorphism is a classic error: From primitive man to Pliny, from Shakespeare to the modern dog fancier, men have ascribed human sentiments and aims to their animal friends and foes. If the brown thrasher sings a long and melodious song at the close of a glorious summer afternoon, he must be rejoicing at being alive on such a day; if the stag and his rival lock horns and struggle until exhausted, it's because even peaceful beasts are willing to kill each other under the influence of jealousy; if the female cat painstakingly washes her kittens, it's because, brimming with mother love, she is taking good care of her babies; if baboons live in primitive oligarchies, it's because they, like us, need family life and friendship and are willing to pay the price of submitting to wise leadership and social regulation.

But all schools of contemporary animal-behavior study try to avoid the anthropomorphic fallacy. They start with the fact that the animals are incapable of symbolic—that is, linguistic—thinking or of emotions based in large part on cultural values. Instead of speculating as to what they might be feeling, the scientists stick to what is empirical and provable: the actual actions of the animals, the measurable changes in their bodies associated with those actions and their demonstrable survival for both the individual and the species.

When one objectively studies the singing of birds under natural conditions, for instance, it becomes clear that one major function of bird song is species recognition; through distinctive songs and calls, the males and females of each species are able to locate one another easily and reliably. An even more important function is the male's use of song to establish his own territory. In many species, male birds attack or avoid one another during the nesting phase, using their characteristic song as the way of warning one another to stay at a distance; the result is a useful spacing out of nesting sites, giving each mating pair a chance to raise its young without interference. It is not as romantic an interpretation of bird song as that of the poets, but it is verifiable—and verified.

Territorial warnings are valuable and common throughout the animal kingdom. Many kinds of male fish wear bright colors that warn their fellows away from their chosen feeding ground; free-roaming dogs and cats urinate in many places to mark their own domain; antelopes rub their faces against branches, releasing scent from facial glands and advertising their ownership of the area. None of the animals has this purpose in mind, as far as anyone knows; the animal may mark in one way or another simply because it feels good, but the survival value of such behavior for the species makes it an evolution-chosen trait.

Animals who intrude upon one another's territory are in for a fight, but it is a fiction that such fights are motivated by fraternal blood lust, like that of Cain. A species that had a tendency to kill its own kind would be at a serious disadvantage in the struggle for survival. A male animal fights an intruding rival of the same species not with murderous intent but merely to drive him away, so that the defender will not have to coexist with him in an area too small for the two of them. Not that the territorial defender thinks this through; as far as ethologists can tell, he fights simply because the rival's size, shape, smell and behavior arouse alarm and anger— some say instinctively, others say partly due to learning in the form of youthful mock combat. In any case, the defender seeks first only to frighten the intruder off by making hostile gestures and noises; if this fails, the two do fight—usually in a ritualized fashion that means neither death nor even harm to the loser. Male cichlid fish seize each other by the lips and push and pull for hours, until one gives up, folds his fins and swims away. Stags, wild goats and male mountain sheep engage in ferocious combat, but neither combatant uses its sharp horns to pierce the other, instead, they smash their horns against each other and push, butt, strain and struggle, until one is exhausted and gives up, the victor making no effort to inflict a wound when the loser turns to leave.

So it is throughout most of the animal world: The same animals that will fight other species to the death will engage each other in fierce but primarily ceremonial and harmless struggles ending either in flight, with the victor not pursuing, or in surrender, with the beaten one giving some sign of appeasement—a cringing posture, the turning away of the head, a rolling over on the back or some other form of exposing himself to the mortal blow. But it is never delivered; the act of appeasement ends the fight.

The appeasement gesture itself is a particularly important evolutionary development among animals that live in groups where the loser cannot run away except at the cost of isolation. Among baboons, for instance, a defeated male will "present"—that is, offer his rump, like a female, to the victor; the latter may choose not to use the proffered rear, but the gesture alters his mood and ensures peace. The sending out of a sexual signal is, in fact, the most effective of all neutralizers of the aggressive impulse. If the female of the species looks much like the male, then she must offer stimuli that bring about changes in the emotional status of the male territorial defender, so that he does not attack her but mates with her. Whether the female does so by means of a sound, an odor or a series of movements, one need not assume conscious intent on her part—most certainly not at the lower levels of evolution and probably not even at the higher ones.

An example: A small tidal-zone fish known as the goby stoutly defends his territory against intruding males by turning dark, opening his mouth threateningly and puffing out his throat; these failing, he attacks and bites the interloper. But if a gravid female comes near, her condition provides him with various stimuli that modify his behavior, the most important being a chemical she exudes due to her gravid state. The scent of it radically changes his reactions: He turns light, rather than dark, and instead of attacking, he fans the water with his tail, making grunting noises and leads her to a shelter he has built, where she lays her eggs and he then releases sperm over them. Without her chemical signal and his response to it, the species would perish, but neither the signal nor the response is intentional or deliberate. Both are purely automatic, as Dr. William Tavolga, a zoologist at the American Museum of Natural History in New York, proved by plugging up the noses of male gobies—who thereupon attacked gravid females just as if they were rival males. But let no one sneer at the dimwitted goby; do we not continually read in advertisements that such and such a perfume will inspire passion, or even love and marriage, in the gentleman of one's choice?

Even territorialism and courtship seem commonplace before the miracle of animal mother love. As we said earlier, which of us has not marveled at the mother cat, who knows without training that she should wash her newborn kittens and also knows when they are old enough to be on their own and therefore cuffs them away as if to help them get started? But those who have analytically studied mothering in cats have less romantic explanations of their behavior. The mothers lick their newborn young not because they know it's a good and healthful thing to do but because the young are drenched in placental fluids containing chemicals the mother has just lost and needs to replace and that, therefore, probably taste good to her. Nor does she "know" when her young are ready to be on their own; the young simply get so large that their suckling and playing are uncomfortable to her and she reacts naturally to pain and irritation.

Similarly, the group life of baboons superficially resembles life in primitive human societies; moreover, watching baboons tend their young, fight, play, fornicate and defend themselves, it is difficult not to attribute human feelings and ideas to them. But dispassionate scientific observation dispels the anthropomorphic fallacy. Baboon mothers do care for their young, but baboon society ignores sick or wounded adults; they are simply abandoned as the troop moves on. Dominant males pair off briefly with females in heat, but there are no long-lasting alliances and nothing like family life, not even of the polygamous variety. Communication is largely a matter of gestures and deals only with immediate situations (there is no passing on of ideas or history); and the major social activity is not work, play nor sexual behavior but grooming—the picking of insects and dirt out of one another's hair. And this is probably an instinctive impulse based on biological need. Observers have noted that a baboon who is away from his group even for a day or two will return heavily infested with ticks and other parasites he cannot remove and that would soon seriously affect his health.

On the importance of studying animal behavior functionally and without anthropomorphism, all sides agree. They disagree sharply, however, about the actual mechanics underlying the behavior they see and about the implications of that behavior for mankind. At one pole, as we have already seen, are the ethologists. The word ethology has caught on with the public (almost as much as ecology) and has come to mean almost all kinds of animal-behavior studies; but among professionals, it still signifies, in Lorenz' own words, "the study of innate behavior; the study of species-specific drive activities." Lorenz, codirector of the Max Planck Institute for Behavioral Physiology in Seewiesen, Bavaria, virtually founded the specialty of ethology two generations ago and remains its principal figure.

The basic tenet of ethology is that by far the largest part of what animals—including man—do is instinctive. For each bit of behavior, there is a blueprint stored away in the nervous system and passed on within the genes of that species. External stimuli and experiences do play a part—but mostly as releasers, or actuators, of the fixed action patterns genetically programed within the animal.

In the years between the two World Wars, Lorenz and his students, reacting against the limitations and artificiality of laboratory experiments in rat psychology, turned to the study of many other species under natural conditions, where each has a repertoire of complicated acts specific to its own kind—acts that seem to appear automatically when the animal needs them and without having learned them in any sense comparable with that of behavorist psychology.

The female digger wasp of the species *Pepsis marginata,* for example, when ready to lay an egg, goes in search of a host for it and unerringly picks out a tarantula of the species *Cyrtopholis portoricae* (no other species of insect, not even any other species of tarantula, will do) and digs a hole in front of it, attacks it and finds a chink in its armor through which she stings it into immobility, then drags it into the hole and lays her egg in its abdomen, finally covering the hole over—all without ever having seen any of this done.

A complicated procedure such as this is made up of many small separate acts, and the ethologists think it is the separate acts that are specifically gene-produced and inheritable. As proof, they point out that in hybrids, these small acts are recombined, even as are colors, markings and other hereditary traits. Lorenz' own favorite subjects of study have been ducks and geese, each species of which goes through a courtship procedure involving a whole series of gestures and signs (the bill shake, the head flick, the tail shake, the grunt whistle and others). In each species, the sequence of acts is specific and invariable; but in hybrids, the sequence is altered, some acts appearing earlier or later, some disappearing, some changing form, all in predictable ways—presumably corresponding to the altered configuration of gene loci in the chromosomes.

Each species, therefore, has a complete set of genetic blueprints for behavior that serves to satisfy its four great drives—hunger, fear, sex and aggression. Circumstances may modify somewhat the precise behavior of the creature, but they cannot change its essential nature; the deer will never be a tiger, the hawk will never be a cow.

The aggression of animals toward their own kind, however, is held in check by inhibiting mechanisms such as the ritualization of fighting, appeasement gestures and the like. In man, unhappily, the brain has outstripped the rest of his biology; appeasement is no safeguard when killing is too quick, too easy and too impersonal to be stopped by the animal gesture. The beast within us is incompetent to handle the tools of murder the man within us has invented.

From such evidence and theorizing, ethologists are almost bound to draw gloomy and misanthropic conclusions, for the dismal record of history and the sorry state of the present world must be direct reflections of man's innate nature. Here, for instance, are the acerbic comments of Eckhard H. Hess, a distinguished animal psychologist at the University of Chicago. "As an ethologist," he says, "I believe that man is an animal—not a better kind of animal but merely a more complicated one. A lot of liberals and intellectuals—even in the biological sciences—try to deny this evidence, because it contradicts their ideological notions about the equality and the perfectibility of all men. In the do-gooder way of thinking, any discussion of the genic constitution of human beings and their behavior is supposed to smack of racism, and that's very bad, while anything that blames environment is very good. But to deny the biological basis of man's behavior, you have to overlook or deny 99 percent of what we know about biology today."

At the pole opposite the ethologists are those students of animal behavior who take their direction from the late Dr. T. C. Schneirla of the American Museum of Natural History. His disciples, who can be found at Rutgers, Johns Hopkins, the University of North Carolina and other institutions, espouse the developmental view. They disagree with Lorenzian instinct theory almost *in toto;* they regard the idea that the genes incorporate fixed action patterns as primitive and simplistic. Even in low-level creatures, they claim, behavior patterns arise out of a continuing dialectic between biological tendencies and experience; they develop out of the interaction between genotype and environment and do not exist preprogramed within the genotype, awaiting only the signal of the right releasers to turn them on. Schneirla studied tropical army ants at close range and noticed that even though the ant's behavior is largely metabolic and automatic, the newly hatched workers stay close to the colony for a few days and seem to flounder around; it takes a while before they become proficient at following trails and performing tasks. Even for them, therefore, behavior is not totally instinctive.

Everyone knows, moreover, that cats "instinctively" kill mice, but one researcher observed the behavior of growing kittens and concluded that this so-called instinct is the complex end product of an almost inevitable series of learning experiences based on biological tendencies. The kitten automatically pays attention to moving objects; this leads to playful chasing, which leads to seizing and biting, which leads, in turn, to tasting blood—each experience providing new gratifications and building toward the mouse-killing pattern. If, however, a kitten is carefully conditioned not to chase or bite mice, or misses the crucial steps at the critical period of its development, it may never become a mouser but remain indifferent toward mice all its life.

Much the same is true of mother love. In several laboratories, researchers have been studying mothering in rats and cats and find it to be a complicated phenomenon assembled out of earlier experiences, physical needs and elemental gratifications yielded by the mothering acts themselves. The mother cat, for instance, licks her own nipples and genitals during pregnancy, because they are swollen and feel uncomfortable. This not only helps the mammary glands develop but prepares her to lick her newborn young, who taste the same as her genitals and are, as we saw earlier, wet with the fluids she needs to restore her own chemical balance. The initial licking is an essential first step that leads to others: It stimulates movement and internal functions in the young and conditions them positively to her, and vice versa. The young, now aroused and hungry, begin random and reflexive nuzzling and sucking of the mother and only accidentally come upon her teats; they learn, however, and day by day get better at it. Their suckling relieves the mother's own congestion and continues to make them pleasing to her; she, too, learns, grows perceptibly more adept at caring for her young as time goes by and is distinctly more skillful with a second litter than with the first.

Summing up these and other experiments by developmentalists, Dr. William Tavolga—the zoologist who played tricks on the male goby fish—says, "The whole concept of instinct is superfluous. Certainly, we see plenty of stereotyped behavior in every species, typical of that species, that seems to appear automatically as the creature grows up in its normal environment. But is it instinctive? Not in the way Lorenz means; for at every level of organization, from the amoeba to man, behavior develops out of the interaction between the cytoplasm and the environment. You cannot go directly from the DNA molecule to a specific piece of behavior, and there is no special or separate category of behavior that can be called instinctive."

On the basis of such evidence and theorizing, the developmentalists draw radically different conclusions from the ethologists about the grand design of animal behavior and especially about the nature of man. In a review of Ardrey's *The Territorial Imperative,* the distinguished psychologist J. P. Scott wrote that it presents a "simpleminded," "uncritical," "adolescent," "oversimplified" and "largely erroneous" picture of human nature. In another book review, Schneirla wrote that Lorenz' *On Aggression* is based on "dubious assumptions" and presents a "naïve" and "outdated" view of human nature. Ashley Montagu, editing a volume of rebuttals of ethology, goes furthest of all: "Man is man because he has no instincts," he writes; "everything he is and has become he has learned, acquired, from his culture." This view is shared by some very unlikely bedfellows: anti-Communist liberals and anti-liberal Communists, pacifist intellectuals and violence-addicted Maoists, pot-smoking hippies and bespectacled scholars, all of whom believe that man is not inherently aggressive or selfish and that his present character is wholly a product of a bad system; to change him, one need only change it. They disagree only about what changes to make. Some "only"!

Most of the people working today in the field of animal behavior take positions somewhere between these two poles of thought. The emerging view of animal-behavior researchers is that the entire nature-nurture, innate-learned, instinct-experience issue is outmoded, if not meaningless; some behavior is purely innate, some entirely learned, but by far the largest part of it results from interactions between genotypic tendencies and environmental influences.

Young squirrels. for example, begin to handle, gnaw and crack nuts by way of natural response to their feel and smell but have to learn by trial and error how to put these several activities together in a useful sequence. Many birds make the right nest-building movements without seeming to require a period of experiment; but they use the wrong materials at first, the right ones later. Songbirds, as they reach maturity, will sing their characteristic song, but inaccurately and incompletely, unless they hear others of their species singing. Monkeys reared in isolation climb and swing like other monkeys but cannot socialize, play or mate, because these complex patterns require much learning. Learning is not all, however: Such monkeys cannot be socialized later on, because they have passed a critical period, during which certain maturational changes take place in the nervous system that are essential to the socialization process.

To understand how the genotype and the environment interact and, therefore, to understand the emerging answer to the ancient nature-nurture puzzle, one has to look closely at animals; even then, he may miss it unless he is lucky. Dr. William Dilger, the Cornell ethologist, regards the nature-nurture issue as a nonquestion but is himself a perfect example of a man who has found an answer to it in one species, partly by years of dedicated observation and partly by accident.

Long ago, in studying another problem altogether. Dilger was using as his laboratory animal a species of tiny green African parrot known as the peach-faced lovebird, which, along with the unusual "loving" behavior of mated couples, has another curious trait: The female of the species cuts out strips of leaves or thin bark with her bill, tucks the strips in among the feathers of the lower part of her back and carries them in this fashion to the place where she is building a nest, Dilger says:

> Every female lovebird does it the same way, whether or not she's ever seen other females doing it. I had a rather naïvely instinctivist view of things in those days and it looked to me like a perfect example of an innate, fixed action pattern, a part of the animal's genotype. I even used it in my lectures as a classical example of instinctive behavior.
>
> Then a kind of accident happened in the lab here about ten years ago. We were raising a bunch of females and a young lab assistant of mine took care of them and gave them food, water, grit and whatever they needed. Lovebirds don't build nests when they're young, so he didn't bother to give them nesting materials and didn't think to mention it to me. But although young birds

don't build nests with the material, they *play* with it—they run under it, pull it around, peck at it and other things of the sort. Finally, they reached breeding age and we paired them—and, to our surprise, not one of those birds could cut out strips and tuck them into her feathers. Not one of them ever managed it. They were simply incapable of it. They showed a great deal of *interest* in the stuff, but all they managed to do was demolish it. Something hadn't happened to them, between the ages of six months and a year, that should have happened. They had missed experiences they needed to have in order to form what I had taken to be a completely innate behavior pattern. They have only a core of response to the situation—a crude, imperfect action with the nesting material that requires experience to modify. They improve their behavior a little the next time and this leads them to modify it a little more the time after that, and so on, until they have acquired the final pattern.

I did some modifying of my own—this whole experience was a key factor in my shift away from the strict ethological viewpoint. I've been studying lovebirds ever since and seeing things I had never noticed before. I've been able to break down tucking behavior into nine separate neuromuscular components—all of them innate—and do things to the birds to see which of the nine are modifiable by experience, which need experience to result in useful behavior and which are essential to other components. I've deprived them of nesting materials at different stages of their lives, I've given them materials but shaved the feathers off their back and rump, so they can't learn to tuck, I've let them learn to tuck and go through nesting and *then* shaved off their feathers. From it all, I've gotten a clear idea of the way in which one specific piece of behavior, in one species of bird, is constructed out of crude genotypic tendencies as they are modified, perfected and pieced together by experiences gained from the environment.

Recently, I've been studying the same interplay in the case of the lovebirds' courtship procedures. Ethologists have generally considered courtship rituals of birds to be strictly instinctive, and it is true that all male lovebirds do the same things when courting females, even without having seen them done by others. The male has to give the female a lot of signals and get certain positive signs back from her before she'll accept him. We have descriptive names for the things he does —"switch sidling," "squeak twittering," "displacement scratching," "head bobbing" and so on—and every male does them, and they always work. But if you really live with the birds, you begin to see differences. I had cages of them right here in my office for years, so that I could see them all day long, no matter what else I was doing. After a long while, I began to see that the novice male makes a lot of mistakes. He does all the things he should do and they look perfect, but he doesn't know *when* to do them; his timing is no good. The female looks as if she's just sitting there; but actually she's giving him very subtle signals that mean "Stop!" or "Not now!" or "Come on!" If she fluffs her cheek feathers slightly, she's agreeable; if she compresses them, she isn't—tiny things like that. It's very hard to recognize—hard for the male bird as well as the human observer. But he has to learn, because if he rushes in when he shouldn't, he'll get nipped. An experienced male won't make that mistake. So, once again, even in a seemingly innate and rigid pattern of behavior, there's a lot of genotype-environment interaction.

Lovebirds vary their response a little; men vary theirs a great deal. More so than any other animal, we are able to modify our reactions to the stimuli we encounter; indeed, we build entire cultures out of those modifications. Less so than any other animal are we provided with ready-made fixed action patterns to satisfy our drives or forced by metabolic processes to respond to stimuli in predictable ways. Each animal has its own diet; men have scores of them. Each animal has its own coital position; we have 10, 20, 100. Each animal preens or grooms itself in a species-specific fashion; we have innumerable ways of doing so. Each of the social animals has a relatively unvarying form of group life; we, in our brief time on earth, have created everything from Athenian city-state to communistic dictatorships.

It is true that, like other animals, we are impelled to action by hunger, fear, anger and sexual desire. But we are not directed by instinct to take specific actions in order to satisfy those drives. The actions one might call instincts in the clam are not only simpler but different in quality from those one might call instincts in the lovebird and radically unlike those often referred to as instincts in man. This is not to say that the study of animal behavior can teach us nothing about ourselves. It can and will, even as the study of animal physiology can and does contribute much to human medicine. But even if one thoroughly studies the skeleton, nervous system, blood and tissue of the rabbit, he is not qualified to diagnose and heal the ills of man; their similarities are instructive, but their differences are crucial.

Above all else, we have learned from animal-behavior studies that the more complicated an animal is, the less its behavior is rigidly programed by the genotype, the more its behavior is developed through experience. The conclusion that man's instincts are very much like those of lower animals is unjustified and misleading. What the evidence justifies instead is the conclusion that man's instincts operate on a level very different from those of most animals and do not result in specific, predictable, stereotyped behavior patterns.

The clinical experience of every psychotherapist and psychoanalyst since Freud indicates that human beings have only the most amorphous and undifferentiated kinds of instincts and that our training within the family and outside it is what makes us either heterosexual or homosexual, monogamous or polygamous, sybaritic or ascetic, convivial or reclusive, combative or passive. We do not automatically become any of these things; we express our sexual "instinct"—one wishes there were another word for it when referring to man— in whatever way we are taught. And without teaching we can do almost nothing: In some orphanages, where children get almost no individual attention other than feeding and changing, many of them are unable even to *walk* by the age of three or four. So much for man's instincts.

Yet for want of a better word, let us agree to call man's genotypic tendencies instincts—while insisting that this means something very different from instincts in lower animals. Man may be innately and instinctively aggressive in the sense that he is chronically restless and irritable; in need of change and excitement, challenge and difficulties; quick to anger when frustrated, and to strike out—or feel the desire to do so—at whatever limits him, threatens him or presses in upon him. But man is not programed and his aggressive drive can be directed in many ways and serve many different ends. One man uses it to become Nero but another to become Marcus Aurelius; one man's aggressive instinct makes him Hitler, another's makes him Gandhi.

The record of man's inhumanity to man is horrifying, when one compiles it—enslavement, castration, torture, rape, mass slaughter in war after war. But who has compiled the record of man's kindness to man—the trillions of acts of gentleness and goodness, the helping hands, smiles, shared meals, kisses, gifts, healings, rescues? If we were no more than murderous predators, with a freakish lack of inhibition against slaughtering our own species, we would have been at a terrible competitive disadvantage compared with other animals; if this were the central truth of our nature, we would scarcely have survived, multiplied and become the dominant species on earth. Man does have an aggressive instinct, but it is not naturally or inevitably directed to killing his own kind. He is a beast and perhaps at times the cruelest beast of all—but sometimes he is also the kindest beast of all. He is not all good and not perfectible, but he is not all bad and not wholly unchangeable or unimprovable. That is the only basis on which one can have hope for him; but it is enough.

LEONARD BERKOWITZ

Simple Views of Aggression

The theme of this essay will be drawn from a dust jacket. On the back of the book, *Human Aggression,* by the British psychiatrist Anthony Storr, we find the following comment by Konrad Lorenz, widely renowned as the "father of ethology": "An ancient proverb says that simplicity is the sign of truth—and of fallacy. . . . However, if the simple explanation is in full agreement with a wealth of data, and quite particularly, if it dovetails with data collected in altogether different fields of knowledge, simplicity certainly is indicative of truth." Four of the books reviewed here offer essentially simplistic messages. With the writers represented in the fifth work, I shall argue that the conceptual simplicity advocated by these volumes is definitely *not* "indicative of the truth." All of the books deal with man's capacity for violence, a problem deserving—no, demanding—careful and sophisticated consideration. The four volumes I shall concentrate on, those by Lorenz, Ardrey, Storr and Morris—and especially the first three—provide only easy formulas readily grasped by a wide audience rather than the necessary close analysis. Being easily understood, their explanation for human aggression helps relieve the anxiety born of the public's concern with war, social unrest, race riots and student protests, but is an adequate, and perhaps even dangerous, basis for social policy.

From *American Scientist,* 57, 1969, pp. 372–83. Reprinted by permission.

All four voice essentially the same message: Much of human behavior generally, and human aggression in particular, must be traced in large part to man's animal nature. Aggression often arises for innately determined reasons, they say. The authors differ somewhat, however, in how they believe this nature leads to aggression. For Lorenz, Ardrey, and Storr (whom I shall refer to as the Lorenzians), a spontaneously engendered drive impels us to aggression, even to the destruction of other persons. Morris, on the other hand, views many of our aggressive acts as genetically governed responses to certain environmental conditions and to signals sent to us by other people. Nonetheless, over and above their similarities and differences, all four volumes present a highly simplified conception of the causes of and possible remedies for human aggression, and I think it would be well for us to look at a number of these misleading oversimplifications.

Facing the writers at their own level, one misconception I shall not deal with here is their relative neglect of the role of learning in human aggression. Our behavior is influenced by our experiences *and* our inherited biological characteristics. I have argued in other pages that innate determinants do enter into man's attacks on others, primarily in connection with impulsive reactions to noxious events and frustrations. These constitutionally governed impulsive responses can be modified by learning, however. The Lorenzians do not appear to recognize this kind of modification in these volumes. They draw a very sharp distinction between learned and innately determined responses, thus ignoring what is now known of the complex interplay between nature and nurture. Lorenz has admitted this on occasion, and the journalist, Joseph Alsop, has recently reported him as saying, "We ethologists were mistaken in the past when we made a sharp distinction between 'innate' and 'learned.'" Of course, there is also an experience-is-all imperialism at the opposite extreme. In sharp contrast to many ethologists and zoologists, social scientists typically have long ignored and even denied the role of built-in, biological determinants. Ashley Montagu's critical discussion of Lorenz in his introduction to *Man and Aggression* is illustrative. "The notable thing about human behavior," he says, "is that it is learned. Everything a human being does as such he has had to learn from other human beings."

Some book reviewers for the popular press, aware of these opposing stances, have approached the present volumes in terms of this kind of polarization. *If* human aggressiveness is learned, Lorenz *et al.* are obviously incorrect, but on the other hand, innate determinants to aggression presumably must operate as described by Ardrey, Lorenz, Morris and Storr. Ardrey, Lorenz and Storr pose the issue in these simple terms. Critics dispute their views, they maintain, primarily because of a misguided "American optimism"; American social scientists, psychologists and psychiatrists, having a liberal belief in the perfectibility of man, want to attribute social ills —including violence—to environmental flaws which might be remedied rather than to intractable human nature. The critics certainly would recognize the existence of man's innate aggressive drive if they could only shed their honorable but mistaken vision of Utopia.

There are other alternatives, however. Some of human aggressiveness might derive from man's biological properties, characteristics which he shares to some degree with the other animals. He might even be innately "programmed" to respond violently to particular kinds of stimulation, much as other animals do. But his animal characteristics do not have to function the way Lorenz and his associates say they do. The Lorenzian analysis of aggression can be criticized on a logical and empirical basis independently of any general assumptions about the nature of man.

The volume *Man and Aggression,* edited by Montagu, serves as a counterpoise to the Lorenzian books. A number of journalist-reviewers have assumed that Lorenz's views are shared by virtually all students of animal behavior. The Montagu volume clearly shows that there is not the unanimity of support that the laymen believe exists. Many eminent zoologists, as well as comparative psychologists, have taken Lorenz's analysis of aggression seriously to task. *Man and Aggression* is a compilation of generally damning criticisms of the Lorenz and Ardrey books by such authorities as S. A. Barnett, J. H. Crook, T. C. Schneirla, and Sir Solly Zuckerman, as well as Lorenz's old opponent, J. P. Scott. For those people who have read only the Lorenzian analyses, Lorenz may speak for all ethologists; Lorenz is equated with all ethology in the Storr book, *Human Aggression.* Yet he is not all of the science of animal behavior, and there are many good reasons in the animal as well as human research literature to question the over-all thrust of Dr. Lorenz's argument on grounds besides the "overbold and loose" nature of the Lorenzian contentions generally recognized by many readers.

We need not here review the many objections to the Lorenz and Ardrey volumes that are summarized by the critics included in *Man and Aggression*. However, some of the oversimplifications and errors of reasoning and fact that are characteristic of these two books are prevalent in the Storr and Morris works, and I think it is important to point out several of these common weaknesses in the extension of popular biology to human aggression.

As nearly every critic of these Lorenzian books has pointed out, the writers are excessively free-wheeling in their use of analogies. They frequently attempt to explain various human actions by drawing gross analogies between these behaviors and supposedly similar response patterns exhibited by other animal species. Attaching the same label to these human and animal behaviors, the writers then maintain that they have explained the actions. For Lorenz, man is remarkably similar to the Greylag goose. The resemblances (that occur to Lorenz but not necessarily to other observers) are supposedly far from superficial ones, and he believes that they can only be explained by the operation of the same mechanisms in man and goose. ". . . Highly complex norms of behavior such as falling in love, strife for ranking order, jealousy, grieving, etc. are not only similar but down to the most absurd details the same . . ." and therefore, all of these actions must be governed by instincts.

The analogy emphasized by Ardrey, of course, is based on animal territoriality. Man's genetic endowment supposedly drives him to gain and defend property, much as other animals do, presumably because this territorial behavior provides identity, stimulation and security. Basing part of his argument on a study of the lemurs of Madagascar, Ardrey contends that there are two types of societies, noyaux (societies said to be held together by the inward antagonism of the members) and nations (societies in which joint defense of territory has given rise to in-group leadership and cooperation). The examples of noyaux listed by Ardrey include, in addition to the

Madagascar lemurs, herring gull colonies, certain groups of gibbons, and Italy and France.

Morris' analogy, needless to say, is between humans and apes. His theme is that *"Homo sapiens* has remained a naked ape . . . in acquiring lofty new motives, he has lost none of the earthy old ones." We cannot understand the nature of our aggressive urges, he says, along with Ardrey, Lorenz and Storr, unless we consider "the background of our animal origins." Unlike the Lorenzians, however, he doubts the existence of an innate, spontaneous aggressive drive, and emphasizes, to the exclusion of such a drive, the genetically determined signals he believes both apes and people send to their fellows. All four authors make much of the control of aggression by supposedly innate appeasement gestures, although Morris seems to have greater confidence in their efficacy than do the others. He even tells us how we should respond to an angry traffic policeman on the basis of this analogy between human and animal behavior: The policeman's aggression can (theoretically) be turned off automatically by showing abject submission in our words, body posture, and facial expressions. Moreover, it is essential to "get quickly out of the car and move away from it towards the policeman." This prevents the policeman from invading our territory (our car) and weakens feelings of territorial rivalry. The looks people give each other are very important signals. Morris maintains in accord with a rapidly growing body of experimental-social psychological research, but, in contrast to these investigators, he oversimplifies greatly. Morris contends that prolonged looking at another is an aggressive act. In reality, persistent eye-contact can also be a very intimate, even sexual, encounter, or may arise from a search for information or social support.

This type of crude analogizing is *at best* an incomplete analysis of the behavior the writers seek to explain. Important data are neglected and vital differences are denied. J. H. Crook's excellent paper in *Man and Aggression* (which should be read by every person who has written a favorable review of the Lorenz and Ardrey books) notes the many important considerations omitted by the Lorenzians in general and Ardrey's treatment of territoriality in particular. Where Ardrey, following Lorenz, maintains that territorial behavior is a highly fixed, species-specific action pattern produced by energy accumulating in certain centers in the nervous system, the truth cannot be packaged as easily as this. Many different conditions enter into animal territoriality. The outcome is a complex interaction of ecological and social conditions with internal states so that territorial behavior is far from inevitable as a species characteristic. Territorial maintenance, furthermore, involves different components, such as attack and escape. These components are probably governed by somewhat different, although often interrelated, mechanisms, and appear to be susceptible to different environmental and internal conditions. Given these complexities and the multiplicity of factors involved in the territoriality displayed by birds, we cannot make simple statements about the functions and causes of territoriality even in these species, and it is highly unlikely that human concern with property is controlled by the same processes. Crook's conclusion is certainly reasonable: "The likelihood that the motivation control of territorial behavior is at a different level from that of fishes and birds suggests that human resemblances to the lower animals might be largely through analogy rather than homology." Sixteen years ago, Daniel Lehrman remarked, in an outstanding critique of Lorenzian theory, "it is not very judicious, and actually is rash . . . to assume that the mechanisms underlying two similar response characteristics are in any way identical, homologous, or even similar," merely because the actions of different species or entities seem to resemble each other (in the eyes of the writer, we might add).

The same comment can be made about the analogizing involved in Lorenz's and Storr's use of the notion of ritualization. Theorizing that there are evolutionary changes in behavior as well as structure, and that particular action patterns, such as appeasement gestures, have evolved from other behaviors, Lorenz argues that responses originally serving one function can undergo alteration in the course of evolution so that they come to have a different function as well. The drive or energy motivating the original action presumably still powers this altered behavior. According to Lorenz, the appeasement or greeting ceremonies performed by humans and animals alike have become ritualized in this manner through evolutionary developments but still make use of transformed aggressive motivation. Lorenz thinks that the smile of greeting, as an example, might have "evolved by ritualization of redirected threatening." Storr, adopting Lorenz's reasoning, also speaks of "ritualizing the aggressive drive in such a way that it serves the function of uniting" people. For both of these writers, diverted aggressive energy powers the social bonds which tie individuals together in affection and even love. Now, we must ask, is there really good reason to contend, as Lorenz does so authoritatively, that the human smile, the appeasement gesture of the macaques (baring the teeth), and the triumph ceremony of the geese must have evolved in the same way from some original aggressive display? The supposed similarity between the human, monkey, and goose behavior does not mean, as Lehrman pointed out, that the processes underlying these actions are "identical, homologous, or even similar." Elaborating further, in his essay in *Man and Aggression*, Barnett says there is no justification for the "confident, dogmatic assertions" Lorenz and his followers have made about the hypothetical process, 'ritualization.' " Harlow's observations regarding monkey development are also troublesome for the Lorenzian analysis of the genesis of social bonds. Affectional patterns generally emerge *before* aggressive ones in these animals, making it unlikely that the earlier, affectional-social acts are "driven" by aggressive motivation.

The dangers of unwarranted analogizing can also be illustrated by referring to another example of "ritualization" mentioned by Storr. It appears that the Kurelu, a primitive people in the heart of New Guinea, engage in frequent intertribal warfare. But instead of killing one another, the warriors shoot arrows at each other from a distance just beyond arrow range and rarely hit each other. Although this type of warfare seems to resemble the threat ceremonies exhibited by a number of animal species, we certainly cannot argue that the Kurelu behavior and animal threats have evolved in exactly the same manner or are based on similar biological mechanisms. Furthermore, both action patterns may ultimately lead to a cessation of attacks—but probably for very different reasons. It is also improper to insist, as the Lorenzians do, that competitive sports are the same type of ritual as the Kurelu warfare and animal threats merely because some writers have applied the same label to all three sets of phenomena; the surface resemblances do not guarantee that all have the same evolutionary causes and that all operate in the same or even in a similar way.

When we come right down to it, there seems to be a kind of

"word magic" in this analogizing. The writers appear to believe that they have provided an adequate explanation of the phenomenon at issue by attaching a label to it: a person's smile is an *appeasement gesture;* athletic events are *rituals* comparable to certain animal displays, etc. Storr shows just this kind of thinking in the "proof" he offers for the notion of a general aggressive drive. Aggression is not all bad, Storr insists (in agreement with Lorenz); aggression is necessary to the optimal development of man. It is "the basis of intellectual achievement, of the attainment of independence, and even of the proper pride which enables a man to hold his head high amongst his fellows." The evidence he cites for this statement is word usage: ". . . the words we use to describe intellectual effort are aggressive words. We *attack* problems, or *get our teeth* into them. We *master* a subject when we have *struggled with* and *overcome* its difficulties. We *sharpen* our wits . . ." (Italics in the original.) Waving his words over the particular behavior (in this case, striving for independence and achievement), he has thus supposedly accounted for these actions—and has also swept aside the many studies of achievement motivation by McClelland and his associates suggesting that there is very little similarity between the instigation to aggression and achievement motivation.

Popular discussions of the role of evolution in behavior can also be criticized on this basis. Even if it can be shown that a given behavior pattern has "evolved," such a demonstration does not explain the performance of that action by a particular individual in a specific setting. The application of the word "evolution" does not really help us to understand what mechanisms govern the behavior in this individual or what stimulus conditions affect these mechanisms.

The Lorenzians (and Morris as well) also display this same word magic in the ease with which they refer to human actions as instinctive. Without taking the trouble to specify the criteria they employ in making their designations, they go scattering the label "instinct" around with great relish. As an illustration, in his book *On Aggression,* Lorenz talks about people's having an "instinctive need to be a member of a closely knit group fighting for common ideals," and insists that "there cannot be the slightest doubt that militant enthusiasm is instinctive and evolved out of a communal defense response." Doubts must exist, however. The Lorenzians offer neither a precise definition of what they mean by "instinct" or any substantial evidence that the behavior in question, whether human aggression or militant enthusiasm, is innate even in their vague usage of this term. Several of the writers in *Man and Aggression* (e.g., Barnett and Schneirla), as well as other scientists such as Lehrman, criticize Lorenz severely for his excessively casual employment of the instinct concept. Lorenz elsewhere has acknowledged this imprecision in his popular utterances (see, for example, the previously mentioned article by Alsop), saying that he has used the word only in a shorthand sense.

Nevertheless, the oversimplification regarding "instincts" so prevalent in the Lorenz-Ardrey-Storr writings is difficult to excuse as only shorthand. To say this is not to deny the role of innate processes in human behavior; such determinants apparently exist. Psychologists, together with other students of behavior, have shown, as an example, that human babies have a built-in preference for certain visual stimuli, and do not start with blank neural pages, so to speak, in learning to see and organize complex visual stimulation. The difficulty is that ideas such as Lorenz's "instinctive need to be a member of a closely knit group fighting for common ideals" are, in actuality, extremely drastic departures from the more precise instinct concept found in technical ethological discussions. When they write for an audience of their peers, ethologists generally describe instincts, or better still, instinctive movements, as behavioral sequences culminating in "fixed action patterns." These patterns, which are at the core of the instinct concept, are thought of as rigid and stereotyped species-specific *consummatory* responses generally serving to end a chain of ongoing behavior. Can this definition be applied to "militant enthusiasm??" What is the rigid and stereotyped action that unerringly unfolds to consummate the hypothetical enthusiasm pattern?

We now come to the most important part of the Lorenzian instinct conception, and the feature that has the gravest social implications: the supposed spontaneity of the behavior. The stereotyped instinctive action is said to be impelled by a specific energy that has accumulated in that part of the central nervous system responsible for the co-ordination of the behavior. The energy presumably builds up spontaneously and is discharged when the response is performed. If the instinctive activity is not carried out for a considerable period of time, the accumulated energy may cause the response to "pop off" *in vacuo*. Aggression, according to Lorenz, Ardrey, and Storr—but not Morris—follows this formula. "It is the spontaneity of the [aggressive] instinct," Lorenz tells us, "that makes it so dangerous." The behavior "can 'explode' without demonstrable external stimulation" merely because the internal accumulating energy has not been discharged by aggressive actions or has not been diverted into other response channels as, for example, in the case of such "ritualized" activities as sports. If violence is to be lessened, suitable outlets must be provided. Lorenz believes that "present-day civilized man suffers from insufficient discharge of his aggressive drive," and together with Ardrey and Storr, calls for more athletic competitions—bigger and better Olympic games. (Denying the Lorenzian formulation, Morris maintains that we do not have an inborn urge to destroy our our opponents—only to dominate them—and argues that the only solution is "massive de-population" rather than "boisterous international football.")

This conception can be discussed at various levels. Neurologically, for one thing, Lorenz bases his assertions on observations regarding cardiac and respiratory activities and simple motor coordinations. With such critics as Lehrman and Moltz, we must question whether or not these findings can be extended to more complex neural organizations, to say nothing of human aggression. (The Lorenzian interpretation of these observations can also be disputed, as Moltz has shown in the 1965 *Psychological Review*.)

There are empirical difficulties as well as this problem of the long inductive leap. Basing their arguments on a number of studies, Hinde and Ziegler (the latter in an important 1964 *Psychological Bulletin* paper) have proposed that many apparent demonstrations of internally-driven spontaneity can be traced to external stimuli and the operation of associative factors. The responses evidently are evoked by environmental stimuli rather than being driven out by spontaneously accumulating internal excitation. Moltz has also summarized evidence disputing the Lorenzian notion that response performance is necessary if there is to be a reduction in elicitability of the instinctive action pattern. As Hinde has suggested in several papers, stimulus satiation rather than a response-produced discharge of instinctive action-specific energy may cause a lessening in response elicitability.

Going from the simple motor coordinations of the lower animals to the more complex aspects of animal and human aggression, the available data are even less kind to the Lorenzian formulation. Of course Lorenz maintains that his ideas are supported by a substantial body of observations. They are upheld, he says, by the failures of "an American method of education" to produce less aggressive children, even though the youngsters have been supposedly "spared all disappointments and indulged in every way." However, as I have pointed out elsewhere in discussing this argument, excessively indulged children probably expect to be gratified most of the time, so that the inevitable occasional frustrations they encounter are actually relatively strong thwartings for them. There is little doubt that these frustrations can produce aggressive reactions, and Lorenz's criticism of the frustration-aggression hypothesis is a very weak one. Belief in this hypothesis, by the way, does not necessarily mean advocating a completely frustration-free environment for children. Child specialists increasingly recognize that youngsters must learn to cope with and adapt to life's inescapable thwartings, and thus must experience at least some frustrations in the course of growing up. Nor do most contemporary psychologists believe that frustration is the only source of aggression. Violence can have its roots in pain as well as in obstacles to goal attainment, and can also be learned as other actions are learned.

Aggression, in other words, has a number of different causes, although the Lorenzians seem to recognize (or at least discuss) only one source. Here is yet another erroneous oversimplification: their notion of a unitary drive that is supposedly capable of powering a wide variety of behaviors from ritualized smiling to strivings for independence or dominance. This general drive conception is very similar to the motivational thinking in classical psychoanalysis, but is running into more and more difficulty under the careful scrutiny of biologists and psychologists. Indeed, contrary to Storr's previously cited argument, there is no single instigation to aggression even in the lower animals. Moyer recently has suggested (in the 1968 *Com-*

munications in Behavioral Biology), on the basis of many findings, that there are several kinds of aggression, each of which has a particular neural and endocrine basis.

Also like the traditional psychoanalysts, the Lorenzians speak loosely of aggressive energy flowing from one channel or behavior to another. This hypothetical process, mentioned earlier in conjunction with "ritualization," must be differentiated from the more precisely defined response-generalization concept developed by experimental psychologists. Reinforcements provided to one kind of reaction may strengthen other, similar responses. Rewarding a child for making aggressive remarks can increase the likelihood of other kinds of aggressive reactions as well. The reinforcement influence generalizes from one kind of response to another because the actions have something in common. (The actor might regard both types of responses as *hurting* someone). It is theoretically unparsimonious and even inadvisable to interpret this effect as an energy transfer from one response channel to another. The Lorenz-Storr discussion of ritualization, and the related psychoanalytic concept of sublimation as well, employ just this kind of energy-diversion idea. We cannot here go into the conceptual pitfalls of this analytical model. (The interested reader might wish to read Hinde's article on energy models of motivation in the 1960 *Symposia of the Society for Experimental Biology*.) But there is a fairly obvious flaw in the Lorenzian statement that pent-up aggressive energy can be discharged in competitive sports. Rather than lessening violence, athletic events have sometimes excited supporters of one, or both, of the competing teams into attacking other persons. This has happened in many countries: in England, as Crook points out and as Storr should have recognized, in this country at times when white and Negro high school basketball teams have competed against each other, and most dramatically, in March 1969 in Czechoslovakia when the Czechs defeated the Russians in hockey. In these cases, the team supporters were so aroused, even when their team won, that they were extremely responsive to aggressive stimuli in the environment.

Experimental tests of the hostility catharsis hypothesis also argue against the energy-diversion idea inherent in both Lorenzian and psychoanalytic theorizing. This well-worn notion maintains, of course, that the display of aggressive behavior in fantasy, play, or real life, will reduce the aggressive urge. Although there is no explicit reference to a catharsis process in Storr's book, his belief that aggressive energy can be sublimated certainly is consistent with the catharsis doctrine. Lorenz comes much closer to a frank acceptance of this idea in his contention that "civilized man suffers from insufficient discharge of his aggressive drive," and in a bit of advice he offers to people on expeditions to the remote corners of the world. Members of socially isolated groups, he says in *On Aggression*, must inevitably experience a build-up of aggressive drive; outsiders aren't available to be attacked and thus provide an outlet for the accumulating aggressive energy. If a person in such an isolated group wishes to prevent the intra-group conflict that otherwise must develop (Lorenz insists), he should smash a vase with as loud and resounding a crash as possible. We do not have to attack other people in order to experience a cathartic reduction in our aggressive urge; it's enough merely to destroy inanimate objects.

Summarizing (and simplifying) a great many studies, research results suggest that angry people often do (a) feel better, and (b) perhaps even experience a temporarily reduced inclination to attack their tormentors, upon learning that these persons have been hurt. This phenomenon seems to be quite specific, however; the provoked individual is gratified when he finds that the intended target of his aggression has been injured, and does not appear to get the same satisfaction from attacks on innocent bystanders. Besides this, the apparent reduction in the instigation to aggression following an attack is probably often due to guilt- or anxiety-induced restraints evoked by the attack and/or the arousal of other, nonaggressive motives, and is not really the result of an energy discharge. Standard experimental-psychological analysis can do a far better job than the energy-discharge model in explaining the available data. Recent experiments indicate, for example, that the lessening of physiological tension produced by injuring the anger instigator comes about when the aggressor has learned that aggression is frequently rewarded. This tension reduction, or gratification, is evidently akin to a reinforcement effect, and is not indicative of any long-lasting decline in the likelihood of aggression; people who find aggression rewarding are more, not less, likely to attack again in the future. This reinforcement process can also account for the appetitive behavior

Lorenz and Storr seem to regard as prime evidence for the existence of a spontaneous aggressive drive. Provoked animals will go out of their way to obtain suitable targets to attack, while youngsters who are frequently aggressive toward their peers generally prefer violent T.V. programs to more peaceful ones. But this search for an appropriate target or for aggressive scenes probably arises from the reinforcing nature of these stimuli rather than from some spontaneous drive, and again, does not mean that there has been an energy discharge when these stimuli are encountered. Quite the contrary. There is some reason to believe that the presence of such aggression-reinforcing stimuli as other people fighting can evoke aggressive responses from those who are ready to act aggressively—much as the sight of food (which is a reinforcement for eating) can elicit eating responses from those who are set to make such responses.

In the end, the Lorenzian analyses must be questioned because of their policy implications as well as because of their scientific inadequacies. Their reliance on casual anecdotes instead of carefully controlled, systematic data, their use of ill-defined terms and gross analogies, and their disregard of hundreds of relevant studies in the interest of an oversimplified theory warrant the disapproval generally accorded them by technical journals. But more than this, the Lorenz-Ardrey-Storr books can also have unfortunate social as well as scientific consequences by impeding recognition of the important roles played by environmental stimuli and learning in aggressive behavior, and by blocking awareness of an important social principle: Aggression is all too likely to lead to still more aggression.

REFERENCES

Ardrey, Robert, *The Territorial Imperative.* New York: Atheneum 1966.
Lorenz, Konrad, *On Aggression,* New York: Harcourt, Brace & World, 1966, p. xiv, 306. $5.75.
Montagu, M. F. Ashley (ed.), *Man and Aggression,* New York: Oxford University Press, 1968, pp. xiv, 178. $5.00.
Morris, Desmond, *The Naked Ape,* New York: McGraw-Hill, 1968, p. 252. $5.95.
Storr, Anthony, *Human Aggression,* New York: Atheneum, 1968, p. 127. $5.00.

LEON EISENBERG

The *Human* Nature of
Human Nature

Understanding the nature of man and his works has become a precondition for the survival of our species, as well as for the enhancement of the flowering of human individuality. The search for that understanding is the central purpose of the university and the source of its relevance to society. After a period of public worship that verged on idolatry, universities have become the target of sustained and bitter attack. Yesterday's idolatry may have been a worship of false gods: credentials to an affluent life, technological virtuosity with little concern for its ends, and a meritocracy that excluded ethnic and linguistic minorities. But today's exorcism is aimed at false devils: the freedom to explore unpopular ideas, the transmission of our cultural heritage, and the support of fundamental research. The young excoriate universities for their corruption by the Establishment, the Establishment for their receptivity to the new, and governments for their failure to guarantee docile citizens.

The criticism, if indiscriminate and shrill, is not without substance; it must be heeded if the universities are to excise the accretions of age. Like others, those connected with the university find it easiest to do what they have done before. Yet, if there is a single

From *Science*, vol. 176, pp. 123–28, 14 April 1972. Copyright 1972 by the American Association for the Advance of Science. Reprinted by permission.

leitmotiv of our time, it is a constantly accelerating rate of change. With each decade, scientific findings translated into technology radically reshape the way we live. Technical capacity has been the ruling imperative, with no reckoning of cost, either ecological or personal. If it could be done, it has been done. Foresight has lagged far behind craftsmanship. At long last we are beginning to ask, not *can* it be done, but *should* it be done? The challenge is to our ability to anticipate the second- and third-order consequences of interventions in the ecosystem before the event, not merely to rue them afterward. The power of our technology so foreshortens the time between its application and the possibility of its correction that we must learn to think through before we act out (*1*).

If we were to understand each other even half as well as we comprehend the energy of the stars, we might yet spare ourselves the horrors we face from traducing those energies into weapons that endanger all life. If psychiatry cannot yet provide a firm basis for that understanding, it may nonetheless be of service if it dispels the myths and the pseudoknowledge that obscure the search for truth.

Self-fullfilling Prophecies

The title of this article implies its conclusion: that there is to human nature a nature that is other than naked ape, actuated by territorial imperatives and impelled by aggressive instincts. Such a conclusion must seem outrageously optimistic in an era in which Americans "waste" Vietnamese, in which West Pakistani massacre their countrymen to the East—but there is no need to retell the litany of violence. How, in the teeth of this "evidence," can we disbelieve Morris, Ardrey, or Lorenz (*2*)? How can we challenge Freud, his illusions of civilization shattered by the barbarities of World War I when he wrote (*3*): "The very emphasis of the Commandment: Thou shalt not kill, makes it certain that we are descended from an endlessly long chain of generations of murderers whose love of murder was in their blood as it is perhaps also in our own . . ."? Or again (*4*): "The tendency to aggression is an innate, independent, instinctual disposition in man . . ."? How, indeed?

This is no mere academic exercise, of concern only to students of behavior. The planets will move as they always have, whether we adopt a geocentric or a heliocentric view of the heavens. It is only the equations we generate to account for those motions that will be more or less complex; the motions of the planets are sublimely indifferent to our earthbound astronomy. But the behavior of men is not independent of the theories of human behavior that men adopt. One example may serve to explicate this thesis.

So long as the "nature" of insanity was thought to be violent, and so long as the insane were chained, beaten, and locked in cells, madmen raged and fumed. With the introduction of the "moral treatment" of the insane at the beginning of the 19th century, violence in mental asylums markedly abated (5). A century later, the "nature" of insanity was perceived as social incompetence; the sick were "protected" from stress, and the institution assumed responsibility for all decision-making. Misguided benevolence stripped the patient of adult status and generated automation-like compliance; the result was the chronicity of the back wards of our state hospitals. A generation ago, the concept of the therapeutic environment, with its rediscovery of self-government and personal responsibility as the bases of attaining competence, began to reverse the cycle of self-perpetuating hospitalization. This led to a decline in what had been a steadily rising population in U.S. mental hospitals, a decline that began before the era of psychotropic drugs (6). Do not mistake me. Psychosis is no mere social convention; it has a psychobiological existence independent of systems of belief. But its manifestations and its course are profoundly influenced by the social field in which the patient and his caretakers operate. Belief systems act no less profoundly on the remainder of mankind. The doctor's very presence relieves pain. Teachers' expectations govern pupils' performance. The citizens' confidence in the benevolence of the social order maintains its stability.

What we believe of man affects the behavior of men, for it determines what each expects of the other. Theories of education, of political science, of economics, and the very policies of governments are based on implicit concepts of the nature of man. Is he educable? Is he actuated only by self-interest? Is he a creature of such dark lusts that only submission to sovereign authority can save him from himself?

What we choose to believe about the nature of man has social consequences. Those consequences should be weighed in assessing the belief we choose to hold, even provisionally, given the lack of compelling proof for any of the currently fashionable theories. In insisting on an assessment of potential outputs in addition to a critique of inputs, I do *not* suggest that we ignore scientific evidence when it does not suit our fond wishes. Any hope of building a better world must begin with a tough-minded appraisal of the facts that are to be had. The thrust of my argument is that there is no solid foundation to the theoretical extrapolation of the instinctivists, the ethologists, the behaviorists, *or* the psychoanalysts, despite the special pleading that often is so seductive to those eager for a "real science" of behavior. Further to the point, belief helps shape actuality because of the self-fulfilling character of social prophecy. To believe that man's aggressiveness or territoriality is in the nature of the beast is to mistake some men for all men, contemporary society for all possible societies, and, by a remarkable transformation, to justify what is as what needs must be; social repression becomes a response to, rather than a cause of, human violence. Pessimism about man serves to maintain the status quo. It is a luxury for the affluent, a sop to the guilt of the politically inactive, a comfort to those who continue to enjoy the amenities of privilege. Pessimism is too costly for the disenfranchised; they give way to it at the price of their salvation. No less clearly, the false "optimism" of the unsubstantiated claims made for behavioral engineering, claims that ignore biological variation and individual creativity, foreclose man's humanity.

What is known about the power of the social-psychological determinants of human behavior compels the conclusion that the set of axioms for a theory of human nature must include a Kantian categorical imperative: men and women must believe that mankind can become fully human in order for our species to attain its humanity. Restated, a soberly optimistic view of man's potential (based on recognition of mankind's attainments, but tempered by knowledge of its frailties) is a precondition for social action to make actual that which is possible.

Innate Schemata and Racial Purity

Some readers may object to "politicizing" what should be a "scientific" discussion. My contention is that it is necessary to make overt what is latent in treatises on the "innate" nature of man. Consider, for example, Lorenz. Surely, those who have been charmed by his film of himself leading, like a mother goose, a brood of greylag geese about the farmyard will recoil from identifying his works as political. What is political about inborn schemata, innate releasing mechanisms, species-specific mating patterns, and the like? A great deal, as his own writings make clear, when such concepts, of dubious applicability to animal behavior itself (7), are transposed directly to man without attending to species differences and to phyletic levels. Lorenz found it possible to write, in 1940, that the effects of civilization on human beings parallel those of domestication in animals (8). In domesticated animals, he argued, degenerative mutations result in the loss of species-specific releaser mechanisms responding to innate schemata that govern mating patterns and that serve in nature to maintain the purity of the stock. Similar phenomena are said to be an inevitable by-product of civilization unless the state is vigilant (8, pp. 56–75).

> The only resistance which mankind of healthy stock can offer . . . against being penetrated by symptoms of degeneracy is based on the existence of certain innate schemata. . . . Our species-specific sensitivity to the beauty and ugliness of members of our species is intimately connected with the symptoms of degeneration, caused by domestication, which threaten our race. . . . Usually, a man of high value is disgusted with special intensity by slight symptoms of degeneracy in men of the other race. . . . In certain instances, however, we find not only a lack of this selectivity . . . but even a reversal to being attracted by symptoms of degeneracy. . . . Decadent art provides many examples of such a change of signs. . . . The immensely high reproduction rate in the moral imbecile has long been established. . . . This phenomenon leads everywhere . . . to the fact that socially inferior human material is enabled . . . to penetrate and finally to annihilate the healthy nation. The selection for toughness, heroism, social utility . . . must be accomplished by some human institution if mankind, in default of selective factors, is not to be ruined

by domestication-induced degeneracy. *The racial idea as the basis of our state has already accomplished much in this respect.* The most effective race-preserving measure is . . . the greatest support of the natural defenses. . . . We must—and should— rely on the healthy feelings of our Best and charge them with the selection which will determine the prosperity or the decay of our people . . . [italics added].

Thus, it would appear, science warrants society's erecting social prohibitions in order to replace the degenerated innate schemata for racial purity. Lorenz's "scientific" logic justified Nazi legal restrictions against intermarriage with non-Aryans. The wild extrapolations from domestication to civilization, from ritualized animal courtship patterns to human behavior, from species to races, are so gross and unscientific, the conclusions so redolent of concentration camps, that further commentary should be superfluous. Perhaps it is impolite to recall in 1972 what was written in 1940, but I, at least, find 1940 difficult to forget; indeed, I believe it should not be forgotten, lest we find ourselves in Orwell's *1984* for the very best of "scientific" reasons.

My position should not be misconstrued as condemning the study of comparative psychology or the search for biological determinants of human behavior as though such efforts were inherently fascist. What I do inveigh against is the formulation of pseudoscientific support for a priori social ideologies that are projected onto, not "found" in, nature. Such pseudoscience ignores species differences and phyletic levels and misrepresents analogy as homology. For example, attack behavior can be observed in organisms as varied as insect, bird, carnivore, ape, and man. In the first, it may be triggered by trace chemicals; in the second, by territorial defense, but only during the breeding season; in the third, by prey, but only if the appropriate internal state of arousal is present; in the fourth, by the appearance of a predator, if escape routes are unavailable and if the troop is threatened; and in man, by a mere verbal slur, if the social context and prior individual experience indicate attack as the socially appropriate response. The mere observation in divergent species of similar behavioral outcomes that fit the generic label "attack" justifies no conclusion about an underlying aggressive instinct, without detailed study of the conditions evoking, and the mechanism governing, the behavior of each. Such "explanations" reify a descriptive label that has been indiscriminately applied to markedly different levels of behavioral organization, as though naming were the same as explaining.

Teleology or Ontogenesis

Indeed, reports on animal behavior (9) fail to support the concept of an aggressive instinct as an independent motivational force analogous to hunger. That is, there is no predictable periodicity, no measurable changes in internal parameters (such as glucose concentrations in the blood), and no evidence of a "need" to attack in the absence of provocative stimuli. This is not to deny that the ease with which, and the circumstances under which, attack is elicited differs among species, nor that hormones, notably androgens, may have a profound impact on the probability of a fight rather than a flight response in higher organisms (10). The characteristics of the species, the genetic endowment of the individual organism, its prior experience, and the immediate stimuli interact to produce the behavioral outcome. Similar outcomes may result from quite different underlying mechanisms; meaningful comparisons become possible only when the mechanisms have been identified.

Examples could be multiplied. At the most general level, the problem stems from a telic orientation: behavior is "explained" by its outcome, rather than by an analysis of its ontogenesis. The cause is assumed to exist preformed in the organism as an "instinct" or innate pattern of behavior. The Platonic ideal is immanent in the organism. But where is it, when does it appear, and how does it come into being? Not even the most ardent instinctivist would any longer argue that the "instinct" for aggression or courtship rituals or nest building is *in* the fertilized egg. Yet it is confidently asserted that it must have been precoded and ready to go because it appears without any apparent requirement for prior learning.

Let us agree: behavior, like structure, is under genetic control. Animals of two species, reared in an identical environment, will nonetheless behave differently. The argument for innateness—in the sense of an inherited component—is compelling when the distribution of a given characteristic in an offspring generation can be predicted from knowledge of its distribution in the parent generation and the pattern of mating in that generation. However, the genetic evidence does not warrant the other sense in which innate is used—that is, developmental fixity, an imperviousness to environmental influences. Environment influences development by mechanisms that need have nothing to do with learning. For example, certain mutations in wing and eye structure of drosophila are temperature sensitive; if the eggs are maintained at 18°C, the wing or eye develops normally, despite the presence of the mutant gene. This is hardly "learning," but it is evidence that expressivity depends on the environment. It does not make the characteristic any less genetic that its phenotypic expression is modified by temperature. But, by having discovered an array of such factors, the investigator has made a start at identifying the biochemical mechanisms underlying the action of genes. The central issue in the study of development is the problem of the interactions among the programmed but modifiable unfolding of the genome, its cellular envelope, and the surround. If the nucleus of a frog's intestinal cell transplanted into an enucleated frog's egg gives rise to a normal animal (11), then for all of the phenotypic differences between cell types, they share, as we knew they must, the same genetic apparatus, but an apparatus whose expressivity is under cytoplasmic as well as nuclear control.

Even in closely related species, differences are more revealing than similarities in elucidating the principles that govern behavior. Consider the study of bird vocalization, which, beyond its intrinsic fascination, may yet provide important clues to the understanding of sound imitation in man (12). It is a graphic example of a behavioral characteristic that displays remarkable ontogenetic differences in closely related species. Song sparrows. isolated from conspecifics and foster-reared by canaries, nonetheless acquire their own song. Yet meadowlarks, similarly isolated as fledgings, acquire the song of the particular foster species: wood pewees, yellowthroats, or red-winged blackbirds (13). Still different is the whitecrowned sparrow, which must hear the adult model of its song during a "sensitive period" of development in order to acquire it;

nonetheless, if the fledgling white-crowned sparrow is simultaneously exposed to conspecifics and to two sympatric species, it "learns" only its own song. Once learned, the song persists, even if the adult is isolated. In the case of the goldfinch, the adult bird is able to learn new flight songs from other species (*14*). These few examples merely hint at the complexity of a growing field of inquiry. Precise attention to differences among species, the interrelationship of those differences with the ecology of the species, and the ultimate identification of the underlying neuromechanisms are what we will require for models that may have heuristic value in studying imitation behavior in man.

Language: A Universal Human Trait

Man's biological equipment is now, if ever, an essential topic of study. That equipment evolved over the 5 million years which elapsed between the australopithecine hominids and *Homo sapiens;* it provided the means for survival in an environment not yet altered by artifacts. The spread of our species and the rapid multiplication of our numbers in the past five millennia attest to the adaptability to that biological equipment to circumstances that did not exist when it was elaborated. It is becoming painfully evident that the changes we have wrought in the past five decades threaten our continuing survival under conditions of an exponential rate of population growth. It now becomes necessary to ask: How adaptable is man? Is mere perpetuation of the species, without concern for the quality of life, a sufficient criterion for man, even if it has been so for nature? Man's intelligence permits him the conscious choice of goals and so differentiates him from the rest of animate existence.

How, then, to discern the nature of man? Two general approaches suggest themselves—the comparative and the developmental. In the first, we compare and contrast the characteristics of men and women in the diverse societies that people this planet in the hope of extracting common denominators that express man's "essential nature"; in the second, we study the interaction between the infant and his social and biological environment as he grows to adulthood.

One trait common to man everywhere is language; in the sense that only the human species displays it, the capacity to acquire language must be genetic. As Chomsky has pointed out (*15*), among the unique aspects of human language learning are the child's ability to infer syntactical rules from a limited set of input samples and, in consequence, his extraordinary capacity to generate grammatical sentences that he has never heard. The language he speaks is determined by the language he hears, but the capacity for language must be a consequence of the genetic programming of brain networks as these respond to maturation and experience. Languages, insofar as they have been studied, appear to share fundamental structural characteristics, a universality that argues for an as-yet-to-be-identified basis in common structures in the central nervous system. I recall the example of the white-crowned sparrow, which, though it must learn its song, is structured in such a way that its neural networks resonate only to a restricted set of external harmonic sequences. The data of linguistics suggest the possibility of a similar restriction on the form of language and the nature of grammatical structures; they imply limited variability in the neural schemata underlying language structures. Further refinement in our knowledge of these cognitive universals may yet enable us to propose models of neural mechanisms, which must then be sought experimentally.

Benzer (*16*) has brought the tools of genetic analysis to bear on behavioral mutants in drosophila. By the ingenious use of mosaics with phenotypic characteristics that permit the morphological identification of individual cells that carry or lack the mutant gene for phototaxis, he has found the source of the behavioral deviation to be structural abnormalities in the affected eye. In flies in which mosaicism is present within a single eye, histological techniques and single cell recordings can specify the deficit even more precisely. Cellular markers "provide powerful techniques for tracing the details of cell lineage during development, as well as genetic dissection of the functioning nervous system" (*17*). Even the limited complexity of the drosophila's central nervous system defies analysis by current techniques, but an important beginning has been made in relating genetically determined behavioral differences to underlying physiological mechanisms.

The Diversity of Human Culture

If language be one of the common features of human culture, even more remarkable are the diverse behaviors that cultures shape and are shaped by. What is labeled "masculine" in one culture and ascribed to the nature of maleness is regarded as "feminine" in another. Children are permitted uninhibited sexual expression and yet become monogamous adults in one culture; in another, preadult sexuality is heavily censored, whereas adult monogamy is privately violated while it is publicly proclaimed. Child care may be the responsibility of the nuclear family or of the group. The same Netsilik Eskimos who are loving and devoted parents can allow a female infant who is not "spoken for" in a prearranged marriage to die unattended and ignored if she is not given a name and is thus, by definition, not yet human. The phenomenon of war is unknown to one society, appears in a second only under environmental stress, but is a lethal "game" without apparent material benefit in a third. Indeed, if we were to permit ourselves the argument that the more "primitive the society, the more true to man's original nature the behavior displayed therein, we should have to conclude, as did Sahlins (18), that "war increases in intensity, bloodiness and duration . . . through the evolution of culture, reaching its culmination in modern civilization." However agreeable, the argument for the pacific character of natural man, uncorrupted by the social order, is inadmissible; culture is as complete and complex in contemporary hunting and gathering tribes, despite their primitive technology, as it is in our own—man is man only in society.

What is striking in this very partial inventory is the remarkable diversity of the human behaviors evoked by various but viable cultures. If we explain the murderous raids of Brazilian Indians on the basis of an innate aggressive instinct, we shall have to invent an involved theory of repression, reaction formulation, and sublimation to account for the peacefulness of the Eskimo. Would it not be far more parsimonious to begin with the assumption that men are by nature neither aggressive nor peaceful, but rather are fashioned into one or another as the result of a complex interaction between a widely, but not infinitely, modifiable set of biological givens and the shaping influences of the biological environment, the cultural envelope, and individual experience?

The very ubiquity of violence in Western society, however we explain its genesis historically, guarantees that children are surfeited with opportunities to learn violent behavior. The child sees that violence pays off; he is provided with adult models of violent behavior with whom to identify (television pales beside real life). Violence as an appropriate response to the resolution of intergroup conflict is sanctioned by national leaders. Reflect: the President of the United States intervened to prevent the immediate imprisonment of Calley, an officer convicted of mass murder in Vietnam by a jury of combat veterans. Consider: the Attorney General of the United States declined to press charges in the Kent State student murders. What are the ethical values these actions by national leaders convey? When violence is sancitioned, it will increase. It can be expected to generalize to situations not "intended" to come within official pardon. Learning may not account completely for human aggression, but the social forces in contemporary society that encourage its development are so evident (*19*) that preoccupation with hypothesized biological factors is almost quixotic.

Emphasis on the very marked differences among cultures may obscure what has been, until recently, a conservative tradition within each. Children reared within a particular value system could expect to complete their days within that system. Values now change so rapidly that what a child is taught by his parents may no longer be functional when that child becomes an adolescent, let alone an adult. However wide the range of behaviors man can exhibit—evidenced by the comparison of one society with another—the task of developing adaptive attributes is very different when radically changed behaviors are required within an *individual's* lifetime rather than over the history of a people. The question now becomes, not how malleable is man, but how much change can a man undergo and still maintain his psychic integration?

Here we lack empirical data; there is no precedent for such rapid change. We confront the fundamental relevance of studies of child development. In a stable society, the price demanded by acculturation may or may not have been burdensome, but clearly it was bearable, or else that society would not have perpetuated itself. Studies of child development were important even then, if only to learn how to mitigate those burdens. But if we are to enable our children to cope with a world whose present shape we barely comprehend and whose future configurations we can only guess at dimly, then we are embarked on an enterprise that is the very keystone of the sciences of survival.

Man as His Own Chief Product

I will forego detailing what we already know and ignore at the peril of the next generation: that the rapidly growing brain of fetus and infant is excruciatingly dependent on the adequacy of its nutrition (20); surely, no further amassing of scientific facts is needed to justify international commitment to the protection of the unborn and the newly born. What has become equally evident is that the nutriment the growing brain requires is affective and cognitive as well as alimentary. The extraordinary dependence of the human young upon adult care and caring provides both an unparalleled opportunity for mental and emotional development and a period of vulnerability to profound distortion by neglect (21). Infants in orphanages lag markedly in development, despite normal food intake, if denied a responsive human environment. There are indeed gaps in our knowledge of this early developmental sequence: just how much stimulation is optimal, just what balance is to be struck between gratification and denial, just what is the best mix between social interaction and time to be alone? Yet the outlines are clear enough to allow no excuse for what we permit to befall defenseless children, who suffer from the contumely we visit on their parents. Each infant differs from the others: no two, except for identical twins, share a common genome, and even identical twins may differ phenotypically because of gestational inequalities. We do not understand individual variability sufficiently well to fashion optimal environments for each child, but surely this does not mitigate our failure to provide at least those general requirements shared by all children (22).

Ignorance, as well as lack of commitment, becomes a limiting factor when children reach the years of formal education. The shortcomings of available theories of learning constrain our ability to respond to individual differences in the way children fashion their personalities and cognitive styles (23). There may be much to be gained from comparative studies of animal learning—to be sure, we are primates ourselves, but primates of a very special sort. We are no less subject to classical and operant conditioning, to trial and error learning, and the like, but only we have the capacity for superordinate modes of verbal learning, and these require much deeper study than has been devoted to them. Our challenge is no longer transmitting solutions that have been successful in the past, but helping our children to acquire attitudes and sets for problem-solving that will enable them to meet undreamed-of challenges to their capacities.

We have done least well at the task of encouraging the development of humane values based upon the recognition that we are a single species. The idea of brotherhood is not new. but what is special to our times is that brotherhood has become the precondition for survival. It may have sufficed in the past to spur a child to learn for the sheer satisfaction of his own success. If we have listened to what our students are telling us, learning for personal embellishment or for the acquisition of virtuosity no longer satisfies a generation intensely aware of injustice and impermanence. Learning must become a social enterprise, informed by concern for others (24).

This it can become. Man is his own chief product. The infant who discovers that he can control the movements of his own fingers transforms himself from observer into actor. The child who masters reading unlocks the treasury of the world's heritage. The adolescent who insists upon a critical reexamination of conventional wisdom is making himself into an adult. And the adult whose concerns extend beyond family and beyond nation to mankind has become fully human.

By acting on behalf of our species we become men and women. In a world in which wars rage, in which repressive governments subjugate their peoples, in which the pursuit of personal affluence ravages an environment that must be shared by all, there can be no neutrality. Members of the university community carry a heavy measure of responsibility for the privilege accorded them; that responsibility is to pledge themselves to the service of man if knowledge is to be transformed into wisdom.

The study of man takes its meaning from involvement in the

struggle for human betterment. Struggle it is and will be: privilege does not surrender easily; false belief is not readily dispelled. The optimism about man's potential I urge upon you is not the self-comfort of reading history as a saga of progressive liberation which will one day be complete. It matters, and matters dearly, to Vietnamese and to Pakistani, to Americans and to Canadians, whether that day comes sooner or later; whether it comes at all is not determined by history but by the men and the women who make history. This has been eloquently stated by the Cuban poet Padilla:

History's going to save us—we were thinking.
Going to save us—were we dreaming?
It wasn't all just uprisings, barricades, bonfires;
in our heads it was a dress of bubbling foam, a
Rhine maiden with clear eyes, smiling, standing
at the door, hand outstretched
toward a hungry and waiting people.
    But there was no one in the doorway. Nor in the house.
    Instead we stumbled. They shoved us inside. We broke our
        teeth going in, got our jaw smashed.
We found tools and weapons and we
fought, we struggled, we worked and continued
fighting. But it's true, old Marx,
that History is not enough.
    Important occasions,
    man makes them.
    It's a real, live man who does it,
who masters it, who will fight.
History by itself does
    nothing, dear friends.
        It does absolutely nothing.

REFERENCES AND NOTES

1. N. Wiener, *Science* 131, 1355 (1960).
2. D. Morris, *The Naked Ape* (McGraw-Hill, New York, 1967); R. Ardrey, *African Genesis* (Dell, New York, 1961); *The Territorial Imperative* (Dell, New York, 1966); K. Lorenz, *On Aggression* (Harcourt, Brace & World, New York, 1966).

3. S. Freud, *Reflections on War and Death* (Moffat, Yard, New York, 1918), p. 60.
4. S. Freud, *Civilization and Its Discontents* (Hogarth, London, 1930), p. 102.
5. P. Pinel, *A Treatise on Insanity,* D. D. Davis, Transl. (Hafner, New York, 1962); G. Rosen, *Madness in Society* (Univ. of Chicago Press, Chicago, 1968); A. Deutsch, *The Mentally Ill in America* (Columbia Univ. Press, New York, ed. 2, 1949).
6. E. M. Gruenberg, *Amer. J. Orthopsychiat.* 37, 645 (1967).
7. D. S. Lehrman, in *Development and Evolution of Behavior,* L. R. Aronson, E. Tobach, D. S. Lehrman, J. S. Rosenblatt, Eds. (Freeman, San Francisco, 1970); E. Tobach, L. R. Aronson, E. Shaw, Eds. *The Biopsychology of Development* (Academic Press, New York, 1971); L. R. Aronson, E. Tobach, D. S. Lehrman, J. S. Rosenblatt, Eds., *Selected Writings of T. C. Schneirla* (Freeman, San Francisco, 1972).
8. K. Lorenz, Z. *Angew. Psychol. Charakterkunde* 59, 2 (1940).
9. J. P. Scott, *Aggression* (Univ. of Chicago Press, Chicago, 1958).
10. ——, *Amer. J. Orthopsychiat.* 40, 568 (1970).
11. J. B. Gurdon, *Sci. Amer.* 219, 24 (Sept. 1968); —— and H. R. Woodland, *Biol. Rev.* 43, 233 (1968).
12. R. A. Hinde, Ed., *Bird Vocalizations* (Cambridge Univ. Press, London, 1969).
13. M. Konishi and F. Nottebohm, in *Bird Vocalizations,* R. A. Hinde, Ed. (Cambridge Univ. Press, London, 1969), pp. 29–48.
14. P. C. Mundinger, *Science* 168, 480 (1970).
15. N. Chomsky, *Language* 35, 26 (1959); *Language and Mind* (Harcourt, Brace & World, New York, 1968); J. Lyons, *Noam Chomsky* (Viking, New York, 1970).
16. S. Benzer, *Proc. Nat. Acad. Sci. U.S.* 58, 1112 (1967); *J. Amer. Med. Assn.* 218, 1015 (1971); R. J. Konopka and S. Benzer, *Proc. Nat. Acad. Sci. U.S.* 68, 2112 (1971).
17. Y. Hotta and S. Benzer, *Proc. Nat. Acad. Sci. U.S.* 67, 1156 (1970).
18. M. D. Sahlins, *Sci. Amer.* 203, 76 (Sept. 1960).
19. J. L. Singer, Ed., *The Control of Aggression and Violence* (Academic Press, New York, 1971).
20. M. Winick, *Pediatrics* 47, 969 (1971); H. G. Birch and J. D. Gussow, *Disadvantaged Children: Health, Nutrition and School Failure* (Harcourt Brace Jovanovich, New York, 1970); H. G. Birch, C. Pineiro, E. Alcade, T. Toga, J. Cravioto, *Pediat. Res.* 5, 579 (1971).

21. L. Eisenberg, in *The Social Responsibility of Gynecology and Obstetrics*, A. C. Barnes, Ed. (John Hopkins Press, Baltimore, 1965), pp. 53–79.
22. B. M. Caldwell, *Amer. J. Orthopsychiat.* 37, 8 (1967); L. Eisenberg, *ibid.*, 39, 389 (1969).
23. S. H. White and H. D. Fishbein, in *Behaviorial Science in Pediatric Medicine*, M. Talbot, J. Kagan, L. Eisenberg, Eds. (Saunders, Philadelphia, 1971), pp. 188–227.
24. L. Eisenberg, *Science* 167, 1688 (1970); K. Kenniston, *Amer. J. Orthopsychiat.* 40, 577 (1970); S. E. Luria and Z. Luria, *Daedalus* 99, 75 (1970).
25. H. Padilla, "Important Occasions," P. Blackburn, Transl., *N.Y. Rev. Books* (3 June 1971), p. 5.

PETER H. KLOPFER

From Ardrey to Altruism: A Discourse on the Biological Basis of Human Behavior

Extrapolations from the behavior of animals to that of man frequently err when they assume the behavior in question to be a unitary phenomenon. For example, the territorial behavior of vertebrates, which has been cited as providing a biological explanation (and justification) for human property rights, probably has as many different bases as there are species. Extrapolations, if they are to be useful, must be accurate. This requires us to focus upon similarities in evolutionary and physiological processes rather than upon similarities in final appearance.

Ever since the notion of an evolutionary continuity among organisms was broached, extrapolations from animals to man have been used to explain human behavior and institutions. For instance, Darwin's theory of evolution by natural selection was extended to explain and justify a competitive social and economic order. The fact that the popular formulation of Darwinism, "nature red in tooth and claw," is actually an erroneous statement of Darwin's theory was overlooked as easily as the irrelevance of natural selection itself to the establishment of human economic institutions; our lives are filled with examples of maladaptive practices maintained through the force of our conciousness and thus not directly subject to the arbitration of natural selection. Ironically, many of the same facts and lines of reasoning used to support 19th Century

From *Behavioral Science,* vol, 13, 1968, pp. 399–401. Reprinted by permission.

laissez faire were later adduced in support of a cooperative, communal, pacifistic social order, by Prince Kropotkin and Warder C. Allee.

In recent months we have seen another attempt at extrapolation, which, through the sponsorship of a national weekly magazine, has attained an immense commercial success. While its author may claim otherwise, the book itself is largely fiction, and affords a good example of the dangers of analogic reasoning. I refer to Ardrey's *The Territorial Imperative.*

Ardrey's theme is that man's aggressive tendencies are tied to the defense of home and country, his "territory," because man, in common with most other organisms, is biologically a "territorial animal." Ardrey's errors in advancing this proposition are of two sorts: ignorance and reason. With regard to the first, an examination of the relevant biological literature shows there exists a striking diversity in kinds of territorial behavior. It is not quite true to say there are as many kinds of territory as there are kinds of animals, but it is very nearly true. Territories may be defended by single animals, by pairs, by groups; they may serve as staging areas for courtship, for nesting, for feeding; for all of these or none of these. Territories may be defended all year around, for several months, or only a few short weeks. They may be defended against all comers, only those of the same sex and species, or only those indulging in certain activities. In short, territorial behavior is far from being a unitary phenomenon. It is a heterogeneous complex, and to assume a single underlying motive, whether in terms of proximate, physiological, or ultimate, evolutionary forces is to assume too much (P. H. Klopfer, 1969). Significantly among the nonhuman primates, territoriality is hardly less varied in all its aspects—except perhaps, in being less pronounced—than in birds or reptiles. Ardrey conveniently overlooks this "minor" fact, too.

Ardrey's logical error is of no less consequence. As the anthropologist Leach has put it, "if we define the word 'aggression' in a behavioristic [that is, objective] way, . . . then man, like any other animal, has built-in 'innate' ways of exhibiting aggression. What is in dispute is whether man likewise has a built-in tendency to defend his home territory so that the precise circumstances in which he will exhibit this aggressive behavior are predictable." To put it another way, Ardrey confuses a motor act—overt behavior—with its underlying mechanism and evolutionary cause (see P. H. Klopfer and J. P. Hailman, 1967). If we see a bird defending its territory in a particular way, we attach to its behavior the term "aggressive," which implies a particular emotional state. We cannot then argue that because men *feel* "aggressive" when they defend their territories, the biological basis for the two acts must be similar.

None of this should be taken to imply that human behavior cannot be understood by reference to animal studies. Indeed, much research is predicated upon the contrary assumption. But it is necessary to avoid the pitfalls of analogic reasoning. Consider this illustration of such an extrapolation, a speculation upon the biological basis of ethical systems.

By ethics is meant no more than strongly held beliefs regarding "right" and "wrong" conduct. The actual content of any ethical belief, that is, what is considered right or wrong, is for the moment, irrelevant. We are constantly making ethical judgments: sometimes we refuse to consciously acknowledge the moral consequences of our acts, but these consequences are no more likely to disappear than does the lion when the ostrich puts his head in the sand. The question is, why do ethical systems exist? Why do we feel guilt upon the commission or omission of certain acts?

Waddington, in his *The Ethical Animal*, (1960) has provided a reasonable answer. The most distinctive feature of our species is the ability to transmit information in a nongenetic fashion, through the establishment of traditions. This is not an absolutely unique feature: birds may have traditional nesting sites and monkey colonies, traditional preferences for certain foods. The behavior in question is transmitted by the members of one generation training those of the next. Even for some insects this is true (Klopfer, 1962). Man is distinctive in the degree to which sociocultural means have replaced DNA, the genetic material. But, tradition building has one essential element: the young, the infants, must be designed so as to be effective receivers of information. In Waddington's words, "This system of socio-genetic transmission of information from one generation to the next can, like any other system of passing on information, only operate successfully if the information is not only transmitted but is also received. The newborn infant, in fact, has to be molded into an information acceptor. It has to be ready to believe (in some general sense of that word) what it is told. Unless this happens the mechanism of information transfer cannot operate. Once it has happened and the mechanism becomes functional then the socio-genetic system carries out a function analogous to that by which the formation and union of gametes transmits genetic information. And just as the content of heredity transmission becomes modified by natural selection, so the content of socio-genetic transmission can be modified by analogous processes, such as the confrontation of beliefs with empirical evidence and so on."

In this discussion we have so far implied by ethics a system of strongly held beliefs relating to "right" and "wrong" conduct, but without regard to the content of the system. Waddington's argument merely asserts that the development of some sort of ethics is an inevitable concomitant of the evolution of the social species, man. Particular needs of man may also favor the evolution of a particular ethical content. If, for instance, intensive and close inbreeding lower fitness—and by "fitness" is meant the measure of an individual's proportionate contribution to the gene pool of the future—those individuals practicing inbreeding will be replaced by those who do not. This might well be the explanation for the near-universality of incest taboos, even, possibly in Rhesus monkeys (D. S. Sade, personal communication). Consider, too, the altruistic ethic: the belief that to sacrifice oneself for one's fellows is good and noble. If altruists are more likely to die than nonaltruists, how could altruism evolve? The answer lies in the fact that if one parent's death results in the survival of at least two of his or her offspring, that genotype will have a greater representation in future generations than one belonging to nonsacrificial parents who lose their offspring. Similarly, if an altruistic act causes the death of the actor, but saves two siblings, that genotype will be favored. Of course, the more distant the genetic relationship between the altruist and those upon whom his benefice is spent, the more of the latter must be saved before the altruistic genes are favored. This theme has been developed quantitatively by W. D. Hamilton

(1964). Specifically, if the gain to a relative of degree r is K-times the disadvantage to the altruist, K must exceed $1/r$. This explanation for the evolution of altruism, incidently, does away with the necessity of invoking such ill-defined concepts as "group selection" (for example Wynne-Edwards).

At the least, these hypotheses are open to experimental validation. Thus, developmental studies of children should reveal the characteristics of the punitive authority-accepting system. Observations of monkeys show that young and subordinate animals may mimic their superiors, but not the contrary. Is this susceptibility to the influence of others age-dependent? To what degree is it a function of other rearing practices? Questions about ethics can be formulated in a biologically reasonable way so as to provide valid insights into the biological basis of human behavior. This fact alone denies any value to superficial extrapolations like those of Ardrey's.

REFERENCES

Allee, W. C. *Cooperation Among Animals.* New York: H. Schuman, 1938.
Ardrey, R. *The Territorial Imperative.* New York: Atheneum, 1966.
Hamilton, W. D. *The Genetic Evolution of Social Behaviour,* I & II. *J. Theoret. Biol.,* 1964, 7, 1–52.
Klopfer, P. H. *Behavioral Aspects of Ecology.* Englewood Cliffs, New Jersey: Prentice-Hall, 1967.
Klopfer, P. H. and J. P. Hailman. *An Introduction to Animal Behavior.* Englewood Cliffs, N.J.: Prentice-Hall, 1967.
Klopfer, P. H. *Territories and Habitats: A Discourse on the Spatial Distribution of Animals.* New York: Basic Books, 1969.
Prince Kropotkin. *Mutual Aid; A Factor in Evolution.* New York: Alfred Knopf, 1914.
Leach, E. *N.Y. Review of Books,* 1966, 7, 10; and pp. 154–55, present volume.
Sade, D. S. Personal communication.
Waddington, C. H. *The Ethical Animal.* London: Allen & Unwin, 1960.
Wynne-Edwards, V. C. *Animal Dispersion in Relation to Social Behavior.* New York: Hafner, 1962.

S. A. BARNETT

On the Hazards of Analogies

Samuel Johnson once wrote that weekly reviewers do not read books, but "lay hold of a topic, and write chiefly from their own wits." He added: "monthly reviewers are duller men, and are glad to read the books through."

Johnson's comment came to mind on a reading of some of the early reviews of *On Aggression*. These discuss especially the similarities that Lorenz believes exist in animal and human behavior. Joseph Alsop, in the *New Yorker*, detects a conflict between "the ethologists" (that is, Lorenz), on the one hand, and psychoanalysts and social scientists on the other: the latter, he suggests, are likely to regard analogies between ourselves and other species as invalid. By contrast, Anthony Storr, a psychotherapist who writes for the *Sunday Times* of London, accepts Lorenz's views on geese and men without protest. But Arthur Koestler, in the London *Observer*, describes these views as a "lusty gallop on a hobby horse," which it would be churlish to grudge.

Unfortunately, this reviewer finds himself forced to be churlish: a book prominently reviewed by celebrated writers becomes important regardless of its intrinsic merits. The reviews mentioned (all by non-zoologists) agree on one thing: that at least Lorenz's accounts of animal behavior are authoritative and reliable. But *On*

From *Scientific American*, February 1967. Copyright © 1967 by Scientific American, Inc. Reprinted by permission. New material added by author, 1968.

Aggression does not in fact represent the methods or opinions current in ethology (the science of animal behavior).

The main theme is stated in the introduction: "behavioral science really knows so much about the natural history of aggression that it does become possible to make statements about the causes of much of its malfunctioning in man." First, then, let us examine the "natural history of aggression," as Lorenz describes it. In chapter 3, entitled "What Aggression Is Good For," we are told that "we can safely assume that the most important function of intra-specific aggression is the even distribution of the animals of a particular species over an inhabitable area." But should we assume this? Lorenz does not discuss the evidence. The members of many, perhaps most, species are distributed, not evenly, but in quite large groups, crowds, or herds. These include large hoofed mammals and ground-living apes. Of them, Lorenz writes, "intra-specific aggression plays no essential part in the 'spacing out' of the species." He adds that among the herds of hoofed mammals there are no territorial boundaries.

This unsupported statement contradicts the observations of several careful workers. In 1956 William Graf described the territorial behavior of the elk, *Cervus canadensis*. These animals make territorial marks by scraping the bark off trees and rubbing their faces in the scrape. Graf also refers to the similar behavior of the black-tailed deer, *Odocoileus hemionus*. In 1957 Carl B. Koford described the behavior of the vicuna, *Vicugna vicugna,* whose territorial defense depends largely on a characteristic posture, in which the head and tail are held high. More recently there have been accounts of territory in the reindeer, *Rangifer tarandus,* and the Uganda cob, *Adenota kob*. Still other examples could be cited.

Lorenz also tells us that, when birds assemble in flocks outside the breeding season, they "lack aggression." This bare statement certainly needs qualification. For example, A.W. Stokes has described, in great detail, antagonistic behavior among blue tits, *Parus caeruleus,* at a winter feeding station. The work by Stokes is particularly important (and unusual) in that it gives *quantitative* information on the effects of various postures on the behavior of the birds toward which these signals are directed.

Further examples of disregard of evidence come in the account of the social behavior of wild rats, to which Lorenz gives a chapter. He refers to the "bloody mass battles of the brown rat," *Rattus norvegicus*. Nothing of the sort appears in any of the detailed accounts of this species: in fact, serious clashes, when they do occur, consist of an attack by one rat on a single opponent; the latter does not fight back. Nor is there pair formation among wild rats, as Lorenz states: a female in oestrus accepts males indiscriminately; and males do not fight for females. (The only reference in the bibliography to work on rats is to a short paper on the interactions of "brown" and "black" rats. Encounters between these species are not bloody mass battles either.) Rats are also described as "models of social virtue," "cruel to their subordinates" and "horrible brutes." And they are said to transmit by tradition knowledge of the danger of poisons. The last statement is reminiscent of the simple tales, often written by clergymen in earlier times, about animal co-operation and its moral implications. (A popular story was of the old blind rat guided by a younger rat by means of a twig.)

In the same passage there is a reference to a similar transmission of pathfinding, and of recognition of foods and enemies. It is not clear in just which species these abilities are supposed to exist. There are evidently traditions of food choice within monkey colonies. As for pathfinding, young animals often follow older ones of their own species, but this has, as a rule, nothing to do with teaching or learning a tradition: there is a deep gulf between *following*, on the one hand, and *imitation* (or learning by observation) on the other. Any discussion of tradition in other species demands a critical account of this distinction, and of the kind of evidence needed before the existence of imitation may be accepted. This is perfectly practicable even in a popular work, but it is not attempted.

A curious digression concerns "the scene that must have taken place when, for the first time, two enemy Indians became friends by smoking a pipe together." The passage that follows is quite unrelated to anything known about the actual behavior of North American Indians.

Another passage more reminiscent of a moral tract than of ethology asks what has been learned "from the objective observation of animals" on the "ways intra-specific aggression assists the preservation of an animal species." Among the benefits, we are told, is that the community is so organized that "a few wise males, the 'senate,' acquire the authority essential for making and carrying out decisions for the good of the community." Among some species of Primates, elderly males do play a special part in social life: a single, senior baboon, *Papio,* for example, sometimes stops conflicts. But there is no authority for suggesting the existence of anything that can be called a senate (or legislature): not even male apes combine to regulate the conduct of their group, although an assault by an elderly baboon may be checked by a group of younger ones.

These examples of Lorenz's method illustrate a general difficulty which all scientific writers on behavior have to face: the use of colloquial language often makes exact description difficult, and rational explanation impossible. A lexical definition of "aggression," for example, is "assault." Yet the animal behavior commonly called "aggressive" consists usually of displays (or signals) which induce the withdrawal of intruders: it does not often involve a clash. (Even when there is actual contact, in natural conditions there is hardly ever serious injury.) The displays which lead to withdrawal may be postures, noises—such as bird song—or odors, and are often called threats. A lexical definition of "threat" is "a declaration of hostile intent." But it is difficult to give a precise meaning to a statement about what an animal *intends.* The word "threat" could be redefined as a signal which tends to induce withdrawal by a member of the same species. This at least allows the term to be used without ambiguity. An objection is that it ignores the performer's internal state. Among ourselves we think of threat as an index of anger or fear. To speak objectively about the counterparts of anger and fear in other species, we need to know something of the physiology of the behavior observed. This entails exact descriptions of electrical, chemical, and structural changes in the nervous system.

A start has been made in this difficult area, but it is not recognised by Lorenz. Instead, there are many references to "instinctual urges," "aggressive impulses," and similar undefined qualities. One of the difficulties in commenting on this book is indeed that key terms are not defined; much is ambiguous or obscure for this reason alone. The progress of science has depended on the rejection of what Newton called "occult qualities." Descriptions in science are of properties which can be reliably observed: "real is what can be measured." We no longer attribute the motion of the planets to angels; we do not "explain," or even name, the steady temperature of a mammal or a bird by an undefined "innate heat"; nor do we account for disease by the presence of demons.

In one passage Lorenz refers to the uselessness of terms such as "reproductive instinct" as explanations, but he repeatedly uses them elsewhere. The human "aggressive drive" is often mentioned; but, if this or any similar expression has a meaning, it is only that almost any human being *can* be provoked to violence. The crucial question is how the violence arises.

The lack of definition is especially awkward when Lorenz discusses patterns of behavior, such as displays, songs, modes of nest building, and so on, which are common to a whole species. Lorenz refers to these species-characteristic patterns as "hereditary," but this represents a confusion between heredity and development. Only *differences* between individuals may properly be called "hereditary." This confusion is an aspect of Lorenz's failure to take account of the development of behavior during the life history of each individual. Uniformity of behavior within a species has sometimes been thought to indicate complete stability in its development. This is now well known to be unjustified, and the concept of "innate behavior," as it appeared in ethological writings of, say, fifteen years ago, has been much modified.

Rhesus monkeys, *Macaca mulatta,* provide a notable example. These animals, like many others, have a status system or peck order within each group; whenever (as in natural conditions) there is a settled status system, conflict is, at most, trivial and harmless. Such social behavior might in the past have been called "instinctive." But if young monkeys are reared without other monkeys, they fail to develop the ability to take part in a stable society: when given companions later on, they are persistently "aggressive" in the sense that they frequently attack and injure others. These celebrated observations, made by Harry F. Harlow and his colleagues, are, of all studies of animal "aggression," the most relevant to Lorenz's theme. They illustrate the importance of studying how social (and antisocial) behavior *develops.* They are not mentioned in *On Aggression.*

There is much discussion of the *evolutionary* origin of behavior patterns. Great emphasis is put on the "triumph ceremony" of geese and other birds; the birds are described as if they were human beings. This ceremony, also called an "appeasement" activity, is seen in different forms in different species. Lorenz writes: "From this gradation we can form a picture of how, in the course of phylogeny, an anger-diverting gesture of embarrassment has developed into a bond which shows a mysterious relationship to that other bond between human beings and which seems to us the strongest and most beautiful on earth."

This and similar passages assume that evolutionary changes in behavior can be traced just as structural changes are traced, and that displays, such as those of courtship and territorial defense, have gradually evolved from other activities. For instance, birds take care of their body surfaces by preening. The displays of many species include movements which resemble preening, many of which show off in a striking way their characteristic feather patterns. Movements which originally had one function are supposed to have changed during evolution, so that they now have another as well. At the same time, the structures involved have evidently become more conspicuous, sometimes by acquiring bright colors. Julian Huxley named this hypothetical process "ritualization," and Lorenz makes many confident, dogmatic assertions about it. The workers who have contributed most in this field are Niko Tinbergen and his pupils. Tinbergen has written: "Comparative description of signals . . . [has] given us an idea of their evolutionary orgin and . . . leads to a description of their alleged ritualization. Assuming that our reasoning has been correct, can we guess what selection pressures must have been responsible for ritualization? The paucity of experimental work on survival value renders such guesses doubly hazardous." This cautious, critical statement represents the actual position among research workers on behavior today.

There are passages in *On Aggression* about stereotyped behavior in which the development of the behavior of an individual seems to be regarded as the same as evolutionary change in behavior due to natural selection. For instance, there are many rituals in human behavior which we call "superstitious," and in obsessional neurosis, induced by an unfavorable early environment, they become excessive. Lorenz writes of obsessional behavior and of the fixed action patterns of animals: "all these phenomena are related"; and he states: "all human art primarily developed in the service of rituals"; characteristically, instead of discussing the difficult problems raised by these proposals, he precedes the last-quoted statement with the words, "There is hardly a doubt that. . . ."

The emphasis on the stereotyped behavior of species other than man, and the neglect of behavior which can be readily altered by experience, is especially strange when the aim is to throw light on human behavior. Man is the one species whose social behavior (except in infancy) does *not* depend on a uniform set of social signals: all our customs, including language, depend on the training we receive in our own family or community. Hence arises the immense diversity of *mores* within the single species, *Homo sapiens*. Yet Lorenz writes: "human social behavior, far from being determined by reason and cultural tradition alone, is still subject to all the laws prevailing in all phylogenetically adapted instinctive behavior."

This statement is made without supporting argument—unless analogies constitute an argument. The great debate that has long raged on this sort of question is acknowledged only in a few statements such as: "The completely erroneous view that animal and human behavior is predominantly reactive and that, even if it contains any innate elements at all, it can be altered to an unlimited extent by learning, comes from a radical misunderstanding of certain democratic principles: it is utterly at variance with these principles to admit that human beings are not born equal and that not all have equal chances of becoming ideal citizens." Yet in fact there is no school of thought which states that animal, or even human, behavior can be altered to an unlimited extent by learning; and people who work for social justice do not say that all are born equal, but only that all should have equivalent opportunities to develop their abilities to the full. Lorenz may look back nostalgically to "the good old days when there was still a Habsburg monarchy and there were still domestic servants"; but this does not justify him in ascribing to his opponents opinions they do not hold.

What, then, are Lorenz's proposals on the causes and treatment of human "aggression"? What revelation has he in store for his readers? One is that there should be more international sport. This widely acceptable suggestion has often been made without benefit of ethology; which is not surprising, since—as Lorenz himself points out—sport is "specifically human." Lorenz does not, however, discuss whether there is evidence that it would reduce other kinds of conflict between nations or individuals. Another suggestion is that there should be more art, science, and medicine—the pursuits of truth, beauty, and healing; this, of course, is still more readily acceptable, since it has been a familiar notion for several thousand years. We are also urged to laugh more, and to love each other indiscriminately. The last recommendation perhaps accounts for the following sentence: "Not even the most ruthlessly daring demagogues have ever undertaken to proclaim the whole art of an enemy nation or political party as entirely worthless." It would be more appropriate if Lorenz had reminded his younger readers of the attempt by the Nazis, between 1933 and 1945, to destroy, not only the German Jewish community, but also the whole of Jewish culture.

The sentence last quoted strongly suggests that Lorenz lives in a private world, insulated from the real one. The same applies to his prinicipal recommendation for further research. "I believe—and human psychologists, particularly psychoanalysts, should test this— that present-day civilized man suffers from insufficient discharge of his aggressive drive." Never mind now that "aggressive drive" is not defined. This and similar notions have been debated among medical men and psychologists for several decades, and are the subject of a substantial literature, none of which is mentioned by Lorenz. The late Karen Horney, a leader of a prominent psychiatric school which especially emphasises this aspect of psychopathology, has written of "the neurotic person's need for indiscriminate supremacy."

Still more to the point is the research which has been done on the developmental psychology of the bully. In the 1940s H. V. Dicks produced convincing evidence that the personalities of the brutal, bigoted German soldiers, who formed a substantial minority of the Reichswehr, were products of families in which the father was a tyrant and the mother submerged. T. W. Adorno and his colleagues independently published a longer and celebrated work, *The Authoritarian Personality*, which extended and confirmed this analysis. On the development of "aggression" in childhood, Lorenz has little to say except for a reference to "countless unbearably rude [American] children" who, he tells us, were a product of the view that children ought to be "spared all disappointments and indulged in every way."

Being a dull man, in Samuel Johnson's classification, I have "read the book through" more than once. On each reading more self-contradictions, confusions, and questionable statements have emerged. How much more acceptable would have been an unpretentious account of actual behavior! It is sad that so much talent should have been misapplied in this fashion. As it is, since *On Aggression* is presented as authoritative at least on animal behavior, it is liable to bring ethology into disrepute with critical readers, and also to mislead students and laymen. But the scope and implications of the book are far wider. It makes statements on two crucial features of our existence: the growth of social behavior in children, and the prevention of violence and war. These are not topics in which loose thinking can be accepted with a tolerant shrug: such work should be based on a respect for facts, for logic and for the researches of others. Instead, the method of *On Aggression* is essentially anti-rational. This method should be repudiated by all scholars—indeed, by all responsible people.

RENÉ DUBOS

Man's Nature and Social Institutions

On January evening in 1965, I was one of eight persons who spent several hours in a New York hotel discussing the ethical problems arising from man's aggressive behavior. The transcript of our discussions, as edited by our host, Hiram Haydn, was published in the Summer, 1965, issue of THE AMERICAN SCHOLAR under the title, "A Symposium on Morality." "What sort of morality is viable and tenable in our times, taking into account what we now know concerning the nature of man?" was the guiding question.

Most participants in the symposium were primarily interested in the social, philosophical, ethical and theological aspects of man's aggressiveness in the modern world. But I took a different view of the problem. Being an experimental biologist, I thought I should emphasize the biological determinants of behavior, and indicate that morality might have emerged as a social adaptation in the course of man's evolution from his animal origins. Deep in my heart, however, I agreed with Philip Hallie when he passionately stated, ". . . the question of the evolution of morality interests me very little, as little as do questions of the origins, *et cetera*. They may be useful for the sake perhaps of argument, but not for the sake of my own life. When I am making a choice, origins and evolution don't come in, although I'm sure these things are illuminating." And it is true indeed that in real life we are rarely concerned with the biological and historical origins of behavior; rather we base our judgments on the quality of choices and decisions. We may believe that *"tout comprendre, c'est tout pardonner,"* but we also know that understanding and forgiving do not imply approving.

While the transcript of the symposium reveals wide differences of view among the participants concerning the meaning of the word morality, it shows a surprising agreement concerning the fundamental wickedness of man. All of us appeared to agree with David Garnett when he bluntly asserted that man is a killer, and differs from all other animals including apes in that, alone among living things, he practices warfare with the intent to kill. The events of recent years seem indeed to prove that one of mankind's chief occupations is destructive warfare and other forms of violence —deliberately practiced. Men have consciously tortured and killed their fellowmen in Algeria, Vietnam, Biafra, the Middle East, in city streets all over the world and even on college campuses. Destructive violence is as much a part of life today as it was in Homer's time.

Revulsion against violence, however, is also one of the hallmarks of human history. The soul-searching and protests generated by the tragedies of the past few years are almost as impressive as the tragedies themselves. In every part of the world, furthermore, there are countless normal human beings who would find it extremely painful, if not emotionally impossible, to kill another human being or even to exhibit aggressive behavior. It takes a great deal of conditioning to prepare a nation for war, and to train soldiers to kill by hand-to-hand combat. While it is obvious that many men are killers, it is equally true that many more are not. And for this reason it seems hardly justified to state that Man— with a capital **M**—is by nature a killer.

One need not be an anthropologist or a historian to know that violence and conflict have existed in all human societies under many different forms, but opinions differ about the origins of human aggression. Some regard it as purely the consequence of cultural or social conditioning. Others believe that it is the direct and inevitable expression of instincts that are indelibly inscribed in man's genetic code. This polarization of views constitutes in reality a pseudo problem, analogous in all respects to the now worn-out nurture *versus* nature controversy. The potentiality for aggressiveness is indeed part of man's genetic constitution. just as it is part of the genetic constitution of all animal species. But the manifestation of all genetic potentialities are shaped by past experiences and present circumstances. There is no genetic coding that inevitably results in aggressiveness, only a set of genetic attributes for self-defense that can become expressed as aggressiveness under particular sets of conditions.

The philosophers of the Enlightenment believed in the perfectibility of man and therefore expected aggressive violence to subside as society became more just and rational. In contrast, the dominant view in our times is that man's propensity for violence is innate—an inescapable evolutionary consequence of the changes in ways of life that occurred when the Miocene precursors of *Homo sapiens* moved from the forest to the savannah type of country some fifteen million years ago. After our precursors had left the prehominid forest Eden, they progressively acquired, so the story goes, the ways of armed hunters and thus became the killer apes of the Pliocene savannahs.

Just as the eighteenth-century philosophers accepted the theory of the good, happy savage on the basis of limited and onesided accounts of primitive life written by the early explorers of the Pacific islands and of America, so we tend to accept the view of aboriginal depravity and violence on the basis of very sketchy anthropological information. In both cases, scientific knowledge is selected and used only to the extent that it fits an *a priori* view of human nature. In William Golding's *Lord of the Flies,* disagreement over leadership leads to violence and terror among a group of English schoolboys cast away on a small island. The theme of the book, according to the author, is "to trace the defects of society back to the defects of human nature." In fact, however, the behavioral defects described by William Golding may not have their origin in human nature but rather in the system of values taught English schoolboys. Boys from other parts of the world might not behave as William Golding imagined on the basis of his English experience. A few years ago, indeed, a group of Micronesian children (from twelve years of age to toddlers) were actually marooned by accident for several months on an isolated atoll, yet there was no violence or terror among them. They survived the experience without physical or emotional stress. Their fortitude was probably due to the fact that, whereas Western culture is dominated by the competitive spirit, Polynesian culture makes children aware of their dependence on the community and therefore makes them socially tolerant of each other.

Certain men act as killers under certain conditions because social life often distorts the instinctive responses that are essential for self-defense. The instinct for preservation exists in all animals and can generate violent behavior even in the most timid species. Rabbits and mice are readily frightened under ordinary circumstances, but they can fight just as viciously as tigers, wolves, baboons and men whenever any of their fundamental "values" are involved. I have seen a rabbit repeatedly and ferociously assault a huge black snake threatening its nest. Time and time again in the laboratory, I have observed tame white mice—so gentle that a child could handle them—engage in fierce fighting against mice of the same breed and age introduced into their cage from the outside. Violent conflict among these mice occurred even though food and water were abundant, the animals were not crowded, and they did not have occasion to fight for females. It would be silly to say that Rabbit or Mouse is a killer because rabbits and mice will fight to defend their young or their territory, or against a stranger introduced from the outside. In animals as well as in men, many manifestations of the instinct for self-defense result in aberrant forms of behavior that are destructive rather than biologically useful.

In animal life the instinct of self-preservation evolved to deal through short-term responses with situations apprehended by the senses. In man, the expressions of the same fundamental instinct have usually been translated from the plane of nature to the plane of society, from sensual perceptions to symbolic conceptions, from short-term responses to long-range effects. If man behaves more commonly as a killer than do animals, it is because his ways of life, his social history, and his mental processes often place him in situations that differ radically from those under which he evolved and in which he acquired the instinct for self-defense. Comparative observations of animals living in zoos or in their natural habitats help to explain how social forces can make man behave as a killer through aberrations of his instinctive defense responses.

In captivity as well as in the wild, males compete for territory and for the available females especially during the rut season. The savage fights among stags, walrus bulls and seals are part of the wild-life lore. The combat between males, however, is rarely to the death. The weaker combatant turns aside and retreats; the victor lets the vanquished go unmolested. Among animals under natural conditions and often in captivity, fighting presents some analogy to German student duels; certain types of wounds are permissible but most battles are limited to bluffing contests and to confrontations of wits. Furthermore, fighting between animals of the same species is often symbolic rather than real. Animals tend to ritualize their aggression by such attitudes as rearing up, roaring, showing their teeth, or erecting their ruffs, hackles or neck hair. Ritualization of behavior is widespread among higher apes, and also, of course, among men.

Although destructive war is extremely uncommon among animals living in the wild, naturally one finds a few exceptions to the rule of "bluff rather than fight." For example, when an animal enters the home ground of another member of the same species, the latter attacks at once, apparently with the intent to kill the intruder. Such hostile attitudes apply chiefly or only to animals of the same species; other animals with slightly different habits or nutritional needs are usually not considered as competitors, and their presence is tolerated. Thus, the concept of the stranger seems to have had its origins in the fear of losing one's place in the sun to potential competitors for the available food and mates. The concept of foreigner in human life—along with the undertones of mistrust and fear associated with the word in all languages—may well have its biological origin in the hostile reaction of animals to strangers of their own kind moving into their own territory.

When primates live undisturbed under natural conditions in the wild, order and peace are maintained by a hierarchy evolved within the band as each generation grows up. This hierarchy is, of course, subject to rearrangement in accordance with the strength and ability of the leader. But, in general, the bonds of comradeship holding the wild society together are far more prominent in day-to-day life than are occasional episodes of pulling rank.

The mechanisms that secure peaceful interplay within the band under natural conditions commonly break down, however, when the animals find themselves in environments that differ from those under which they evolved. Even in the best-managed zoos, the animals have little or no opportunity for exercising their individual enterprise or for exploring as they normally do in the wild. Their artificial ways of life and environment disturb the operations of the instinctive mechanisms through which hierarchy is established in the wild. In the zoo, some animals try to establish and maintain their authority by threats or actual acts of violence. Quarrels become endemic, and now and then the whole society collapses, the females and the young being indiscriminately slaughtered. As there is no food shortage in the zoos, a primate population in such a disorganized state is in some respects comparable to a non-integrated human population in which material abundance does not prevent social conflicts.

When man emerged from his animal background, he created ways of life and environments in which the social restraints achieved during the early phases of his evolution were no longer effective or suitable. Biological adaptation has not prepared him for the competitive attitudes that prevail in most societies. Man becomes a killer of his own species because he has failed to develop social restraints capable of substituting for the biological wisdom evolved under natural conditions. Violence and internecine conflict are most common in highly competitive societies, particularly during periods of rapid change that upset social order. Man has not yet learned to live in the zoos he has created for himself.

Contemporary events in the prosperous countries of Western civilization leave no hope, unfortunately, that violence can be checked simply by making available to all greater wealth and physical comfort. Even a country as prosperous and economically well-organized as Sweden is not immune to the problems caused by violence.

Eight miles from Stockholm, the Swedes recently created the brand new town of Skärholmen, which was first opened for habitation in 1968 and now counts some twenty thousand inhabitants. Skärholmen was planned to incorporate the most advenced archi-tectural technology but, according to a study reported in the new publication *Europa* (No. 2), modern planning and design have generated their own problems. In particular, the children and teenagers of the new town tend to be withdrawn, restless and aggressive—more so in the case of those living near the center of town in the high-rise buildings than of those living on the out-skirts in detached houses. Psychologists who have studied life in Skärholmen have come to the conclusion—neither original nor necessarily true—that the antisocial attitudes of the young are gen-erated by high population density and by austere urban architec-ture.

Since urbanization is likely to continue increasing for a number of years, the future of mankind would be rather dark if it were really true that aggressiveness is an inescapable accompaniment of crowded urban life. But, in fact, history and the events of our own times offer much evidence that high population density is com-patible with peaceful social relationships. For example, Hong Kong and Holland have been among the most crowded areas in the world for centuries, yet their inhabitants are on the whole ex-tremely sociable and orderly. In contrast, violence has long been a feature of the American social scene, not only in the crowded cities, but perhaps even more in areas of extremely sparse popula-tion.

The history of the South Pacific islands illustrates the limitations of simple biological theories for the understanding of violence in human societies. Some three thousand years ago, the Polynesian people began to evolve social systems in response to ecological and social problems similar to ours today. Until the time of the European explorations, these islands constituted small isolated worlds; their inhabitants had little chance to escape to new fron-tiers or to expand demographically and economically. Many South Pacific islanders adapted to confined places by making sociability an essential aspect of their life-styles and by cultivating social and ecological practices that minimized deprivations and conflicts. Be-fore the arrival of the white man, life on Tahiti, Samoa and Hawaii was sufficiently comfortable, safe and happy to generate among the Enlightenment philosophers the pleasant illusion that primitive life proved the fundamental goodness of man and gave the hope that modern societies could re-create the living conditions that had made possible the good, happy savage.

There were, of course, many examples of violence among primitive societies. While Tahiti, Hawaii and Samoa appeared to the European explorers as the blessed islands, the neighboring Marquesas Islands harbored ill-tempered cannibals, and the Easter Group Islands were the sites of destructive revolutions. The various Indian tribes of the North American continent also differed greatly one from another in their attitudes toward violence. Some cultivated it as a virtue; others developed complex social mechanisms to prevent or at least to control its manifestations.

To minimize the destructive effects of violence, we might find it profitable humbly to take a lesson from the animal world and try systematically to ritualize our conflicts. War games among primitive people, the jousts of medieval knights, and some of the later gentlemanly conventions of military behavior had in fact some similarities to the sham fights so common among animals, not only in the wild but also in tame populations. If modern societies could develop effective techniques for the ritualization of conflicts— by global Olympic games, for example, or by space exploration— they might achieve something like what William James called the moral equivalent of war. Battles of bravado might go far toward averting the destructive effects of violence.

Man's propensity for violence is not a racial or a species attribute woven in his genetic fabric. It is culturally conditioned by history and the ways of life. The instinct for self-defense exists throughout the animal kingdom and can exhibit aberrant manifestations in animals as well as in man—more frequently in man only because he always lives under conditions that differ profoundly from the ones under which he evolved. We cannot escape from the zoos we have created for ourselves and return to wilderness, but we can improve our societies and make them better suited to our unchangeable biological nature. I do not have much faith in the nineteenth-century version of the perfectibility of man, but I believe deeply in the perfectibility of human institutions.

HERMANN HELMUTH

Human Behavior: Aggression

Anthropologists who concern themselves with the physical aspect of man are to a great extent in agreement nowadays that the human body shows no *principal* differences from the body of animals, especially from that of higher primates. Yet there does not exist this unanimity of view with regard to the psychic aspect, the evolution of human behavior from that of animals. Konrad Lorenz (1964), who has endeavored to prove such an evolution, interprets intraspecific aggression as a behavioral drive whose origin is deeply rooted in man's biology. In his work, *On Aggression* (New York, 1963) he writes: "Just as both the eye of a cuttlefish and that of a vertebrate can be termed with the same justification, with regard to function and construction, as an eye, without any quotation marks, with the same justification we can omit these quotation marks when we speak of the social modes of behaviour of higher animals which are analogous to those of man, i.e., that the forms of behaviour—in this case aggression between animals of the same kind—have developed as the result of a convergent adaptation of the animals. Due to intraspecific selection, the aggressive instinct has been developed in Neolithic times under environmental con-

Translated and revised by the author from "Zum Verhalten des Menschen: die Aggression," and reprinted by permission from *Zeitschrift für Ethnologie,* vol. 92, 1967, pp. 265–73.

ditions which were peculiar to that period and is thus part and parcel of human biology."

At this point brief mention must be made of the environment as a factor which determines aggression or behavior in general. The activity of both man and animals in principle has, in the main, referred to, and expresses itself only in, the environment. (The different attitudes to nature of man and animals will be discussed later.) If one were to equate the variety of human cultures and their relationship to one another with the community order of organisms, one could apply Darwin's ideas on the struggle for existence to the cultural world of man. Struggle of one biological species against another can be seen reflected in the struggle of cultures, peoples, nations or even smaller cultural units, against one another. The cultures of peoples of the earth can thus be interpreted as an environmental factor which determines aggressive behavior.

It is beyond the scope of this article to discuss such physical factors as geology, geography or climate, biological influences such as the animal and plant worlds, and the sociological factor, man as environmental factor of man.

According to Marx and Engels, human history is the history of inevitable conflict between classes, of aggression therefore of one social stratum toward another. This conflict is determined by the difference in degree in the ownership of property and by socio-economic differences as environmental factors. These environmental factors, private property and the socioeconomic basis, can be traced back in their origin and their form to their specific culture. Thus culture represents an environmental factor both in a wide concrete as well as an abstract sense.

Further, even the data registered by human senses are—complicating even further what has been said—invested with different value. A study of obedience and disobedience toward an authority has led to this conclusion (Milgram, 1965). Distinctly differing reactions in the degree of obedience were registered, depending on whether the person in authority demanding respect was present directly or indirectly, behind a glass partition, visually and acoustically present, or only present acoustically by telephone, or only there on tape recordings. The form of the environmental conditions represented by the senses and their proximity to the subject are therefore also of significance.

But let us return once more to the "aggressive instinct." What Lorenz means by aggression or aggressive drive is injury to or the attempt to injure another animal of the same kind or species, or the fighting behavior of animals and humans directed against members of the same species. But it is still not clear whether he means a general attitude toward individuals of the same kind, or only certain actions or, especially in the case of humans, linguistic expressions of aggression.

To attempt a description or even an explanation of life one would not restrict oneself to chemistry or physics. One could certainly describe the material bases and yet not be able to penetrate to the essence of life. Likewise, no biologist concerned with general biology would merely study mammals since certain important areas would remain untouched—for example, methods of eating (Strudler, Filtrierer), procreation (parthenogenesis, metagenesis, heterogony), or the structure of the body (exoskeleton, endoskeleton). Since no humans exist whose behavior has not been shaped culturally, any science of human behavior must take into account man's culture, and the ways in which this has affected his behavior. In addition, any such science must take as its starting point the forms of behavior of all humans and not simply of one specific group. A partial presentation, for example, of the behavior of humans from only one cultural group, can make no claim to general validity since human conduct is extremely variable.

An answer to the question whether the aggressive behavior of man is of a biological-genetic nature can be arrived at by different methods. It would first have to be ascertained whether this behavior is common to all men, whether it can lay successful claim to being valid in the case of all men. If it were only characteristic of man in Western culture, then this alone would suffice to negate the question. In order to prove the biological origins of the aggressive drive, it would also be necessary for this to be present where there is no cultural conditioning. One possibility of studying human behavior unprejudiced by cultural influences would be to raise man in isolation. This is not only out of the question, but also meaningless since in all probability, as a result of this pathogenic environment, pathological modes of behavior would also be created. Thus there remains only the attempt to observe small children before their acculturation and socialization begin. However, for the study of typically human forms of behavior a child which is less than six months of age is unsuitable. It cannot be ascertained whether a negative answer is conditioned by a natural process of maturing which has not yet taken place or by cultural education which has not yet begun (Lévi-Strauss, 1959). Even the twin method developed by Galton (1876) does not offer a conclusive solution to the problem of the aggressive drive, and yet it does bring the problem much nearer to solution. Investigations carried out by the twin method (Newman, 1937; Shields, 1962) revealed that monozygotic twins who had grown up and been educated in different environments, when compared with twins brought up in the same environment, possessed certain, though slight, differences in the degree of specific qualities despite great similarities in personality, intelligence and talent which had been ascertained by the same means. I know of no studies with twins who grew up in completely different ethnic cultural environments. Through studying twins it has, however, been clearly shown that a substratum of human behavior can be regarded as biologically inherited. This has been put forward recently by Eibl-Eibesfeldt (1972) in his study, *Love and Hate*. And, more specifically, experimental endocrinological research on rhesus monkeys and *Homo sapiens* proved that the male hormone testosterone can influence the strength of aggressive behavior (Hamburg, 1971).

A fresh possibility of throwing light on the problem as to whether human aggressive behavior is biologically conditioned or socially learned is the study of primate behavior, especially of those primates which are most closely related to man. However, Japanese and American researches, especially, call to mind, even in the case of primates, nonbiological—that is, socioculturally learned or patterned, modes of behavior. Or expressed in neutral terms, one can speak of protocultural modes of behavior, as observations of Japanese macaques living in natural surroundings suggest (Kawamura 1959; Kawai 1963; Kawai, Tsumori 1963). Therefore, for further knowledge of the nature of the behavior, biological or cultural, reference would be required to experiments carried out with specimens in isolation (Harlow 1959, 1962) or observations of different subgroups of the same species.

Of particular significance for questions such as the former are the behavioral studies undertaken by Japanese primatologists (Itani 1959; Yamada 1963) of macaques (*Macaca fuscata*) living wild on Japanese islands, those of Washburn and DeVore, 1961, of wild olive baboons, those of Schaller 1963, of the mountain gorilla, in their natural habitat, likewise those of Goodall, 1963, V. and F. Reynolds, 1965, and Nishida 1970, on chimpanzees from various areas.

While observing a group of Japanese macaques, whose natural bonds of relations were known to one another, Yamada noticed a form of behavior which he called co-feeding. This co-feeding was very common between mother and child or children, between aunt and cousins, in a descending order of relation, between macaques which were not related. The social position in the scale was of secondary importance. Itani's observation showed that male monkeys holding a high position, carried around with them older children, that is those who were between one and two years of age, and engaged in social grooming. This behavior, which was termed paternal care, (although the natural father was not known) can be clearly set apart from the care which was shown to the youngest infants. Itani speaks of the universality of this behavior in the case of the Japanese macaques. Since it is here a question of care for the older offspring, and no preference for the females was shown, it can neither be a question of behavior in conformity with the "infant scheme," nor a form of sexual attraction. Thus aggression does not appear to play an important role in the case of the closely related and among the higher ranking males towards the older children. More recently, Lahiri and Southwick (1966) showed that this mode of behavior not only existed among Japanese macaques, but also among Barbary "apes" (*Macaca sylvana*) living in a zoo in Washington. That this happens not only in captivity had been proven by Crook (1970). The Barbary macaques in Morocco, Crook suggests, use this form of cooperation to avoid "patterns of constraint regulating social mobility and that it has arisen with the context of competition for access to both physical and social commodities."

The social behavior of olive baboons living wild in the Amboseli Game Reserve was described in detail by Washburn and DeVore. If the monkeys of several troops happened to meet in the afternoon at the only water hole within a wide radius, no forms of enmity were to be observed among them; likewise nothing happened which might have suggested aggressive behavior when two troops were eating near one another. Troops which rarely met were very interested in one another. According to the authors, sexual attraction did not play an all-important role in keeping the group together. "It is the intensely social nature of the baboon . . . that keeps the troop together." Is it not possible that where sexual bonds were lacking, the supposed aggression had become overpowering and led to a dissolution of the group?

Encounters too between different troops of mountain gorillas proceeded quite peacefully according to Schaller. Only in one of twelve encounters, which lasted a lengthy period (maximum three days) and which were more or less close, did two adult males of different troops stare at one another, and yet no hostile actions of any kind were engaged in. On one occasion an animal was seen to beat its chest as the result of slight excitement. The behavior of the animals within a troop is likewise peaceful. The members of one group behave extremely tolerantly toward each other, although they spend most of the day very close together. Even the sexual act of two low-ranking males with a female of the group did not result in any aggression on the part of the leader. Even when there was brief aggressive behavior among the females, Schaller was unable to observe any disputes of serious nature. Thus in the case of the mountain gorillas. too, aggression has no distinct influence on the social life of the animals. On the contrary, the peacefulness of gorillas within their troop and between different troops is impressive.

The same is substantiated by studies made by V. and F. Reynolds on chimpanzees in the Budongo forest. The chimpanzees live together in a more loosely structured society than gorillas and baboons and among them even the absence of a strong hierarchy is stressed as a regulator of behavior. These chimpanzees in no way exhibit aggressive behavior when they encounter other groups; several troops feed peacefully together in a very restricted area. When several males copulated with the same female, there were no signs of aggressive behavior among the males. "Within 300 observations hours, 17 cases of arguments with signs of anger or threats as well as real fighting were registered, and none lasted longer than a few seconds." Of these, only four cases concerned old males; in seven cases young and old chimpanzees and young chimpanzees among themselves were involved in disputes; there were rarely disputes between old chimpanzees of the same sex, and only once did it come to a short struggle between one female and another with a child, but both were soon afterwards sitting on the same branch and eating. In the light of these observations, an aggressive "instinct" or "drive" cannot be clearly discerned among these chimpanzees from the Budongo forest, despite the absence of a "pecking order" amongst them.

The observations of Jane Goodall on chimpanzees of the Gombe River corroborate the findings of the Reynolds'. Goodall too remarks on the loose social structure within the group and thinks in this respect that the interaction of aggressiveness and submissiveness is rare among individual animals. Despite the differences between the social structure of the group of chimpanzees and that of the baboons and macaques with their distinct hierarchy of dominance, the chimpanzees reveal a great deal of tolerance in their behavior toward one another, and this is especially remarkable among the males. "Threatening behaviour was found in 4 cases (during an observation period of twenty-four months), and only then when a subordinate wanted to take food before a higher ranking male. Three of these cases occurred under artificial conditions." Cases of one animal attacking another were very rarely noticed, and only once did an actual fight occur. Therefore, among the chimpanzees of the Gombe River, too, the aggressive drive has little significance. Nishida (1970) observed a group of 6 adult males, 10 adult females and 13 immature chimpanzees in the Mahali Mountains of Tanzania. During his twenty-eight months of more general, and thirteen months of more specific observations, he saw 102 cases of aggression, which were classified into 10 degrees of severity, from 1 (swinging one arm sideways up or down) to 10 (kicking or stamping on the object). Only in 15 cases did attackers actually catch and hit their object and only in one case did two males participate in a joint attack. Such interaction with regard to food was listed in 27 cases. "One of the characteristics" Nishida says," is the decrease of true attacks and the corresponding increase of threats in aggressive behavior" of chimpanzees, with "agonistic interactions" being infrequent (Nishida 1970, p. 73).

Most recently, Hamburg (1971) lists circumstances under which aggressive behavior of nonhuman primates is most likely to occur; these are grouped into two larger categories: defense (mostly against other species, but also a mother defending her child against a member of the same species) and "access to valued resources" (Hamburg, 1971, p. 20). These valued resources might be food objects, sleeping places, social status or a female in estrus, but not the defense of a fixed territory.

The isolation experiments of Harlow (1959) showed that rhesus monkeys which had been brought up isolated or with substitute mothers were in no way aggressive in spite of their disturbed socialization.

On the basis of what has been said, an aggressive drive seems to play a rather insignificant role among those monkeys and especially apes observed in their natural environment or under experimental conditions. With respect to *Homo sapiens,* the aggressive drive could at the earliest have been developed during a late period of human evolution, since it is not at all strongly developed among the great apes. Bearing in mind that *Homo sapiens* is one species, such a drive would have to be encountered in all humans in all cultural groups. Is this what is, in fact, encountered? For an answer, the findings of comparative ethnology will have to be examined.

It immediately becomes apparent on reading works which are concerned with the social life of so-called "primitive" peoples to what great extent conflicts and disputes, larger incidents and wars, are stressed in field researches. And yet, presumably, the normal way of life was much more peaceful than descriptions so frequently suggest. Since a peaceful way of life, as presented in travelogues and descriptions of the life of exotic peoples, offers the reader little that is sensational and attractive, works which deal with peaceful communal life appear relatively rarely and occupy a minor place in the literature of ethnology.

A few reports will now be cited which deal with the peaceful and communal life of so-called "primitive" peoples. In his work, *The Pygmies of the Congo: Past and Present* Martin Gusinde draws our attention to the fact that "although on the whole harmony does prevail both in the single family and within the tribe very often disputes are engaged in, but without any serious effect or lasting discord . . . Bambuti pygmies are not lacking in mutual consideration . . . like the desire to live on agreeable terms with one another, it is a natural social virtue, despite common and yet brief disputes. Aggressive enmity is really not to be found amongst members of the same tribe." Relations between tribes appear to be even more peaceful: "Since penetration into foreign territory could be the occasion for disputes and fights . . . everyone seeks from the very beginning to avoid such a confrontation . . . and the Bambuti are anything but bellicose . . . they are not threatened by their own kind." Likewise, Turnbull (1965) sees the life of the more modern pygmies as peaceful in general, despite a great number of quarrels about domestic affairs like food (67 cases), sex (37 cases), village life (11 cases), theft (5 cases), or territory in the village (4 cases). Attempts by persons not directly involved to settle the issues are very rare. Trespassing on some other band's hunting territory may lead to club-fighting, although Turnbull did "not come across . . . a solitary instance" of "such open hostilities taking place between two bands" (p. 220). On the other hand, "there is considerable latent antagonism between band (Mbutis) and village (Negroes)" (Turnbull, 1965, p. 223).

We also know of the peaceful communal life among the Eskimos. Rasmussen (1929, 1932) reports that Eskimos do in fact accept one man's killing another under certain circumstances, but for an Eskimo a war of one settlement against another is something quite unthinkable. Kaj Birket-Smith (1959) also mentions the general love of peace, the lack of social tensions found among the Eskimos, and the same thing is reported by Ruth Benedict (1934) with regard to the Mission Indians of California. The latter author has also written a detailed report on the principles of conduct of the Zuni Indians of the Pueblos of the southwest of North America. Even though different interpretations exist depending on different personal points of view with regard to the way of life of the Zuni—organic or by means of repression (termed Apollonian by Ruth Benedict—see J. W. Bennett, 1946), one can maintain that both the representatives of the organic and the repressive view are agreed in recognizing that the communal life of the Zuni is shaped by common sense and a desire to live together amicably. The ideal of the men is not war, not personal distinction through warlike deeds and outstanding achievement, not authority in the domestic sphere, but the desire alone of the individual to become one of his group. Since strong outbursts of emotion would disturb this harmony in the community, moderation is the first duty. Nothing in Benedict's description of the life of the Zuni suggests the extent and intensity of aggression among them as we know these in Western European peoples. This does not mean an aggressive drive is not there as a biological potentiality: yet as the result of the cultural conditioning of the Zuni, it does not appear.

Most recently, Eibl-Eibesfeldt (1972) studied the "bonding behavior and aggression control" in one Bushmen group. This contribution to the scientific study of aggressive behavior in a tribe which was always believed to be particularly peaceful is of special interest. Looking for "innate behavior patterns" in man, Eibl-Eibesfeldt claims to have found it in aggression. For lack of space, it is impossible here to enter into the old discussion on nature-nurture. However, the author's introduction to this problem does not offer more than a superficial discussion of it, and is more polemical than enlightening. Admitting (Eibl-Eibesfeldt 1972, p. 15) that innate behavior patterns are modifiable, one is eager to find this concept applied to the Bushmen, but later on there is no further mention of it. Most disappointing and incomprehensible is the lack of a definition of aggression—what he understands by it and what he interprets as aggression. One finds defensive acts, explorations, play and "show-off" behavior tacitly included, with which, I am sure, not all ethologists-psychologists will agree. A point not considered is that the presence of observers and their gifts may have caused disturbances in the group's behavior. Other questions untouched are aggressiveness in relation to age and sex differences. There are only a few pages about aggression among adults. Therefore, one is tempted to argue that the author is indirectly admitting that their life is actually quite peaceful. The evidence collected relating to territorial conflicts, e.g., life of adult Bushmen, seems to be rather ambiguous and is not as clear as the author would apparently have wished it to be. If the impression that only the children are aggressive is right, then how is the change in behavior being brought about? What are the changing forces? The term "culture" has no place in Eibl-Eibesfeldt's vocabulary.

In my original paper (1967) I did not maintain that aggression never occurs among Bushmen, Pygmies, Eskimos, etc. However, the modifiability of human behavior by means of culture seems to me to be so great that the term "aggressive drive" (Lorenz, 1963) is misapplied. Eibl-Eibesfeldt's new study only serves to convince me that aggressive acts do occur (perhaps more often among children than I formerly believed); nevertheless, his arguments for an "innate aggressive behavior pattern" in man, as exemplified in the case of Bushmen, are too weak for me to accept.

Margaret Mead (1935) draws a picture of the Arapesh of New Guinea which is essentially the same as Benedict's portrait of the Zuni. Contrary to the prevalent view that only head-hunters and cannibals are to be found in New Guinea, "the profession of war is as good as unknown" among the Arapesh. "They have no tradition of head-hunting, and it is not regarded as proof of any outstanding courage when a man kills his opponent. Whoever has already killed is regarded almost as abnormal." However, if conflicts do occur between different tribes "then the dispute can be ended after a few sharp words." "In a society to whom violence is foreign, which considers all men gentle and helpful, there are no compulsory measures vis-à-vis the violent man."

The attitudes in the social life of such different people as Pygmies, Eskimos, Indians and Melanesians as described here only show how different human conduct can be, especially if one takes into account the well-known aggressive events of our own European history (Freeman 1969). The examples given make clear, I think, how one human behavioral characteristic, man's aggressive conduct, is influenced by ideals which are immanent in different cultures. It is also obvious, not only that the view which a man has of his own tribal brothers is a product of his own culture, but that further, as in the case of the Arapesh, the same view of man which prevails in one culture is regarded as valid for all men everywhere, that the Arapesh regard all men as good and peace-loving. Yet even Europe offers an example of an extreme love of peace and complete renunciation of force. In the eyes of the Mennonites, who originated in Central Europe and whose thought is Christian, peace with all men, renunciation of all kinds of force, and hope and love in the Christian sense are the ideals which determine life with their fellow men. During the French Revolution of 1789 they were relieved from military duties, and crimes are practically unknown among them. Their tolerance in questions of faith and their active love of their fellow men were acknowledged even then, in 1789.

This example shows that even Dutch, Germans and Swiss, from whom the Mennonites were in the main composed, and whose racial, hereditary structure is the same as ours, are freed by a religious ideal from the aggression which, according to Lorenz, controls us all. One might almost think that religion does indeed re-educate its followers into new beings. For it is not nature which makes new men of the Mennonites but their religion, their ideal of peace, and of renunciation of force. This is therefore just as true in the case of Indians or Melanesians as it is in the case of Europeans, and shows how human nature, as a basis of behavior, is formed, permeated, and directed by the form of the culture, modes of behavior which are socially evaluated. There is rather a mutual penetration and conditioning of the biological stratum of behavior by the variety of cultures than a crass opposition of biology and culture. Psychobiological studies will further elucidate this important problem, To cite only the results of psychological studies on children exposed early in life to aggressiveness, Hamburg (1971, p. 22) for example came to the conclusion that "biological predispositions to learning aggressive patterns and exposure to specific social learning situations may interact to produce great differences in aggressiveness during later life." Thus this seems to confirm the case of other rather exceptional peoples who, in comparison with our Western society, are on the other end of the aggressive scale. The perpetual exposure to aggression of one generation after another leads western-civilized peoples, not surprisingly, to the concept of a natural drive, e.g., the aggressive drive.

The problem which keeps cropping up in this respect is that of ethnocentrism or racism. Different kinds of human behavior are interpreted in this light as having different values. Both the ethnocentric and racial overestimation of one's own culture or race toward other cultures which are so often regarded as inferior, is made on the one hand exclusively on the basis of cultural factors such as religion, language, technology, etc., which therefore can be altered and improved, and on the other hand on the basis of biological factors such as genes or gene complexes which are inherent in races, and which in contrast are relatively unchangeable. Though the ethnic cultural viewpoint can be regarded as the only one, as for example in the UNESCO statement on race, 1952, the representatives of the biological approach have material too to support their arguments. Since it would necessitate an article in its own right, no attempt is made in this context to offer a solution to this extensive problem. However, this question does lead us to the evaluation of facts, already stressed, which can be different for different ethnic groups and is yet characteristic of human thought, thereby leading us also to the different views on man. When applied, both extreme views can react, thereby forming and directing man himself. The same can be said with regard to the views on aggressive behavior.

Depending on whether one is indifferent to the aggression of one human being toward another, or values it highly as a sign of definite manliness and approves of it because it promises success, or one rejects it as being negative for communal life, one can refer to human nature as peaceful, childlike, harmonious, or as aggressive and warlike. But the selection and generalization of only one mode of behavior, namely of aggression, out of the pool of all biologically possible modes of behavior which lie at the root of every action, is an artificial construction. If one were to continue the analysis of behavior in the same manner as Lorenz, one would have to, as was shown with examples from anthropology, oppose the acceptance of an aggressive instinct in man with an equally rigidly abstract sociability drive.

Freud's "sexual instinct" in its relationship to the "aggressive instinct" cannot be discussed here. In a generalized form, the acceptance of the "sexual instinct" as a factor which alone determines human behavior has already been rejected by comparative anthropology (Malinowski, 1927). An attempt will be made to offer another dynamic solution to the problem, which would do more justice to the totality and variety of human behavior and which has the advantage of greater simplicity.

According to J. von Uexküll (1928), the form of the eye and of the brain, which processes the sense data, of the species *Homo sapiens* determines the shape and size of his optic horizon. No matter where we are situated on earth, no matter where we go, we are always accompanied by a visual horizon about 8 kilometers in radius, and we are the center of the dome which surrounds us always and everywhere. Optically therefore, the horizon remains principally the same. This state of affairs is altered by the typically human. Biologists (Koehler 1943, Simpson 1966) as well as anthropologists (Spiro 1954) and philosophers (Cassirer 1953–57) are very much of the opinion that the symbolic language of man (image, model and language) in contrast to the emotional language of animals, has decisively formed his ability to think. The propositional language of man alone allowed the creation of a symbolic world between the natural world of perception ("Merkwelt") and affect ("Wirkwelt") (Cassirer 1960). By virtue of this symbolic thought, which can be distinguished from practical thought, as we understand this, for example, in the case of chimpanzees (Yerkes 1953, Ferster 1964) and also macaques (Harlow 1949, Kawamura 1963), man alone is placed in a position not only to broaden his horizon but, depending on significance, to perceive new dimensions of reality (Cassirer 1960), to constantly create other, qualitatively new horizons around himself as the central point. This ability to create allows man to construct completely new and different images which can be diametrically opposite to one another, from out of the spectrum of his possibilities. Only as a result of the symbol and ability to think in symbols is man capable of making a polar distinction between "I" and "you," love and hate. The polarity of the human ability to act and create (Rothacker 1965) has been realized in all the diversity of cultures and is likewise to be found in the individual. Just as in human cultures it is possible to put the accent on mutual love, respect and friendship or enmity, disrespect and hate, it is equally possible for the individual to act according to diametrically opposed decisions, whereby cultural, individual-psychic life-historical influences play a role.

To all intents and purposes, this offers a possibility to overcome aggression, for it is not to be disputed that this occurs in primates and in man. However, observations reveal that aggression in the behavior of primates, for example, especially of the apes which are most closely related to man, have no great significance. Here in nonhuman primates, since individualistic behavior is the result of observations and imitations of the forms of behavior of other individuals and of one's own experience, one can already say that there is some "protocultural" conditioning. In addition to the biological means of overcoming hostile actions alone suggested by Lorenz in the form of "ritualization" and "reorientation," it seems to me that in the case of human behavior a new way, that of cultural conditioning and reconditioning, is of greater significance. The positive possibility which is offered by culture of a higher estimation and idealization of peaceful communal life, projected by culture onto the biological basis of behavior, ought therefore to be given special emphasis.

REFERENCES

Benedict, R., 1934: *Patterns of Culture.* Houghton Mifflin Co., Boston and New York.

Bennett, J. W., 1946: "The Interpretation of Pueblo Culture: A Question of Values." *Southwestern Journal of Anthropology* 2, 1946, p. 361–74.

Birket-Smith, K., 1959: *The Eskimos.* Methuen, London.

Cassirer, E., 1953–57: *The Philosophy of Symbolic Forms.* 3 vols. Yale University Press, New Haven.

——., 1944: *An Essay on Man.* Yale University Press, New Haven.

Crook, J. H., 1970: "Social Organization and the Environment: Aspects of Contemporary Social Ethology." *Animal Behaviour,* vol. 18, p. 197–209.

Eibl-Eibesfeldt, I., 1972: *Love and Hate.* Holt, Rinehart, & Winston, New York.

——., 1972: *Die !Ko-Buschmann-Gesellschaft,* Piper.

Ferster, C. B., 1964: "Arithmetic Behavior in Chimpanzees." *Scientific American,* vol. 210, no. 5, May 1964, pp. 98–103.

Freeman, D., 1964: "Human Aggression in Anthropological Perspective." *Natural History of Aggression.* Institute of Biology Symposia No. 13, Academic Press, London and New York.

Galton, F, 1876: "The History of Twins as a Criterium of the Relative Powers of Nature and Nurture."' *Journ. Roy. Anthrop. Inst.,* vol. V, p. 391–406.

Goodall, J., 1965: "Chimpanzees of the Gombe Stream Reserve," in I. DeVore, (ed.) *Primate Behavior.* Rinehart & Winston, New York.

Gusinde, M., 1942: *Die Kongo-Pygmäen in Geschichte und Gegenwart.* Nova Acta Leopoldina. N. F. Bd. 11, no. 76, Halle/S.

Hamburg, D. A., 1971: "Psychobiological Studies of Aggressive Behavior." *Nature,* vol. 230, no. 5288, p. 19–23.

Harlow, H. F. and M. K. Harlow, 1949: "Learning to Think." *Scientific American,* Aug. 1949.

——., 1962: Social Deprivation in Monkeys. *Scientific American,* Nov. 1962.

Harlow, H. F., 1959: "Love in Infant Monkeys." *Scientific American,* June 1959.

Itani, J., 1959: "Paternal Care of the Wild Japanese Monkey, *Macaca fuscata fuscata." Primates, Journ. of Primatology.* vol. 2, no. 1, p. 61–93.

Kawai, M., 1963: "On the Newly-acquired Behaviors of the Natural Troop of Japanese Monkeys on Koshima Island." *Primates,* vol. IV, no. 1, p. 113–15.

—— and A. Tsumori, 1963: "A Confirmatory Analysis of the Newly-acquired Behaviors of the Japanese Monkeys on Koshima Island." *Primates,* vol. IV, no. 1, p. 115–16.

Kawamura, S., 1959: "The Process of Sub-culture Propagation among Japanese Macaques." *Primates, Journ. of Primatology,* vol. 2, no. 1, p. 43–54.

Koehler, O., 1943: *Die Aufgaben der Tierpsychologie*. Halle/S.

Kropotkin, P., 1902: *Mutual Aid: A Factor of Evolution*. Heinemann, London.

Lahiri, R. K. and C. H. Southwick, 1966: "Paternal Care in *Macaca sylvana*." *Folia primatologica*, vol. 4, p. 257–64.

Lévi-Strauss, C., 1949: *Les Structures élémentaires de la parenté*. Paris, Ed. Mouton et Co., Den Haag.

Lorenz, K., 1963: *On Aggression*. Harcourt, Brace & World, New York.

——, 1964: "Ritualized Fighting," In: *Natural History of Aggression*. Institute of Biology Symposia No. 13, Academic Press, London and New York.

Malinowski, B., 1927: *Sex and Repression in Savage Society*. Kegan Paul, London.

Mead, M., 1935: *Sex and Temperament In Three Primitive Societies*. William Morrow, New York.

Milgram, S., 1965: "Some Conditions of Obedience and Disobedience to Authority." *Human Relations*, vol. 18, no. 1, p. 57–76.

Newman, H. H., F. N. Freeman and K. J. Holzinger, 1937: *Twins: a Study of Heredity and Environment*. University of Chicago Press, Chicago.

Nishida, T., 1970: "Social Behavior and Relationship among Wild Chimpanzees of the Mahali Mountains." *Primates*, vol. II, no. 1, p. 47–87.

Radin, P., 1927: *Primitive Man as Philosopher*. Appleton & Co., New York and London.

Rasmussen, K., 1929/32: Report of the Fifth Thule Expedition, vol. VII, VIII, IX.

Reynolds, V. and F. Reynolds, 1965: "Chimpanzees of the Budongo Forest," in I. DeVore (ed.), *Primate Behavior*, Holt, Rinehart & Winston, New York.

Rothacker, E., 1695: *Probleme der Kulturanthropologie*. Bouvier and Co. Verlag, Bonn.

Schaller, G. B., 1963: *The Mountain Gorilla: Ecology and Behavior*. University of Chicago Press, Chicago.

Shields, J., 1962: *Monozygotic Twins*. Oxford University Press, New York & London.

Simpson, G. G., 1966: "The Biological Nature of Man." *Science*, vol. 152, no. 3721, p. 472–78.

Spiro, M. E., 1954: "Human Nature in its Psychological Dimensions" *American Anthropologist*, vol. 56, no. 1, p. 19–30.

Turnbull, C. M., 1965: *Wayward Servants: The Two Worlds of the African Pygmies.* Natural History, New York.

Uexküll, J. von, 1928: "Gibt es ein Himmelsgewölbe?" *Archiv für Anthropologie,* N. F. Bd. XXI, S. 40–46.

Washburn, S. L. and I. DeVore, 1961: "The Social Life of Baboons." In: *Primate Social Behavior,* C. Southwick, ed. Van Nostrand Co., Princeton, N.J.

Yamada, M., 1963: "A Study of Blood Relationship in the Natural Society of the Japanese Macaque." *Primates, Journ. of Primatology,* vol. 4, no. 3, p. 43–65.

Yerkes, R. M. and A. W. Yerkes, 1953: *The Great Apes.* Yale University Press, New Haven.

DAVID PILBEAM

An Idea We Could Live Without: The Naked Ape

Last fall CBS Television broadcast a National Geographic Special, in prime time, called "Monkeys, Apes, and Man." This was an attempt to demonstrate how much studies of primates can tell us about our true biological selves. In a recent *Newsweek* magazine article, Stewart Alsop, while discussing problems of war, stated that nations often quarrel over geo-political real estate when national boundaries are poorly defined: his examples were culled from areas as diverse as the Middle East, Central Europe, and Asia. One of his introductory paragraphs included the following:

"The animal behaviorists—Konrad Lorenz, Robert Ardrey, Desmond Morris—have provided wonderful insights into human behavior. Animals that operate in groups, from fish up to our ancestors among the primates, instinctively establish and defend a territory, or turf. There are two main reasons why fighting erupts between turfs—when the turfs are ill-defined or overlapping; or when one group is so weakened by sickness or other cause as to be unable to defend its turf, thus inviting aggression."

Here Alsop is taking facts (some of them are actually untrue facts) from the field of ethology—which is the science of whole animal behavior as studied in naturalistic environments—and extrapolating

From *Discovery*, 7 (2). Spring 1972. Reprinted by permission.

directly to man from these ethological facts as though words such as *territoriality, aggression,* and so forth describe the same phenomena in all animal species, including man.

Both these examples from popular media demonstrate nicely what can be called "naked apery." When Charles Darwin first published *The Origin of Species* and *The Descent of Man,* over 100 years ago, few people believed in any kind of biological or evolutionary continuity between men and other primates. Gradually the idea of man's physical evolution from ape- or monkey-like ancestors came to be accepted; yet the concept of human behavioral evolution was always treated with scepticism, or even horror. But times have changed. No longer do we discriminate between rational man, whose behavior is almost wholly learned, and all other species, brutish automata governed solely by instincts.

One of the principal achievements of ethologists, particularly those who study primates, has been to demonstrate the extent to which the dichotomy between instinct and learning is totally inadequate in analyzing the behavior of higher vertebrate species—especially primates. Almost all behavior in monkeys and apes involves a mixture of the learned and the innate; almost all behavior is under some genetic control in that its development is channelled—although the amount of channelling varies. Thus, all baboons of one species will grow up producing much the same range of vocalizations; however, the same sound may have subtly different meanings for members of different troops of the same species. In one area, adult male baboons may defend the troop; those of the identical species in a different environment may habitually run from danger. Monkeys in one part of their species range may be sternly territorial; one hundred miles away feeding ranges of adjacent groups may overlap considerably and amicably. These differences are due to learning. Man is the learning animal par excellence. We have more to learn, take longer to do it, learn it in a more complex and yet more efficient way (that is, culturally), and have a unique type of communication system (vocal language) to promote our learning. All this the ethologists have made clear.

Studies of human behavior, at least under naturalistic conditions, have been mostly the preserve of social anthropologists and sociologists. The anthropological achievement has been to document the extraordinary lengths to which human groups will go to behave differently from other groups. The term "culture," a special one for the anthropologist, describes the specifically human type of learned behavior in which arbitrary rules and norms are so important. Thus, whether we have one or two spouses, wear black or white to a funeral, live in societies that have kings or lack chiefs entirely, is a function not of our genes but of learning; the matter depends upon which learned behaviors we deem appropriate—again because of learning. Some behaviors make us feel comfortable, others do not; some behaviors may be correct in one situation and not in another— forming a line outside a cinema as opposed to the middle of the sidewalk, for example; singing rather than whistling in church; talking to domestic animals but not to wild ones. The appropriate or correct behavior varies from culture to culture; exactly which one is appropriate is arbitrary. This sort of behavior is known as "context dependent behavior" and is, in its learned form, pervasively and almost uniquely human. So pervasive is it, indeed, that we are unaware most of the time of the effects on our behavior of context dependence. It is important to realize here that although a great deal of ape and monkey behavior is learned, little of it is context dependent in a cultural, human sense.

In the past ten years there has been a spate of books—the first of the genre was Robert Ardrey's *African Genesis* published in 1961— that claim first to describe man's "real" or "natural" behavior in ethological style, then go on to explain how these behaviors have evolved. In order to do this, primate societies are used as models of earlier stages of human evolution: primates are ourselves, so to speak, unborn. *African Genesis, The Territorial Imperative, The Social Contract,* all by Ardrey, *The Naked Ape* and *The Human Zoo* by Desmond Morris, Konrad Lorenz's *On Aggression,* the exotic, *The Descent of Woman,* by Elaine Morgan, plus Antony Jay's *Corporate Man,* without exception, for some reason approach the bestseller level. All purport to document the supposedly surprising truth that man is an animal. The more extreme of them also argue that his behavior—particularly his aggressive, status-oriented, territorial and sexual behavior—is somehow out of tune with the needs of the modern world, that these behaviors are under genetic control and are largely determined by our animal heritage, and that there is little we can do but accept our grotesque natures; if we insist on trying to change ourselves, we must realize that we have almost no room for maneuver, for natural man is far more like other animals than he would care to admit. Actually, it is of some anthropological interest to inquire exactly why this naked apery should have caught on. Apart from our obsessive neophilia, and the fact that these ideas are somehow "new," they provide attractive excuses for our unpleasant behavior toward each other.

However, I believed these general arguments to be wrong; they are based upon misinterpretation of ethological studies and of the rich variety of human behavior documented by anthropologists. At a time when so many people wish to reject the past because it has no meaning and can contribute nothing, it is perhaps a little ironic that arguments about man's innate and atavistic depravity should have so much appeal. The world *is* in a mess; people *are* unpleasant to each other; that much is true. I can only suppose that argument about the inevitability of all the nastiness not only absolves people in some way of the responsibility for their actions, but allows us also to sit back and positively enjoy it all. Let me illustrate my argument a little.

Take, for example, one particular set of ethological studies—those on baboons. Baboons are large African monkeys that live today south of the Sahara in habitats ranging from tropical rain forest to desert. They are the animals that have been most frequently used as models of early human behavior; a lot of work has been done on them, and they are easy to study—at least those living in the savannah habitats thought to be typical of the hunting territories of early man. They are appealing to ethologists because of their habitat, because they live in discrete and structured social groups, and because they have satisfied so many previous hypotheses.

Earlier reports of baboon behavior emphasized the following. Baboons are intensely social creatures, living in discrete troops of 30 to 50 animals, their membership rarely changing; they are omnivorous, foraging alone and rarely sharing food. Males are twice as big as females; they are stronger and more aggressive. The functions of male aggression supposedly are for repelling predators, for maintaining group order, and (paradoxically) for fighting among themselves. The adult males are organized into a dominance hierarchy, the most dominant animal being the one that gets his own way as far as food, grooming partners, sex, when to stop and eat, and when and where the troop should move are concerned. He is the most aggressive, wins the most fights, and impregnates the most desirable females. Females, by the way, do little that is exciting in baboondom, but sit around having babies, bickering, and tending to their lords. Adult males are clearly the most important animals—although they cannot have the babies—and they are highly status conscious. On the basis of fighting abilities they form themselves into a dominance hierarchy, the function of which is to reduce aggression by the controlling means of each animal knowing its own place in the hierarchy. When groups meet up, fighting may well ensue. When the troop moves, males walk in front and at the rear; when the group is attacked, adult males remain to fight a rearguard action as females and young animals flee to safety in the trees.

Here then we have in microcosm one view of the way our early ancestors may well have behaved. How better to account for the destructiveness of so much human male aggression, to justify sex differences in behavior, status seeking, and so forth. I exaggerate, of course, but not too much. But what comments can be made?

First, the baboons studied—and these are the groups that are described, reported, and extrapolated from in magazine articles, books, and in CBS TV specials—are probably abnormal. They live in game parks—open country where predators, especially human ones, are present in abundance—and are under a great deal of tension. The same species has been studied elsewhere—in the open country and in forest too, away from human contact—with different results.

Forest groups of baboons are fluid, changing composition regularly (rather than being tightly closed); only adult females and their offspring remain to form the core of a stable group. Food and cover are dispersed, and there is little fighting over either. Aggression in general is very infrequent, and male dominance hierarchies are difficult to discern. Intertroop encounters are rare, and friendly. When the troop is startled (almost invariably by humans, for baboons are probably too smart, too fast, and too powerful to be seriously troubled by other predators), it flees, and, far from forming a rearguard, the males—being biggest and strongest—are frequently up the trees long before the females (encumbered as they are with their infants).

When the troop moves it is the adult females that determine when and where to; and as it moves adult males are not invariably to be found in front and at the rear. As for sexual differences, in terms of functionally important behaviors, the significant dichotomy seems to be not between males and females but between adults and young. This makes good sense for animals that learn and live a long time.

The English primatologist Thelma Rowell, who studied some of these forest baboons in Uganda, removed a troop of them and placed them in cages where food had to be given a few times a day in competition-inducing clumps. Their population density went up and cover was reduced. The result? More aggression, more fighting, and the emergence of marked dominance hierarchies. So, those first baboons probably were under stress, in a relatively impoverished environment, pestered by humans of various sorts. The high degree of aggression, the hierarchies, the rigid sex-role differences, were in a sense abnormalities. In one respect, troop defense, there is accumulating evidence that male threats directed toward human interlopers occur only after troops become habituated to the observers, and must therefore be treated as learned behavior too.

Studies on undisturbed baboons elsewhere have shown other interesting patterns of adult male behaviors. Thus in one troop an old male baboon with broken canines was the animal that most frequently completed successful matings, that influenced troop movements, and served as a focus for females and infants, even though he was far less aggressive than, and frequently lost fights with, a younger and more vigorous adult male. Here, classical dominance criteria simply do not tie together as they are supposed to.

The concept of dominance is what psychologists call a unitary motivational theory: there are two such theories purporting to explain primate social behavior. These are that the sexual bond ties the group together, and that social dominance structures and orders the troop. The first of these theories has been shown to be wrong. The second we are beginning to realize is too simplistic. In undisturbed species in the wild, dominance hierarchies are hard to discern, if they are present at all; yet workers still persist in trying to find them. For example, Japanese primatologists describe using the "peanut test" to determine "dominance" in wild chimpanzees by seeing which chimp gets the goodies. Yet what relevance does such a test have for real chimp behavior in the wild where the animals have far more important things to do—in an evolutionary or truly biological sense—than fight over peanuts? Such an experimental design implies too the belief that "dominance" is something lurking just beneath the surface, waiting for the appropriate releaser.

Steven Gartlan, an English primatologist working in the Cameroons, has recently suggested a different way of analyzing behavior, in terms of function. Each troop has to survive and reproduce, and in order to do so it must find food, nurture its mothers, protect and give its young the opportunity to learn adult skills. There are certain tasks that have to be completed if successful survival is to result. For example, the troop must be led, fights might be stopped, lookouts kept, infants fed and protected; some animals must serve as social foci, others might be needed to chase away intruders, and so on. Such an attribute list can be extended indefinitely.

If troop behavior is analyzed in a functional way like this, it immediately becomes clear that different classes of animals perform different functions. Thus, in undisturbed baboons, adults, particularly males, police the troop; males, especially the subadults and young adults, maintain vigilance; adult females determine the time and direction of movement; younger animals, especially infants, act as centers of attention.

Thus a particular age-sex class performs a certain set of behaviors that go together and that fulfill definite adaptive needs. Such a constellation of behavioral attributes is termed a role. Roles, even in nonhuman primates, are quite variable. (Witness the great differences between male behaviors in normal baboon troops and those under stress.) If dominance can come and go with varying intensities of certain environmental pressures, then it is clearly not innately inevitable, even in baboons. Rigid dominance hierarchies, then, seem to be largely artifacts of abnormal environments.

What is particularly interesting in the newer animal studies is the extent to which aggression, priority of access, and leadership are divorced from each other. Although a baboon may be highly aggressive, what matters most is how other animals react to him; if they ignore him as far as functionally important behaviors such as grooming, mating and feeding are concerned, then his aggression is, in a social or evolutionary sense, irrelevant.

I want to look a little more closely at aggression, again from the functional point of view. What does it do? What is the point of a behavior that can cause so much trouble socially?

The developmental course of aggressive behavior has been traced in a number of species: among primates it is perhaps best documented in rhesus macaques, animals very similar to baboons. There are genetical and hormonal bases to aggressive behavior in macaques; in young animals males are more aggressive, on the average, than females, and this characteristic is apparently related to hormonal influences. If animals are inadequately or abnormally socialized, aggressive behaviors become distorted and exaggerated. Animals that are correctly socialized in normal habitats, or richly stimulating artificial ones, show moderate amounts of aggression, and only in certain circumstances. These would be, for example, when an infant is threatened, when a choice item is disputed, when fights have to be interrupted, under certain circumstances when the troop is threatened, and occasionally when other species are killed for food.

Under normal conditions, aggression plays little part in other aspects of primate social life. The idea that the function of maleness is to be overbearingly aggressive, to fight constantly, and to be dominant, makes little evolutionary sense.

How about extrapolations from primates to man that the "naked-apers" are so fond of? Take, for example, dominance. Everything that I have said about its shortcomings as a concept in analyzing baboon social organization applies to man, only more so. Behaviors affecting status-seeking in man are strongly influenced by learning, as we can see by the wide variation in human behavior from one society to another. In certain cultures, status is important, clear-cut, and valued; the emphasis placed on caste in Hindu society is an obvious example. At the opposite extreme, though—among the Bushmen of the Kalahari Desert, for example—it is hard to discern; equality and cooperativeness are highly valued qualities in Bushman society, and hence learned by each new generation.

I've used the term "status-seeking" rather than "dominance" for humans, because it describes much better the kind of hierarchical ordering one finds within human groups. And that points to a general problem in extrapolating from monkey to man, for "status" is a word that one can't easily apply to baboon or chimp society; status involves prestige, and prestige presupposes values—arbitrary rules or norms. That sort of behavior is cultural, human, and practically unique.

As we turn to man, let's consider for a while human groups as they were before the switch to a settled way of life began a mere—in evolutionary terms—10,000 years ago. Before that our ancestors were hunters and gatherers. Evidence for this in the form of stone tool making, living areas with butchered game, camp sites, and so on, begins to turn up almost 3 million years ago, at a time when our ancestors were very different physically from us. For at least 2½ to 3 million years, man and his ancestors have lived as hunters and gatherers. The change from hunting to agricultural-based economies began, as I said, just over 10,000 years ago, a fractional moment on the geological time scale. That famous (and overworked) hypothetical visiting Martian geologist of the 21st century would find remains of hunters represented in hundreds of feet of sediments; the first evidence for agriculture, like the remains of the thermonuclear holocaust, would be jammed, together, in the last few inches. Hunting and gathering has been a highly significant event in human history; indeed, it is believed by most of us interested in human evolution to have been an absolutely vital determinant, molding many aspects of human behavior.

There are a number of societies surviving today that still live as hunters and gatherers; Congo pygmies, Kalahari Bushmen, and Australian Aborigines, are three well-known examples. When comparisons are made of these hunting societies, we can see that certain features are typical of most or all of them, and these features are likely to have been typical of earlier hunters.

In hunting societies, families—frequently monogamous nuclear families—are often grouped together in bands of 20 to 40 individuals; members of these hunting bands are kinsmen, either by blood or marriage. The band hunts and gathers over wide areas, and its foraging range often overlaps those of adjacent groups. Bands are flexible and variable in composition—splitting and reforming with changes in the seasons, game and water availability, and whim.

Far from life being "nasty, brutish, and short" for these peoples, recent studies show that hunters work on the average only 3 or 4 days each week; the rest of their time is leisure. Further, at least 10% of Bushmen, for example, are over 60 years of age, valued and nurtured by their children. Although they lack large numbers of material possessions, one can never describe such peoples as savages, degenerates, or failures.

The men in these societies hunt animals while the women gather plant food. However, women often scout for game, and in some groups may also hunt smaller animals, while a man returning empty-handed from a day's hunting will almost always gather vegetable food on his way. Thus the division of labor between sexes is not distinct and immutable; it seems to be functional, related to mobility: the women with infants to protect and carry simply cannot move far and fast enough to hunt efficiently.

Relations between bands are amicable; that makes economic sense as the most efficient way of utilizing potentially scarce resources, and also because of exogamy—marrying out—for adjacent groups will contain kinsmen and kinsmen will not fight. Within the group, individual relations between adults are cooperative and based upon reciprocity; status disputes are avoided. These behaviors are formalized, part of cultural behavior, in that such actions are positively valued and rewarded. Aggression between individuals is generally maintained at the level of bickering; in cases where violence flares, hunters generally solve the problem by fission: the band divides.

Data on child-rearing practices in hunters are well known only in Bushmen, and we don't yet know to what extent Bushmen are typical of hunters. (This work on Bushman child-rearing, as yet unpublished, has been done by Patricia Draper, an anthropologist at the University of New Mexico, and I am grateful to her for permitting me to use her data.) Bushman children are almost always in the company of adults; because of the small size of Bushman societies, children rarely play in large groups with others of their own age. Aggression is minimal in the growing child for two principal reasons. First, arguments between youngsters almost inevitably take place in the presence of adults and adults always break these up before fights erupt; so the socialization process gives little opportunity for practicing aggressive behavior. Second, because of the reciprocity and cooperativeness of adults, children have few adult models on which to base the learning of aggressiveness.

Thus, the closest we can come to a concept of "natural man" would indicate that our ancestors were, like other primates, capable of being aggressive, but they would have been socialized culturally in such a way as to reduce as far as possible the manifestation of aggression. This control through learning is much more efficient in man than in other primates, because we are cultural creatures— with the ability to attach positive values to aggression-controlling behaviors. Thus Bushmen value and thereby encourage peaceful cooperation. Their culture provides the young with non-violent models.

Other cultures promote the very opposite. Take, for example, the Yanomamö Indians of Venezuela and Brazil; their culture completely reverses our ideals of "good" and "desirable." To quote a student of Yanomamö society: "A high capacity for rage, a quick flash point, and a willingness to use violence to obtain one's ends are considered desirable traits." In order to produce the appropriate adult behaviors, the Yanomamö encourage their children, especially young boys, to argue, fight, and be generally belligerent. These behaviors, I should emphasize, are learned, and depend for their encouragement upon specific cultural values.

Our own culture certainly provides the young with violent, though perhaps less obtrusive, models. These I should emphasize again, are to a great extent learned and arbitrary, and we *could* change them should we choose to do so.

So far we have seen that fierce aggression and status-seeking are no more "natural" attributes of man than they are of most monkey and ape societies. The degree to which such behaviors are developed depends very considerably indeed upon cultural values and learning. Territoriality likewise is not a "natural" feature of human group living; nor is it among most other primates.

As a parting shot, let me mention one more topic that is of great interest to everyone at the moment—sex roles. Too many of us have in the past treated the male and female stereotypes of our particular culture as fixed and "natural": in our genes so to speak. It may well be true that human male infants play a little more vigorously than females, or that they learn aggressive behaviors somewhat more easily, because of hormonal differences. But simply look around the world at other cultures. In some, "masculinity" and "femininity" are much more marked than they are in our own culture; in others the roles are blurred. As I said earlier, among Bushmen that are still hunters, sex roles are far from rigid, and in childhood the two sexes have a very similar upbringing. However, among those Bushmen that have adopted a sedentary life devoted to herding or agriculture, sex roles are much more rigid. Men devote their energies to one set of tasks, women to another, mutually exclusive set. Little boys learn only "male" tasks, little girls exclusively "female" ones. Maybe the switch to the sedentary life started man on the road toward marked sex role differences. These differences are almost entirely learned, and heavily affected by economic factors.

So much of human role behavior is learned that we could imagine narrowing or widening the differences almost as much or as little as we wish.

So, what conclusions can be drawn from all this? It is overly simplistic in the extreme to believe that man behaves in strongly genetically deterministic ways, when we know that apes and monkeys do not. Careful ethological work shows us that the primates closely related to us—chimps and baboons are the best known—get on quite amicably together under natural and undisturbed conditions. Learning plays a very significant part in the acquisition of their behavior. They are not for the most part highly aggressive, obsessively dominance-oriented, territorial creatures.

There is no evidence to support the view that early man was a violent status-seeking creature; ethological and anthropological evidence indicates rather that pre-urban men would have used their evolving cultural capacities to channel and control aggression. To be sure, we are not born empty slates upon which anything can be written; but to believe in the "inevitability of beastliness" is to deny our humanity as well as our primate heritage—and, incidentally, does a grave injustice to the "beasts."

SALLY CARRIGHAR

War Is Not in Our Genes

There are still men and women living who can remember the horror which greeted Darwin's theory that we are "descended from apes." That phrase probably accounted in part for the revulsion because "descended from" was generally used in a more personal way—"I am descended from Scottish ancestors," that is, I am one of them, I am like them. Darwin meant, of course, "We have evolved from apes," with apes standing in for the whole range of evolved animals, but the unfortunate phrase had caught on.

That we have *evolved* from apes—and are, therefore, obviously different from them—is an unemotional, scientific assertion, harmless enough, it would seem, except that it does leave Adam and Eve stranded without progeny and raises an unresolved question about men's souls. If each human being has been created with his own unique soul, then so have all animals—wolves, rabbits, mice, water bugs. To many people that thought was, and still is, intolerable, although the concept does not seem very difficult if one thinks of soul as *life,* the bit of animation temporarily lent from the great source of all life.

The first, grudging acceptance of evolution was in connection with physical structures: it was hard for anyone to deny such evidence as the development of a thinking cortex on top of a simpler

From *The New York Times Magazine,* September 10, 1967. Copyright © 1967 by The New York Times Company. Reprinted in revised form by permission.

brain. The idea of the evolution of *behavior,* however, has been slower to win support, for there is no "fossil behavior." From fossil bones, guesses can be made as to the ways that the bones were used, but how can anyone ever reliably know the origins of the habits of today's animals—or of our own?

Nevertheless, the evolution of behavior is now inspiring one of biology's hottest debates.

Darwin himself laid the groundwork for it when he wrote "The Expression of the Emotions in Man and Animals," and showed how closely alike the signs of emotion are. This book was largely ignored, at least in its implications, for the mechanical age had arrived and there was more interest in putting captive animals into pieces of apparatus, in testing their reflexes, their ability to find their way out of mazes, to count, and to discriminate between colors and forms—problems like these.

About 1950, however, a group calling themselves ethologists broke out of the laboratories, declaring that the most reliable facts about animal behavior are secured by watching animals in their natural habitats. From the discoveries made by these thoughtful observers, it soon became clear that we really don't know very much about how most animals lead their lives, about what animals do. Dr. William H. Thorpe of Cambridge University was one of the first to stride boldly onto the battlefield with the statement: "There is hardly any aspect of the behavior of animals which may not have some reference to problems in human behavior."

Some ethologists fell on that battlefield and went back to the laboratories. The ones who stayed in the field had to endure some ridicule; they were called Boy Scouts and taunted with the criticism that their work could not be a science since most of it was done without experimentation. Some of this obviously stung, for few ethologists are now simply trying to fill in the great gaps in our knowledge about the daily lives of wild animals. Work in the field must now include experimentation, and some ethologists are even confining the animals that they study in artificial environments which they call "semi-wild."

Meanwhile, the behavior of animals has fascinated the non-scientific public. Readers devour Joy Adamson's Elsa books, George Schaller's reports of his gorilla companions and those of Jane

Goodall about the chimpanzees with whom she and her husband live. An increasing number of popular films and television programs about animals whet this interest. And if orthodox biologists hold out against assuming any lines of descent in human behavior, from all sides laymen are asking what we can learn from living animals.

What about the relationship between the sexes? What about care of the young and their training, about the health of animals and how they maintain it, their feeding habits, how they relax and the ways in which they play? Above all, with war so great a threat in our lives, what about animal aggression?

This last has been the subject of two recent and readable books: "On Aggression," by Konrad Lorenz, and "The Territorial Imperative," by Robert Ardrey. Both authors declare that fighting is an instinct which demands expression in virtually all higher animals—and also in ourselves because, they claim, we have inherited this compulsion. Before examining their arguments, however, it is first necessary to define exactly what is meant by aggression.

Most laymen would think at once of predatory attacks on prey for food: the pursuit, the pounce, the kill. The biological definition, however, excludes this kind of slaughter because it involves no malice. A wolf bringing down an ill or aged caribou (a strong caribou can outrun a wolf) is no more angry than we are when we buy meat at the butcher's shop. He is merely hungry, as are other predators when prey is there and vulnerable.

Nor is there any true aggression, any malice, between members of different species going about their separate ways in the wilderness they share. They seem to recognize that each has different needs and perhaps, in their inarticulate way, they even recognize that other species have rights. On a path used by many or at a water hole or salt lick, the weaker and smaller animals await their turn, letting the stronger go first without argument.

Aggressiveness in its strict biological sense, and in the sense that Lorenz and Ardrey use the word, is expressed between two members *of the same species* when both want the same thing. With the great majority of animals, this same thing will be living space in which to raise the young of the year—an animal's homesite, also known as his territory.

Sometimes aggressiveness is aroused over possession of a desired female or over rank in a hierarchy. Biologists often call the space around a disputed female a territory. It moves when she moves and the male, going along, will not allow another male to approach within a certain well-understood distance.

Lorenz and Ardrey both tie their definition of aggressiveness in mankind to home territory. They call attention to properties marked with "No Trespassing" signs and—this is their ominous and essential theme—they extend the concept of farms or suburban lots to the nation, claiming that men fight to preserve or expand their national boundaries almost as involuntarily as they would their homes. They fight the soldiers of other nations because their remote animal ancestors once instinctively fought for nesting site, burrow, hunting range or the space which encircles a female.

Thus both Lorenz and Ardrey are convinced that war is an instinctive compulsion. Lorenz says that the most important function of animal aggression "is the spacing out of individuals of one species over the available habitat, in other words, the distribution of 'territories.'" He concludes: "There cannot be any doubt, in the opinion of any biologically minded scientist, that intra-specific aggression is, in man, just as much of a spontaneous instinctive drive as in most other higher vertebrates."

Ardrey, for his part, says: "If we defend the title to our land or the sovereignty of our country, we do it for reasons no different, no less innate, no less *ineradicable* than do the lower animals" (italics added). He also says: "All of us will give everything we are for a place of our own." And: "I believe man's innumerable territorial expressions are human responses to an imperative lying with equal force on mockingbirds and men."

Now, a widespread belief that human wars are instinctive, by which biologists mean inevitable, would of course tend to make them inevitable. Therefore it seems worthwhile to inquire whether aggression is universal in animals and just how insistent an urge it is. If aggression, as these authors insist, is a doom carried in human genes, we are predestined to wage wars and hopes for peace would seem to be slim. Lorenz does plead with some eloquence for an effort to replace competition for living space with competition in sports and other sublimations—but he already has made the urge to fight for territory seem so over-powering that the final impression left by "On Aggression" leans toward the depressing view that fighting for territory is, in Ardrey's word, "ineradicable." That this is the lasting message gained from both books is shown by the comments of many reviewers and readers. The publicity for both, including pictures of viciously snarling animals, helps to promote this conviction.

It must be agreed that during mating seasons, at least, disputes over territorial boundary lines are prevalent. Spring, when most animal young are born and many conceived, is a time of much sparring for areas on which to raise them and find their food. But for some species, late summer and fall are the rutting season, and that is the time when the "territories" surrounding females are fought for.

In most cases, such aggressive behavior is related to reproductive needs. A territory, as space, can be as small as the single nesting tree defended by a woodpecker, or the range, nine miles or more in diameter, believed necessary to feed an average family of wolves.

To the creatures themselves, territory probably means home in the same way that home, for us, means more than house. To them the need may be temporary but it is not surprising that they instinctively fight for it.

But how universally and how desperately? The doom of eternal war would not seem so inescapable for us if some animals—indeed, if *any* of them—can escape the compulsion.

Caribou have no territories; neither do elephants. Sea otters don't. They copulate in the water and raise their young in fronds of seaweed. Whales are not likely to have individual homesites, although no one knows definitely. Lemmings live in villages, shallow excavations in the Arctic frost mounds, with several lemmings sleeping together in each nest until a gravid female is about to give birth, when she makes a nest of her own.

These could be called colonies. There are numerous animals in the temperate zone who have communal dwellings: gophers, prairie dogs, marmots. What goes on in their hidden worlds, at each stage of the annual cycle, is imperfectly known for most species. Some colonies defend the territory shared by all; it appears that others do not. Within the burrow it is customary for an individual family to defend its own unit.

What of cowbirds, which lay their eggs in other birds' nests and then are off to live on the backs of cattle (formerly bison), feeding on the parasites in their hosts' fur? It is amusing to speculate on whether individual cowbirds claim certain cows as their territory. It seems unlikely.

Among primates, most monkeys live in groups. In some there is a hierarchical social organization. Usually the dominant male has first choice when a female is in oestrus and discord often prevails. Other groups are sexually promiscuous and among them fighting often seems abhorrent. If youngsters are too aggressive, the adult males will separate them.

Howling monkeys claim possession of their communal areas but defend them generally with only vocal protests—as do gibbon families. When their screams fail to drive away intruders, gibbons may bite, but such occasions are rare.

The English ethologist J. H. Crook discussed the question of territory in The Listener, April 6, 1967. He explained the very flexible attitude of some birds and animals usually thought to defend territories. A territory "allows an individual to develop a close familiarity with a locality. This increases its food-finding efficiency and the speed of finding refuge from enemies." But some ducks that mate on their wintering grounds, or on migration, will accompany a new spouse to its homesite instead of returning to their own.

Species may change territories in response to local conditions. In drier years, certain marsh-dwelling weaver birds will disperse their nests over a large ground area; in wetter years, they may congregate in a large tree islanded in a flood pool. Harem groups of the gelada baboon wander independently in poor feeding years but "congregate in large herds of variable size under conditions of plenty. They have no territories, their disposition directly reflecting the local food availability."

Chimpanzees, says Dr. Crook, vary the size of their parties. As a rule individual and small groups wander over large home ranges and "territorial behavior appears to be absent." The facts are complex he says. "The dispersion pattern itself must depend largely on learning and tradition, and this is particularly so when we are talking about advanced mammals such as the monkeys. The sort of territory-holding present is more likely to be determined by the commodities for which the higher mammals compete than by any species characteristic directly determined by the genes. Thus in different ecologies, territorial systems will vary or even be absent altogether." These conclusions regarding the animals closest to us in the evolutionary scale seem very significant.

How unreliable are rigid definitions of territory was emphasized on Britain's BBC Third Program in August 1967 by Dr. Paul Layhausen, director of the Max Planck Institut at Wuppertal and described as "one of the world's foremost experts" on the subject of animal behavior. Territoriality is not just the static demarcation of an area, he said; it is part of a much more complex working out of a system of relationships in time as well as space—the very subtle and fluid pattern of "destiny tolerance." He continued: "There's much more to it still, of course: the difference between the ways in which mammals and birds 'survey' their territory . . . ; the interlacing of the routes by which animals go about their affairs, and the interrelation of the times at which they do things . . . Density tolerance is a matter of time as well as space."

One thinks of the fact that many bird parents will tolerate the trespassing of neighbors after their young are out of the nest: the time factor here seems more important than that of space.

Since most birds and animals which defend territories do limit this strongly emotional response to the reproductive season, a point to be considered is whether human beings, too, only feel animosity toward aliens while they are of the child-bearing age. Much depends on the individual, but that is the time, granted, when many homes are first established. If the most intense "territorial" feelings are typical of the young adults, how does it happen that most countries have to resort to conscription in order to raise their predominantly youthful military units? As is well known, those who enter the services voluntarily often do so to escape from conditions which seem stifling at the parental home. Others marry at about the same age and set up their own households. Some biologists, as an argument for territoriality, make much of the fact that animal young may be "driven out" in their second year. Observations in the wild suggest that few have to be driven. When they are ready to mate, they wish to form their own families and in order to do so, they leave.

Ardrey is not a biologist, as he himself explicitly and creditably states in his book. In reporting the work of professionals, he seems simply to have misjudged the emphasis that they put on territories and territorial aggression.

Lorenz, of course, is an ethologist of world repute, but his experience with animals is limited in a different way. He has done most of his research with tamed animals, such as geese induced by guard fences and food to live in a human environment, and with captive cichlid fishes in tanks. All creatures so confined have their aggressiveness heightened enormously.

As Lorenz himself explains, these two types of animals, fish and birds, are among those which demand "individual distance," meaning that they do not welcome, at any time, anywhere, the close approach of their con-specifics (the biological term for others of one's own species). Lorenz's fish and geese, disturbed by the enforced intimate association with their mates, have worked out rather elaborate rituals for "redirecting" their aggression—from mates to neighboring males. Since these are only symbolic attacks, the adjacent male seldom is injured, and the spouse, with his aggression now neutralized, returns to his mate triumphant.

Rituals *of the same sort* are not employed by our own class of animals, mammals, for mammals are "contact" species—that is, they seek and enjoy the touch of their own kind. This distinction between animals who want and those who do not want to be near their con-specifics is only mentioned briefly by Lorenz, but it is actually of the most basic importance.

Lorenz sets out in detail the observation that among all strongly aggressive animals there is a very powerful inhibition against killing con-specifics. Since they do, unavoidably, often annoy one another, however, various behavior patterns have become established to prevent fights with lethal consequences. The redirected aggression of fish and geese is one example; among mammals, a common mechanism is simply the flight of the weaker combatant. The victor does not pursue him; the fact that he gives in is satisfaction enough.

Serving the same purpose are many close-range gestures of submission or appeasement. Lorenz describes the well-known reaction of a defeated wolf. As soon as he recognizes that he will lose a fight, the wolf turns his head away, a movement that the victor immediately understands and accepts. When Lorenz described this wolf behavior in 1952 in "King Solomon's Ring," he spoke of it as the loser "offering his neck" to his opponent—moving evidence of good faith between wolves, inasmuch as the victor always withholds the final bite.

Since that time, Lorenz has more firmly become a "mechanist." In "On Aggression," he describes the loser's behavior as one of the "submissive or appeasing movements [which] have evolved from juvenile expression movements persisting into adulthood. This is not surprising to anyone who knows how strong the inhibition against attacking pups is in any normal dog." But however defined, the wolf ritual works; it prevents the killing of a con-specific.

Another form of ritualized, harmless fighting is the "tournament," such as the pushing contest between two ungulates (deer or other hoofed quadrupeds) during the rut. If they really wanted to kill each other, they would attack with their hoofs (as they do a predator). Instead they literally lock horns, each trying to make the other give way. As soon as one knows himself to be losing ground, he disengages his antlers, turns and runs, and the winner goes back to his females. It is a contest to see which is the stronger male—and the one, therefore, more likely to father superior fawns and, in those ungulate species in which the bulls defend the herd, more likely to prove a superior warden against predators.

Perhaps from their concentration on the subject, both Ardrey and Lorenz seem to have exaggerated impressions of the amount of conspecific aggression. At the start of Chapter II of "On Aggression," Lorenz writes: "What is the significance of all this fighting? In nature, fighting is such an ever-present process, its behavior mechanisms and weapons are so highly developed and have so obviously arisen under the selection pressure of a species-preserving function that it is our duty to ask this Darwinian question . . . Darwin's expression, 'the struggle for existence,' is sometimes erroneously interpreted as the struggle between different species. In reality, the struggle Darwin was thinking of . . . is the competition between near relatives."

When Lorenz writes of "all this fighting," and fighting as being "such an ever-present process" in nature, he is describing a wilderness that would not be recognized by those who, like myself, have lived there for years at a stretch.

On some mornings one finds blood on the snow where tracks of fox and hare collide, but that is evidence of predation, not the encounter of an animal with another of its own kind. Real aggression, usually reproductive in its origin and purpose, concerns the animals so briefly that most of the several dozen species I am familiar with spend far more than half their time—some of them as much as 11 months in the year—in casual or amiable association with their fellows.

Typical are black bears. After a rather perfunctory but successful courtship, a male returns to a drowsy life, the daytime often spent in a copse with four or five other males. They do, however, show animosity toward one of the off-shade bears that are a color phase of their own species. The forest rangers say that these rejected bears become neurotic. One charged me once, with small provocation. I escaped into my cabin but he stalked me for the next three weeks until, my exasperation boiling over, I attacked him, hurling rocks and language I hardly realized I knew. He left for good—I hope with no new psychological trauma.

Both Lorenz and Ardrey distinguish too briefly between offensive and defensive fighting. Is one who defends his territory "aggressive?" If not, if only an invader is properly so described, how many do thus intrude? Extremely few, except in captivity. Among wolves, one who comes into the territory of another's family may be seeking companionship (a "lone wolf" is usually an orphan). According to most observers, he is not attacked; he is simply threatened and he leaves—and is not pursued to the border. Even the young ungulate bull or buck does not often boldly challenge an older, stronger male. He tries to steal a female, and when he encounters the leader's anger, at once retires to a safer distance.

Those who describe the wilderness from a domestic garden like Darwin's or Lorenz's fenced enclosure and laboratory or Ardrey's library, tend to put the emphasis on a few, dramatic animals like rats, wolves and lions.

Rats are contact species, and to explain some fights he saw among rats, Lorenz suggests that they were not personal confrontations, that rat clans tend to kill all outsiders. Such group aggressiveness would seem especially ominous because of the possible analogy with mankind's national wars. But here, as with geese and fish, Lorenz is presenting evidence provided by captives, and captives held in conditions so unsatisfactory as to stimulate fighting.

As Lorenz describes them: "Steiniger put brown rats from different localities into a large enclosure which provided them with completely natural living conditions. At first the individual animals seemed afraid of each other; they were not in an aggressive mood, but they bit each other if they met by chance, particularly if two were driven towards each other along one side of the enclosure, so that they collided at speed." (Most biologists, incidentally, would not call the conditions provided by any enclosure as "completely natural"—especially not if it were so small that individuals collided when racing along the fence.)

Steiniger's rats soon began to attack one another and fought until all but one pair were killed. The descendants of that pair formed a clan, which subsequently slaughtered every strange rat introduced into the habitat.

During the same years that this study was being conducted, John B. Calhoun in Baltimore was also investigating the behavior of rats. There were 15 rats in F. Steiniger's original population; 14 in Calhoun's—also strangers to one another. But Calhoun's enclosure was *16 times* larger than Steiniger's and more favorable in other ways: "harborages" were provided for rats pursued by hostile associates (such refuges would probably exist in the wild), and all Calhoun's rats were identified by markings.

For 27 months, from a tower in the center of the large area, the movements of all the individual rats were recorded. After a few fights while getting acquainted, they separated into two clans, neither of which tried to eliminate the other. There was a good deal of crossing back and forth unchallenged—so often by some individuals that they were dubbed messengers.

Steiniger has also observed rat clans on a small island in the North Sea. They were rather belligerent in a neutral no-man's-land. But isn't it possible that these rat populations were outgrowing the available living area? The crowdedness of many communities is surely one cause for the dangerous degree of aggressiveness now existing throughout the world. War and the population explosion: these influences must be related—to what extent would seem to be a most promising study of man's belligerent motives. But as for clan-aggressiveness, *per se,* many of us believe that this cannot be identified with any certainty as an evolutionary source of human wars.

Other than rats, wolves, and lions, there is a vast kingdom of little lives absorbed in the business of living. When Lorenz says that "fighting is an ever-present process" in nature, he must be forgetting all the moles, hedgehogs, raccoons, opossums, woodchucks, otters, chipmunks, squirrels of several kinds, rabbits, lemmings, moles, muskrats and beavers—not "eager," as a leisure generation of human beings has facetiously called them, but terribly earnest about creating one of the most complex (and needed) animal "estates" on earth. It is usual for them to respect one another's ownership of these properties.

Lorenz says that only the most aggressive creatures ever form permanent pairs, but beavers mate for life. And although their gnawing teeth would serve as very effective weapons, I have never known any occasion when they were so used against con-specifics. In their cleverly built houses, behind the dams and network of canals they have constructed, they live in notable harmony with one another and with the muskrats, for whom they provide ponds and who may be welcomed into beaver houses—as badgers will receive, and make friends with, coyotes and foxes.

How would such animals have *time* for continual fighting? What the absent biologists do not seem to realize is that a wilderness is a community of workers. Simply finding enough to eat every day is a chancy and tiring task. Think of the vast bulk of a whale to be nourished and the problems of providing for a family of wolves (averaging 12).

One has a mental picture of field mice running around everywhere in sufficient numbers to sustain the predators, but examination of some coyotes' stomach contents showed that, for days, they had eaten nothing but small amounts of berries, carrion, garbage and old scraps of leather.

It may be a surprise to know that many animals also spend a great deal of time keeping themselves clean and, if possible, free of parasites. Primates groom one another for hours every day. One year, one of the small pretty deer-mice came in to share my cabin, and sometimes I wished she would stop washing her fur; she did it so incessantly it was tiring to watch. (When I bathed, sponging water over myself from the basin in which I stood, she always took up a position in front of me and went through her own bathing routine. I used to wonder whether she sensed the analogy. I don't think she did but I enjoyed asking the question.)

Such mammals as these, in rising strata of complexity—these are our ancestors, more recent than the primitive, sexually antagonistic fish and geese. Many mammals have never even developed rituals to prevent the death of con-specifics, because they don't need them. Except when attacked by a predator, they quite simply do not fight.

Our immediate forebears, the apes, seem to have reached something like a summit in nonaggressiveness, since they do not fight either—not as individuals or as clans. Lorenz suggests that they do not attack their associates because they do not have such effective weapons as the teeth of wolves or the paws of lions, but would not the arm of a full-grown male gorilla be as strong as a lion's paw?

We do not know which mammals were the nearest ancestors of primates, but there are sufficient numbers of nonaggressive creatures living today to suggest that co-operation was becoming the habit of evolving mammals even before the primates developed. What, therefore, has happened? Man obviously is an aggressive animal. We have lost both the peacefulness and the inhibition against killing others of our own kind. Is there an explanation?

As Lorenz points out, aggressiveness can be taught. It is also intensified when it is exercised (and atrophies when it is not). When men began to settle in communities, they learned the irritations of being crowded. By then they had probably learned the use of weapons, originally for the purpose of killing game. And since they had already acquired at least a rudimentary speech, they could absorb from one another, and preach, animosity. With words, they could incite hatred against neighboring tribes. A leader, coveting power or property, could, with propaganda, instill in his subjects admiration for warlike attitudes.

Perhaps that is the way—culturally rather than genetically—that human aggressiveness arose. As for sadism, something no animal displays, it is my belief that the trait is psychotic. (In the case of cats' treatment of mice, research indicates that it is pure play—though useful as practice of hunting skills. The cat probably does not realize that it is torturing the mice.)

Nothing could more effectively prolong man's fighting behavior than a belief that aggression is in our genes. An unwelcome cultural inheritance can be eradicated fairly quickly and easily, but the incentive to do it is lacking while people believe that aggression is innate and instinctive with us, as both Ardrey and Lorenz declare.

More than 100 years ago, the philosopher William Whewell wrote: "There is a mask of theory over the whole face of nature." Anyone writing about the wilderness has a great responsibility not to accept too readily a belief that the mask is nature's true face. In a chaotic and perfidious world, nature is all we have that is infallibly real.

If writers assert their own, unproven hypotheses as the truth, civilized people, so isolated from the wilderness that they cannot recognize a fallacy when they hear one, will be deprived in their one lifeline of what may be felt intuitively as sane and good. Then, even the intuition will be lost—what is there left for anybody but madness?

J. P. SCOTT

That Old-Time Aggression

The control of destructive violence between individuals and nations is one of the major practical problems of our times. Its consequences are so great that it deserves a major scientific effort directed toward its solution, and its causes are so many and so various that scientists from almost every discipline, from mathematics through physiology and biological sciences to the social sciences, have something to contribute. *On Aggression* is such a contribution, written by the distinguished European ethologist Konrad Lorenz.

It is a beautifully written and translated book, and follows a line of argument which almost anyone can understand. Lorenz apparently began it as a reaction against Freud's interpretation of aggression as an impulse of destruction directed both toward others and toward oneself. He points out that fighting behavior in the animal kingdom had evolved in many different ways and usually serves some useful function, such as the dispersal of animals throughout their living space and the division of land into breeding territories so that adequate food is available for the young. And he describes human aggressive impulses as probably having had some such constructive function in primitive man. Aggression is therefore not necessarily an evil, but is evil because it has been distorted from its original function.

No modern student of the evolution of animal behavior would

From *The Nation*, January 9, 1967, pp. 53–54. Reprinted by permission.

quarrel with this viewpoint, and this is a major contribution to the understanding of aggressive behavior in animal societies.

Nevertheless, this is a disappointing book, both from a scientific and a practical point of view. Lorenz explains aggressive behavior on the basis of instinct, an idea which was popular around the turn of the century, and his solution for the problem, sublimation, was presented with equal eloquence and greater practicality by William James in his essay on "The Moral Equivalent of War," in 1910.

To understand why a modern biologist would publish a book which leaves out of consideration most of the scientific discoveries of the past 50 years requires some knowledge of Lorenz. He is a very intelligent person who picks up ideas quickly and who has a great deal of verbal and written fluency. He also has the ability to make friends quickly and to communicate a sense of excitement, and by these personal qualities he has been able to inspire a great many people to enter the field of animal behavior, or ethology, as it is sometimes called. He is also kindly and humanitarian, and this comes through in both his personal contacts and his writings.

At the same time he is a very narrow specialist, who primarily knows the behavior of birds, and particularly that of ducks and geese, on which his book has an excellent chapter. He evidently reads very little other than material which is directly related to his own specialty. Consequently, when he began observing the behavior of birds from the viewpoint of native behavior, or instinct, he went back to the writings of other students of bird life, Wallace Craig and Whitman, for his theoretical concepts. Lorenz quotes articles published in 1918, and most of the ideas in them had been worked out years before. This was before modern geneticists had begun to work out the consequences of the facts of Mendelian genetics in relation to evolution, and it was also before the publication of much of the modern work on the physiology of the emotions and appetites. These ideas of instinct are thus pre-Mendelian and pre-physiological, and in this day and age such a classical theory of instinct forms a very incomplete and inadequate explanation of behavior.

One of the major points in Lorenz's theory is the spontaneity of aggression. To him, this is self-evident. But for a physiologist there must be a demonstration of chemical and physical changes within

the body which would lead to such "spontaneous" aggressive behavior. A series of these changes are well known in the case of
hunger, where the cells use up blood sugar, which in turn stimulates
certain centers of the brain which then cause hunger contractions in
the stomach, thus making one more ready to eat. The situation with
respect to the emotion of anger is quite different. Beginning with
the studies of the American physiologist Walter B. Cannon, whose
book *Bodily Changes in Pain, Hunger, Fear, and Rage* was published in 1929, it has been shown that the emotion of anger orig-
inates in one portion of the brain, the hypothalamus, and stimulating this area with electrodes in an animal such as a cat will
produce reactions very similar to anger. Without such stimulation
the animal is quiet. Evidence obtained from the removal of parts of
the brain shows that certain other areas have a stimulating effect on
anger, and that these are balanced by other portions which inhibit it.
Stimulation from the outside, such as the pain of a blow, will upset
the balance and cause the emotion of anger. Thus we have a
mechanism which prolongs and magnifies the effects of external
stimulation but no mechanism for building up the first stimulation
from within. There is no internal change corresponding to the
change in blood sugar which results in hunger. In short, the physiological evidence is against Lorenz's notion of the spontaneity of
aggression, and indeed, it is difficult to see how such a mechanism
for spontaneity could have evolved. Fighting is an emergency reaction, and it is hard to imagine how natural selection would lead to
the development of a mechanism of continuous internal accumulation of energy which would unnecessarily put an animal into
danger.

This may appear to be a fine technical point, but it has one
important consequence. If Lorenz is right, then man can never lead
a happy, peaceful existence, but must continually be sublimating the
spontaneous "drive" which accumulates within him. If the physiologists are correct, then it is theoretically possible for man to lead a
happy and peaceful existence provided he is not continually stimulated to violence. Sublimation will have its uses, because in any
practical situation there will always be some accidental stimulation
toward violence, but it is only one of the many techniques provided
by modern scientific knowledge for the control of aggression.

As for other major causes of aggression, such as heredity and training, Lorenz simply leaves them out. Heredity has major effects upon the development of aggressiveness, both between animal species and between individuals of the same kind. Training has equally important effects on the higher animals. We know that through appropriate training methods, an animal like a mouse can be converted into an individual which will attack females and even infant mice, something which mice normally never do. A male mouse, by other methods, can be trained to be completely peaceful. Lorenz has also completely missed (and this may be because of his lack of acquaintance with research done on mammals) one of the major recent findings of research on animal behavior. Social organization is not something which is born into an animal, but something which is developed, and if social organization is disturbed, harmless or even beneficial aggressive behavior can be transformed into destructive violence. Thus the violent baboons in the London Zoo studied by Zuckerman were a group of individuals strange to each other and hence a disorganized society. The undisturbed societies of baboons studied by Washburn and DeVore on the South African plains present an entirely different picture. Fighting is present but controlled by a dominance order, and is chiefly directed against predators, and one sees the baboons risking their lives for the benefit of a group. Thus a baboon, in common with many other mammals, has the capacity to develop destructive violence under conditions of social disorganization, whereas under the proper conditions of social organization he has the capacity to develop peaceful and cooperative behavior, to direct fighting into useful channels, and to act in a manner which might well be described as altruistic. One wonders whether the same might not be said of man.

There is an element in human behavior, however, which goes beyond this simple formulation. Man is a tool user, and one of the tools that men have discovered is that they can organize themselves into groups for the purpose of destruction and violence, and that such trained groups will overcome any individual or untrained group. This is one of the major causes of warfare—its usefulness or apparent usefulness for attaining certain ends—and it presents a problem which can only be solved on the level of human social organization.

In brief, fighting is a complex phenomenon, taking many forms, and is stimulated and controlled by many different factors. Any "single factor" explanation, such as that of instinct, is necessarily incomplete. To give Lorenz proper credit, he would probably write a different book if he were to write it today, as in a more recent volume he has begun to incorporate the phenomenon of learning into his theories of the evolution of behavior.

The Territorial Imperative is a very different kind of a book, although Konrad Lorenz is one of Ardrey's heroes. Briefly stated, Ardrey's thesis, carried over from his earlier book, *African Genesis,* is that human aggression has an even simpler basis than that postulated by Lorenz, namely "man's instinct for territoriality." This is presented so naïvely that even an unscientific reader is not likely to take the book seriously, and Ardrey himself realizes that the evidence from field studies of primates goes against his ideas.

Ardrey's book can also be better understood in terms of the history of its author. Ardrey began his career as a dramatist, with little or no formal training in science. In a sentence, *Territorial Imperative* is good theater and third-rate science reporting, full of entertainment and wild analogies.

In the early 1940's I published a scientific paper demonstrating that there were inherited differences between the fighting capacities of two pure strains of mice. Males of the gray strain were irritable and quick to start a fight, whereas those of the black strain were slow to start, but once the fighting began they almost always won over the grays. After its publication, I was interviewed by a newspaper reporter who wanted me to say that this situation was "just like ourselves and the Germans." It took some minutes before I was able to persuade him that the resemblance was purely superficial, that mice are not just like people, and that the differences between the behavior of Germans and ourselves were mostly due to culture, rather than to any profound biological difference.

This unsophisticated level of science reporting has become much rarer than it used to be, but it has survived in full strength in Ardrey's book. To him, a band of lemurs in Madagascar is just like a modern human nation.

Ardrey has read widely in the scientific literature on territoriality, but his ideas, if not always as wildly unsophisticated as my reporter's, are equally uncritical. He has written these down as they come to him, and the result is a sort of intellectual pizza pie, with tasty tidbits of information embedded in a mass of partially baked ideas.

This is too bad, because a good popular account of territoriality could be written. The facts are that territoriality occurs only in the higher animals such as the vertebrates and arthropods and even there in a very spotty fashion. In primates, our closest biological relatives, there are many cases of species which have no real territories. To take one of the more aggressive primates as an example, rhesus monkeys live in a core area and as a group wander out into a more extended range which overlaps with that of other groups by as much as 80 per cent. There are dominant and subordinate groups, and ordinarily the subordinate groups avoid contact. If they meet unexpectedly, the dominant group will attack, no matter where the contact takes place. There is plenty of fighting, but none of it is related to territory. Baboon groups live in similar overlapping home ranges, and DeVore and Hall never saw a group defend a territorial boundary. Unlike the rhesus, groups tolerate each other, and there are few conflicts even when groups come into close contact around water holes. On the other hand, there are some recently described primate groups that apparently defend rather precise territorial boundaries just as some birds do.

We have no knowledge whatever about the territorial behavior of pre-cultural man, and even if we did there has been ample opportunity for genetic change to have taken place within the past several hundred thousand years. We will have to make our judgments on territoriality in human beings on the basis of modern man himself, and here the anthropologists tell us that the importance of territoriality and private property varies enormously between different cultures. To present an extreme example, in none of the Eskimo societies except the Aleut was there any such thing as the defense of "territory," even though the introduction of a strange group into a hunting area might mean starvation and death for the original inhabitants. Other societies have believed that they held rights to certain animals or plants in a territory, but not to others; or they have believed that while the tribe as a whole held rights to a territory, no individual or individual family could claim special rights to any particular piece of ground. In short, there is no evidence that territoriality is or is not a biologically determined universal condition in modern man, but a great deal of evidence of important cultural differences. There *may* be some biological basis for territorial behavior in people, but it is equally possible that it is a human cultural invention.

Will *The Territorial Imperative* have a bad effect? It reminds me of another book that I read when I was fifteen—Albert Edward Wiggam's *The Fruit of the Family Tree*. This book, now happily forgotten, was an attempt to apply what was then known about the science of animal breeding to human affairs. It was the author's simple thesis that all human ills were caused by bad heredity, and that if we were to breed human beings with the same care that we did animals all the world's problems could be solved. To an unsophisticated fifteen-year-old it seemed that if heredity was this important someone would study heredity and behavior seriously and apply the knowledge accordingly. I went ahead to specialize in the science of genetics and, of course, the more I learned about it the more it became obvious that there were other important factors that determined behavior and that heredity was only one of the many causes operating within the extraordinarily complex systems which comprise animal and human behavior.

Ardrey's book may inspire present-day fifteen-year-olds to go and learn more about the science of animal and human behavior and the causes of destructive violence. If so, it will have had a good effect. Unfortunately, fifteen-year-olds have no monopoly on lack of sophistication, and unsophisticated adults sometimes get into positions of power. Simple-minded ideas similar to those of Wiggam concerning racial improvement led Hitler and his friends to try to eliminate one whole section of the human race. I doubt if Ardrey's book has any such serious implication as this, but the erroneous notion that fighting over the possession of land is a powerful, inevitable, and uncontrollable instinct might well lead to the conclusion that war is inevitable and therefore a nation must attack first and fight best in order to survive and prosper. It is to be hoped that the persons in power in our society are too sophisticated to fall for any such adolescent interpretation of world affairs, but history will, as usual, have the last word. Meanwhile, we can say that

Ardrey's thesis is an over-simplified and therefore largely erroneous answer to an extraordinarily complex problem.

The popularization of scientific information in our society is a very important task, as the ultimate usefulness of science depends upon its getting into the minds of as many people as possible. That this can be done in both a readable and scientifically authentic way is demonstrated by such books as Amram Scheinfeld's *You and Heredity*. Trained only as a writer, Scheinfeld set out to present the science of genetics to the general public. However, he worked with a geneticist until he thoroughly understood the material himself, and when he had written the book he submitted it to scientists for criticism. Originally published in 1939, this book became an immediate popular success. As the years went by, Scheinfeld published new editions as the science of genetics changed and developed, and his latest book, under the title of *Your Heredity and Environment* (Lippincott, 1965), is a major resource for any one who wishes to become informed on the science of genetics. In contrast, the reader who wishes to know about territoriality may be attracted by the title of Ardrey's book, but what he will get will be entertainment. For authentic information he will have to go to original sources.

T. C. SCHNEIRLA

Instinct and Aggression

Dr. Lorenz, Director of the Max Planck Institute for Behavioral Physiology in Germany and author of works on animal behavior, has written two new books on important subjects. In *Evolution and Modification of Behavior* (Chicago, 1965) he discusses his theory of animal behavior; in *On Aggression* (a translation of his book *Das Sogennante Böse,* Vienna, 1963) he applies this theory to a problem in social behavior. Both books are based on dubious assumptions.

Aggression is defined as "The fighting instinct in beast and man which is directed against members of the same species." The thesis for man and beast alike is: Aggressive instincts dominate behavior unless curbed. The importance of this point for man is stressed: Someone from another planet, " . . . looking upon man as he is today, in his hand the atom bomb, the product of his intelligence, in his heart the aggression drive, inherited from his anthropoid ancestors, which this same intelligence cannot control, would not predict long life for the species."

The concept of instinctual aggression is of course not new. That such an instinct was paramount in natural selection is an idea Lorenz shares with Herbert Spencer (first to speak of "survival of the fittest") who featured aggression instinct as a major factor in man's evolution, and with Freud. Lorenz finds aggression and

From *Natural History,* December 1966. Reprinted by permission. New material added by author, 1968.

fighting common in lower animals and considers them potent in the evolution of all animals.

On Aggression begins with vivid accounts of observations of strikingly colored coral-reef fishes in tanks and in the sea. Cases are described in which each observed territory-holder, excited by an invader of his own species, attacks and drives off the trespasser.

Although the results of these studies on coral-reef fishes are engagingly presented, and open the statement of evidence in which they are featured, the reader has no means by which to appraise their reliability. The experiments with coral-reef fishes in laboratory tanks were carried out with subjects that were not always in good condition and—as an equally serious drawback—were not so designed as to control crowding as a factor in influencing the behavior described. The author's observations on reactions of these fishes in the sea are eloquently reported; unfortunately, there is no mention of the observational checks and balances that are indispensable to bring recollections of free observations out of the area of subjective impression and into the area of reliability. Hence the conclusions drawn are open to question.

Territorial-defense fighting, common in lower vertebrates, birds and mammals, is then discussed as crucial in natural selection in its role as a basis for food-getting, mating, rearing young, and other behavior promoting species survival. In lower animals, instinctive aggression is viewed as working well; in man, however, the author expresses concern that it has been getting out of hand.

Mechanisms that inhibit fighting, Lorenz holds, are essential to survival in lower animals and man alike. Chief among these are ritualistic displays in which aggressors are warded off with little or no physical contact. In man, however, the inhibitory controls imposed on aggression both through natural selection and through cultural processes may fail in the split-second emergencies created by modern weaponry and related bellicose patterns. Man is " . . . the only being capable of dedicating himself to the highest moral and ethical values . . . " but " . . . whose animal properties bring with them the danger that he will kill his brother, convinced that he is doing so in the interests of these very same high values. *Ecce homo!" Behold man!*—that is, as Lorenz sees him.

Lorenz shares this sombre view with Freud, who also saw conflict and war as inevitable, violent expressions of irresponsible human aggressive instincts. Lorenz, like Freud, considers the social bond and related influences inadequate to inhibit man's dominantly aggressive biological nature in the modern world.

In his chapter, "Avowal of Optimism," Lorenz sugggests that man, under the described threat, must find methods for ritualizing and channelizing instinctive aggressions, must encourage people of differing ideologies and races to get acquainted, must direct "the militant enthusiasms" of youth toward "genuine causes that are worth serving in the modern world," and must improve his understanding of behavioral mechanisms fundamental to aggression, the better to control them. Finally, he must use his resources of humor and of knowledge to these ends. These suggestions, although helpful, seem to reveal an aspect of Freudian sublimation; that is, of making the best of a bad deal.

A different picture of man, however, based on current scientific theory and methodology, is at odds with Lorenz's outdated negative view. Results of research on human group behavior emphasize man's great social potentials arising from his developmental plasticity and his versatility for constructive behavior. At the same time, evidence on the origins of *asocial* behavior suggests that hypotheses in which instinctual aggression is offered to explain the rise of wars are tangential and naïve.

The question is not whether results from investigations of behavior in lower animals are applicable to man, but whether the application is as simple a matter as Lorenz's procedures imply. Responsible scientists must carry out their research on behavior within the broadest perspective and evaluate evidence in terms of the most valid theory possible. Evidence on individual differences, on the conditions of development, and on the state of the population must be featured, for these surely were all crucial in the natural selective background of every animal. The results of research must be presented in comprehensive reports open to searching analysis; not in descriptive, subjective terms as Lorenz does in this book.

The significance Lorenz gives his results is too great to justify his non-experimental, anecdotal treatment of the subject. An appropriately broad, systematic presentation of the behavioral facts would have aided readers to understand, for example, how very differently individual fish may have responded according to the conditions (e.g., stressful crowding in aquaria), and how results from observations of animals in confinement actually compared with the behavior of these same animals under natural conditions.

Studying social phenomena and other behavior under natural conditions is extremely important, and the ethological approach inspired by Lorenz and Tinbergen has aided such work, which ideally goes hand in hand with laboratory research. The field of behavioral development is highly controversial, however, in ways that do not emerge clearly in . . . *Behavior*. Lorenz's critics dispute neither his emphasis on " . . . the great fact of adaptiveness in behavior . . . ," as he implies, nor on correlations between genotypes (empirically described species genetics) and phenotypes (individual patterns developed). Rather, they reject much of his evidence as partial and unreliable, and question on these and other grounds the assumptions he applies dogmatically to these problems.

It is not clear from . . . *Behavior* whether or not science will be aided by Lorenz's terms, "phyletic information" and "individually acquired information," which he confuses consistently with reality. These concepts, notwithstanding the impressive cybernetic aura he gives them and the polemical deftness with which he uses them in explanatory roles, do not differ much from their traditional synonyms, "nature" and "nurture," respectively.

Space precludes discussing here the obfuscations raised in . . . *Behavior* for readers who try to judge the theoretical issues involved in the book. Lorenz admits that the terms "innate" and "learned" used (by "earlier ethologists") to denote mutually exclusive agencies, are fallacious. But at the same time, in speaking of "information" that is either "phyletically acquired" or "individually acquired," he revives the fallacious dichotomy by using the word *information* in two different senses. He repeats his assertion of some years ago that others (whose evidence and ideas he evades) offered "learning in the egg and *in utero*" to explain ontogenesis, although he should know *by now* that this gambit is both an untrue statement and a misrepresentation of important evidence. But Lorenz's positivism often leads him to exclude evidence on behavioral development that is at odds with his assumptions.

Two related devices stand out in the book. One is the term "innate school-marm" for hypothetical genetic agencies presumed to determine what the animal is to learn as it develops. Another is the "deprivation experiment," formerly the "isolation experiment," offered here as *the* method for determining what is innate. The author directs these ideas at the separation of innate and learned elements in behavior with a faith in their soundness hardly justified by available evidence or comprehensive theory. His implication that the genes rigidly "program" the animal's learning is opposed by the results of many experiments, also by evidence from animal training that, under appropriate developmental conditions, animals do many things that species mates never do ordinarily. The deprivation experiment, as he terms it now, is better called the change-of-environment test, as it is widely used to study behavioral differences in young animals raised under conditions other than those presumed to be natural for them. Believing that " . . . it can only tell us directly what is not learned," the author must assume that he knows beforehand the developmental significances of these "natural" conditions. This, however, is precisely the problem needing investigation. Actually, this method is only one part of the behavior investigator's repertoire, now widely used in developmental research of much wider scope than is considered in . . . *Behavior*.

Lorenz's argument is built from the assumption that patterns such as aggression are seated specifically in the genes. It is a long way from the genes to behavior, however, and the books under review do not light the way. This key assumption is not only unsupported; it is also denied by a sizable weight of evidence. As is well known, the frequency and nature of aggressive behavior varies among members of both inter-species and intra-species groups raised together under conditions favorable to one or to another pattern of behavioral development.

Lorenz seems interested neither in the study of individual differences nor in phyletic comparisons in behavioral development; yet these problems are vital to understanding how aggression, for example, arises and varies in widely different types of animals. The question of why, when two fish react to invasions of their territory, one flees whereas the other attacks, or why some people generally are peaceable whereas others are quarrelsome, is not easy. Neither is it the same question for fish and for people. All available methods (including "deprivation tests") must be used for studying such differences in function and in behavior throughout development.

The more scientists study behavioral development and the more they study its properties through the animal series, the less likely are they to follow Lorenz's oversimplified formula which he applies uncritically to all integrative levels. As an example, in certain animals on what I have called the "biosocial level," chemical secretions, according to concentrations, attract or repel species mates, thereby dominating behavior. Ants, bees, and wasps offer good examples of biological processes controlling behavior directly. But insects are not people. On the "psychosocial level," in contrast, structural and physiological factors contribute indirectly to behavior and differently according to the conditions of individual development. In man, adrenalin, a neurosecretory excitatory substance, can arouse fighting, loving, poetizing, preaching, singing or panic according to the individual's background and his current situation. The assumptions underlying the theory expounded in these books are sufficiently open to question for lower animals; their free extrapolation to man is therefore quite doubtful.

It is as heavy a responsibility to inform mankind about aggressive tendencies assumed to be present on an inborn basis as about "original sin"—and this Lorenz admits in effect. A corollary risk is advising societies to base their programs of social training on attempts to inhibit *hypothetical* innate aggressions, instead of continuing positive measures for socially constructive behavior. Major aggressions of history, including Hitler's, may be explained superficially by the easy devices of instinct theory, or studied systematically with evidence known to historians and scientists.

EDMUND LEACH

Don't Say "Boo" to a Goose

As a mine of scientific-sounding misinformation Mr. Robert Ardrey would be hard to beat, but his application of the techniques of TV drama writing to the more musty corners of academic orthodoxy certainly livens things up. Looking up a well-known and easily accessible reference acquires the excitement of a James Bond spy story: "I at last found a copy in the guarded library of today's Royal Anthropological Institute in Bedford Square." Everything is black and white. Conventional professional scientists with whom Ardrey disagrees become criminal conspirators worthy only of the crudest ridicule; for his friends, the ethologists, no praise can be too high: "When Konrad Lorenz's book appears in Britain and America" it will "take its place among the landmarks of our thought." It has now appeared and it is no landmark, but it is modest and wise, while Ardrey's version is only noisy and foolish. The two books have a common central theme—the function of innate aggression in man and other animals. Ardrey concentrates on what ethologists call "territoriality," that is the drive to defend property aggressively, and he operates with very crude nineteenth-century ideas about how the evolutionary process works—"the survival of the fittest"—"Nature red in tooth and claw" and all that. Lorenz, on the other hand, is concerned to show that animal aggression is only a "so-called evil" and that its adaptive consequences are advantageous or at least neutral. Fighting between members of the same species helps to secure an even distribution of the species over its inhabitable area, and "aggression" has been responsible for all the more gorgeously dramatic, but inefficient, products of evolution, such as the Bird of Paradise and the Argus Pheasant. On which point Heinroth has remarked: "Next to the wings of the Argus Pheasant, the hectic life of western civilized man is the most stupid product of intraspecific selection"! For Lorenz, an even more striking virtue of aggression lies in its negation and control. Nature has had to ensure that aggressive animals shall not exterminate themselves by mutual slaughter. Thus behavior which signifies aggressive hostility towards enemies comes to be modified into a "ritualized" form which signals love and amity between friends. If we take fish and birds as our models, then the basic morality which allows a man to love his wife and respect his neighbor's property has the same instinctive source as the basic immorality which leads to war and destruction.

But can we take fish and birds as our models? In observing how animals behave we can only record what they do and the circumstances in which they do it; we know nothing about their feelings and motives. But when we discuss human behavior our objectivity is fogged by subjective private experience. It may be perfectly sensible to describe the action of a baboon in baring its teeth towards an opponent as "an aggressive gesture." For the Chinese Government to authorize the test firing of a nuclear rocket may also be properly described as "an aggressive gesture." But to argue that the two behaviors are comparable in anything except a purely metaphorical sense is just nonsense. Yet this is precisely what both our authors are up to all the time. They want to imply that the political policies of modern states are in some sense predetermined by the genetic constitution of *Homo sapiens*. Ardrey argues quite explicitly that Indian-Chinese border disputes are analogous to squabbles between two varieties of geese sharing the same pool! This is just word-play, and as with any other verbal conjuring trick it can be played in several different ways. Despite Ardrey's praise for Lorenz, the conclusions of the two books are diametrically opposed. Lorenz finds room for limited Christian-Confucian optimism—future salvation will be found in a specific human capacity "to love all our human brothers indiscriminately," Ardrey offers us only a crude Hobbesian war of all against all—"we are predators, of course, and from time to time we shall go out looting and raping and raising general havoc." Ardrey explicitly compares man's "killing propensity" to that of a wolf (p. 340); this precisely is what Lorenz repudiates:

> A wolf can rip the jugular vein of another with a single bite. There would be no more wolves if reliable inhibitions did not prevent such actions. Neither a dove nor a hare nor even a chimpanzee is able to kill its own kind with a single peck or bite. . . animals with relatively poor defense weapons have a correspondingly greater ability to escape quickly, even from specially armed predators who are more efficient in chasing, catching and killing than even the strongest of their own species. (*On Aggression*, 1966, p. 240)

> [The statement that man has a carnivorous mentality] confuses the concepts of the carnivore and the cannibal, which are, to a very large extent, mutually exclusive. One can only deplore the fact that man has definitely not got a carnivorous mentality! All his trouble arises from his being a basically harmless, omnivorous creature, lacking weapons with which to kill big prey, and, therefore, also devoid of the built-in safety devices which prevent "professional" carnivores from abusing their killing power to destroy fellow members of their own species. A lion or a wolf may, on extremely rare occasions, kill another by one angry stroke, but . . . all heavily armed carnivores possess sufficiently reliable inhibitions which prevent the self-destruction of the species. (p. 241)

Although every schoolboy will tell you that it was Charles Darwin who first conceived the notion that Man might be descended from an ape and that he devised this heresy some time around 1859, the truth is that Man's relationship to other animals has been a matter of fascinated conjecture for most of mankind throughout most of human history: The foster-mother of Romulus was a wolf, Helen of Troy was fathered by a swan. More recently the eighteenth-century Neapolitan, Giambattista Vico, imagined the ancestors of modern men to be speechless giants having the attributes of a gorilla; the slightly younger J. J. Rousseau argued that anthropoid apes are real human beings existing in a state of nature. But although Darwin's heresy had long been a commonplace, we are still reluctant to admit its implications. Men indeed are animals, but surely they are more than that? And having imagined that this distinction is clear-cut, we go on to persuade ourselves that it is the non-animal, human, part of ourselves which is by far the most important. In the eighteenth century this distinction was embodied in the word *Reason*. Man possessed Reason, animals did not. The late nineteenth century substituted a more complex idea—*Culture*. The lives of mere animals, it was said, are determined by inherited characteristics, "instincts"; the lives of human beings on the other hand, are determined by habits transmitted by learning within a social context. Human beings are sharply distinguished from all other animals by their sophisticated powers of communication, by consciousness of personal identity, and by their awareness of property rights over things and persons and places. We flatter ourselves. We now know that though rats have not yet got around to nuclear warfare or telemetry, they can learn how to recognize poisoned food *and* pass on this information to their more ignorant acquaintances, and if we systematically investigate just how this might be possible, the classic dichotomy between *instinct* and *culture* becomes very blurred indeed. Certainly we are much more clever than the rats and the possession of spoken language makes a hell of a difference, but just how much difference?

This, essentially, is what these two books are about. Both are attempts to provide "popular," boiled-down versions of the implications of ethology (the study of animal behavior) for the human understanding of human beings. This is tricky country, and Lorenz's naiveté is often quite as misleading as Ardrey's downright error. Ethologists concern themselves with the competition for survival between whole animal species, and they have been particularly ingenious in showing how inbred peculiarities of appearance and behavior are adaptively advantageous in the age-long sequence of genetic evolution. But when ethologists start talking about Man they are inclined to write as if "a whole culture" was somehow comparable to "a whole species," which is really just nonsense. If a *species* "dies out" the individuals concerned cease to exist; if a *culture* "dies out" it may mean no more than that Cowboys and Indians have learned to drive Cadillacs. At one point Lorenz, growing sentimental about the evolutionary advantages of cultural norms, writes:

> The studies of the ethnologist and psychoanalyst Derek Freeman have shown that hunting is so intricately interwoven with the whole social system of some Bornean tribes that its abolition tends to disintegrate their whole culture, even seriously jeopardizing the survival of the people. (p. 261)

In actual fact the abolition of the traditional culture of Bornean head-hunters has been accompanied by an upsurge of population of embarrassing dimensions.

Nevertheless, careful reflection upon just what *is* the distinction between species difference in animals and cultural difference in man is badly needed, and the ethologists' brash comments on the matter should help to clarify the anthropologists' discussions. Even Ardrey's profound confusions, by which he claims to explain the passing fashions of international politics as a simple response to genetic drives, could serve some useful purpose if it leads a more serious author to tackle what is certainly a very serious subject.

Ardrey's argument runs something like this. The ethologists have shown that the phenomenon of territoriality recurs throughout the animal kingdom. Individual members of a particular species identify with a particular territory. All other members of the same species are dichotomized as friends and strangers. Strangers are attacked if they intrude on *our* territory; the deeper the intrusion the more violent the counter aggression. "This vital mode of behavior is not learned by the individual but is innate in the species." Ardrey then makes two kinds of mistake. In the first place he usually writes as if this kind of behavior were found in *all* animals and that, therefore, it *must* be characteristic of man also. This is an error of fact. Secondly he confuses the behavior as such with the circumstances that produce it. He thinks that the statement "aggressive behavior is innate" conflicts with J. P. Scott's proposition that "all stimulation of aggression eventually comes from forces present in the external environment." This is not the case. If we define the word "aggression" in a behavioristic way, as an ethologist should, then man, like any other animal, has built-in "innate" ways of exhibiting aggression. What is in dispute is whether man likewise has a built-in tendency to defend his home territory so that the precise circumstances in which he will exhibit this "aggressive behavior" are predictable. Ardrey is well aware of the weakness of his case. He knows (pp. 220-224) that man's nearest living cousins, the anthropoid apes, show no such tendency, but he blandly assures us that these pacifist animals are "evolutionary failures"! He writes luridly of our "human" ancestors of two million years ago: "Far from being a beginner at the killing game . . . this pygmy sized predator of the high savannah was a skilled and successful hunter of what men today would still call big game . . . we killed animals ten or twenty times our size, did we kill each other?" And, of course, Ardrey's answer is "yes," the whole fantasy resting on a quite uncritical interpretation of a single fossil ape-like skull of a creature whose relationship to modern man is obscure but certainly not close.

Lorenz's comment is much to the point. If proto-man had been at all like the figment of Ardrey's imagination he would have wiped himself out of existence. The survivors in the evolutionary rat-race are of two kinds—those which are disinclined to kill at all and those which are inclined to kill but are inhibited against killing members of their own kind. The uninhibited killer is a non-starter. Natural man, in Lorenz's view, is a pacific creature; pit two unarmed individual men against each other in an unconfined space and the odds are heavy that both will survive. Man only becomes dangerous when he is equipped with weapons, and weapons are a product of culture, not of nature. But this is where the application of ethological arguments to the human situation becomes really interesting. And it is just here that Ardrey misses the point.

Evolutionary theory does not at all suggest that the "successful" species are those gifted with "killing propensity." Very much the reverse. Species become differentiated by specialized adaptation to territorially isolated ecological conditions. The attachment of an individual to its home territory is directly linked up with this process of adaptive specialization. In such cases Ardrey's "territorial imperative" does have important evolutionary consequences. But one of the special peculiarities of the species Homo sapiens is its lack of ecological specialization. No other species can adjust so readily to drastic variations of temperature, humidity, and diet. And this highly advantageous plasticity is tied in with the fact that man, as a species, is almost entirely free from territorial limitations and attachments. It is true that living human beings, both as individuals and as groups, do on occasion exhibit symptoms resembling the "territoriality" displayed by various species of birds and fish, but this human behavior is a cultural not a species characteristic, and this makes all the difference. It is optional not "instinctive" behavior. Sovereignty is not a new idea, but it is not a human universal.

But let us go back to man and his weapons. It begins to look as if man and his proto-human ancestors have been using tools and weapons for several million years. Several crucial peculiarities of man—capacity for speech, upright gait, marked sexual dimorphism, absence of seasonal sexuality, lack of fur, peculiar placement of the sexual organs, etc.—are adaptive peculiarities which have evolved in the context of a natural environment modified by the existence of weapons and tools. Man did not evolve as a complete human being and *then* acquire speech and culture. He developed speech and culture while still evolving as an animal species. And our human predicament is that this process still goes on. Other animals adapt to a specialized environment which is relatively stable. If the environment changes drastically the species usually becomes extinct. In contrast, man's adaptive apparatus includes a technology which changes the environment as it goes along. Man and his environment are thus *always* out of step. As Lorenz puts it, "the extreme speed of ecological and sociological change wrought by the developments of technology causes many customs to become maladaptive within one generation." He finds the pace too hot, and it fills him with anxiety. I find this odd, but it shows up a glaring weakness in current ethological fashion. Students of animal behavior are so accustomed to finding a perfect fit between the innate capacities of a species and its total environment that they are inclined to view as pathological any palpable lack of fit between the state of human society and the state of the geographical space within which it exists. This is the classic fallacy of functionalist sociology all over again. Lorenz's word "maladaptive" turns up in contexts where Durkheim would have written "anomie"; Georg Simmel was making Lorenz's point about the positive function of conflict nearly sixty years ago; for sociologists, Malinowski's notion that, in a healthy society, social norms must always fit with the requirements of ecology and of human biological needs has been a dead duck for nearly a generation.

Certainly the observation of animals may have moral lessons for human beings—"Go to the ant, thou sluggard, consider her ways and be wise"—but we shall only deceive ourselves if we attempt to minimize the differences between human and non-human animal behavior. The development of speech in *Homo sapiens* has completely altered our nature. A goose can communicate with another goose by means of "ritualized" gestures, but the kinds of message it can transmit are very narrowly delimited: "Hostility" and "friendship" are only the observer's labels for simple triggered responses. In contrast, human beings can say an infinite number of things in an infinite number of different ways; responses are intrinsically unpredictable; politicians and historians are what they are precisely because no man can ever know what his "opponent" is going to do next.

Relations of solidarity and opposition, amity and hostility, gift exchange and war, constitute the basic subject matter of sociological enquiry, and only a very simple-minded man could suppose that such complex matters might be readily understood by simple analogy with the habits of the prairie-dog. But this is what Ardrey implies. It is perfectly true that, as members of a common species *Homo sapiens,* we are all predisposed to behave in certain fixed ways which reflect our biochemical constitutions. But this in itself does not tell us very much. We are all naturally endowed with a capacity for speech and all spoken languages have certain features in common—e.g., they convey meaning by means of an alternation of vowels and consonants—but these constraints set no limit on what we say. Likewise the physical gestures of *Homo* are limited in kind by the fact that the actor is a man and not a goose. But what we express by these gestures is not limited at all. Thus any belief that our customs are somehow predetermined in the same sense as are the mating rituals of birds is an illusion.

The argument is in some respects circular. The ethologists interpret particular animal behaviors as *aggressive, amicable, dominant, submissive,* etc., and they use such terms because of what they know intuitively about themselves. That being so, it is quite illogical to reverse the process and pretend that we might understand human aggression better because of its analogic similarity to "animal aggression." Until he reaches Chapter 13 Lorenz only occasionally falls into this fallacy. Most of his book is an entrancing record of how human observers can make objective studies of relationships between animals. But Ardrey's anthropomorphism is of the clumsiest kind. He has a nursery-floor view of human affairs: "The principal cause of modern warfare arises from the failure of an intruding power correctly to estimate the defensive resources of a territorial defender." Ethology apart, this is the Hobbesian notion that if there were no policemen, each of us would immediately set about murdering everyone else in sight, and it is total rubbish.

To sum up, the Lorenz book is delightful and fascinating, as long as the author sticks to his own field; away off when he starts mixing in anthropology or politics or philosophy. In ,the Ardrey version the mixture of extraneous matter is so great that it is best left alone altogether.

GEOFFREY GORER

Ardrey on Human Nature:
Animals, Nations, Imperatives

Almost without question, Robert Ardrey is today the most influential writer in English dealing with the innate or instinctive attributes of human nature, and the most skilled populariser of the findings of paleo-anthropologists, ethologists, and biological experimenters. As a populariser, he covers some of the same material as, for example, Arthur Koestler. He is a skilled writer, with a lively command of English prose, a pretty turn of wit, and a dramatist's skill in exposition; he is also a good reporter, with the reporter's eye for the significant detail, the striking visual impression. He has taken a look at nearly all the current work in Africa of paleo-anthropologists and ethologists; time and again, a couple of his paragraphs can make vivid a site, such as the Olduvai Gorge, which has been merely a name in a hundred articles. His wide readership has been earned, at least in part, by his mastery of the writer's crafts.

His first, almost accidental, encounter with Africa was, he tells us, as a journalist. His two books on scientific themes are largely autobiographical, a fact which is emphasised in the sub-title of each: *African Genesis* (1961) is subtitled "A Personal Investigation into the Animal Origins and Nature of Man"; and *The Terri-*

From *Encounter*, June 1967. Copyright © 1967 by Geoffrey Gorer. Reprinted by permission of Harold Ober Associates Inc.

torial Imperative (1967) "A Personal Inquiry into the Animal Origins of Property and Nations." It would not be unfair to say that he is conducting his adult education in public. In the course of the two books he tells us a good deal about himself.

He was born in Chicago's South Side in 1908, his family being of Scottish origin. He was educated in Chicago, apparently taking some course in social science under Professor Ogburn; he graduated during the depression, and for a short time earned his living as a lecturer in anthropology at the Chicago World's Fair and as a self-described statistician; these were his only contacts with the social sciences for twenty years. He became a playwright who was esteemed, if not markedly successful, was awarded a Guggenheim fellowship, and then moved to Hollywood as a professional scriptwriter. Apart from World War II, when he was in an overseas branch of the Office of War Information, this work continued until 1954. He then became unemployed, his new Broadway play was a flop, and he was engaged by the editor of *The Reporter* to do a series of articles on Africa, particularly the Mau Mau rising. Almost by accident, he was asked to interview the Australian-born South African paleo-anthropologist, Raymond Dart.

In February 1955, Dart gave him a fossilised jawbone of *australopithecus* to hold; this experience became Ardrey's Road to Damascus. In a flash, it would seem, the orientation of his life was changed: his aim in life was no longer to entertain but to educate (in the first place, himself). He had felt immediate conviction of the correctness of Dart's interpretation of his australopithecine and associated fossils; and it became his mission to rescue Dart from the neglect and contumely which his unorthodox interpretations had gained from the academic world of paleo-anthropology. In this he has been markedly successful.

It is a typical sequel to conversion that the convert feels compelled to share his illumination with the benighted; and Ardrey writes with much the same conviction of having achieved access to deeper truths as do converts to the older established religions or to Marxism or psycho-analysis or "psychodelic" drugs; it is this feeling of urgency which helps give Ardrey's books their compulsive readability. But, although the convert feels that he is completely changed, he brings to his new life his old habits and skills. Ardrey was a dramatist; and one of the characteristics of dramatists is to put a very great load of significance on to a few symbols or metaphors, a far greater load than they would bear outside the condensation of a play. Nearly all my criticism of Ardrey's ideas derives from his tendency to overload symbols and metaphors, to use the same phrases in a very wide variety of contexts and with very different significants.

As far as I can check, Ardrey is a first-class conscientious reporter. He looks and listens and notes with care and precision; he is extremely diligent in his reading and research; and he does not distort his authorities beyond what is inevitable in any selection and condensation. One can question his selection of topics to emphasise or to ignore; but, to the best of my knowledge, he never ascribes to a scientist an observation or conclusion he has not made. He has read extremely widely in his selected topics of paleoanthroplogy and ethology; even those familiar with most of the literature are likely to find descriptions of research they had hitherto ignored, particularly in *The Territorial Imperative,* with its bibliography of 245 items.

Unfortunately, Ardrey's diligence and research has so far stopped short at *Homo sapiens.* His views on human behaviour are almost entirely impressionistic, embued with the sophistication of a cosmopolitan writer who reads news magazines. Like most dramatists he writes as though he had an intuitive insight into human motivation; and like most autobiographers he believes that he is a typical example of human nature, but more honest than most. He is reliable when he discusses *proconsul* or *australopithecus,* the birds and the bees, mice and monkeys, for he relies on expert authorities; when he discusses man he relies on himself.

The argument of both books is that we will arrive at a more rational understanding of contemporary man if we study man's instinctual endowment; and that this instinctual endowment can be learned from the study of the remains of pre-hominids and early hominids and the behaviour of other vertebrates. Our knowledge of human evolution and of animal behaviour has increased so enormously in the last thirty years that Ardrey is justified in writing of a "scientific revolution" and he has brought this knowledge to the attention of the literate English-speaking public as no other populariser has done. Konrad Lorenz has a large audience; but, like many another genius, he has paid relatively little attention to independent work done in his field.

Ardrey's moment of illumination came when Raymond Dart demonstrated to him that *Australopithecus africanus*—one of the very early primates—had been a carnivorous predator who was bipedal and selected and used the humerus of one antelope and the mandible of another as weapons. In his 1953 paper, *The Predatory Transition from Ape to Man,* Dart had argued that the hominisation of the pre-hominids had been facilitated by the change, in one line of australopithecines, from a vegetarian to a flesh diet; the use of weapons had led to a bipedal stance, the development of the thumb, eventually the enlargement of the brain. In Ardrey's words:

> Far from the truth lay the antique assumption that man had fathered the weapon. The weapon, instead, had fathered man. The mightiest of predators had come about as the logical conclusion to an evolutionary transition. With his big brain and his stone handaxes, man annihilated a predecessor who fought only with bones. And if all human history from that date has turned on the development of superior weapons, then it is for very sound reason. It is for genetic necessity. We design and compete with our weapons as birds build distinctive nests.

This short quotation shows both the strength and weaknesses of Ardrey's methods. In the study of human evolution Dart's work was both novel and disturbing; it was almost completely neglected when Ardrey first wrote, and is still not universally accepted. It was valuable to bring this material to wider notice.

None of the later sentences is justified by the evidence. There is nothing to suggest that *Australopithecus africanus* and *Homo sapiens* were contemporaries, and that therefore the latter "annihilated" the former. The bones which *Australopithecus* selected were implements for killing other species, not for killing co-specifics. Weapons, in human history, are entirely designed for killing co-specifics; in all societies of any technological complexity there is a distinction between implements for hunting and implements for war; rarely do the two overlap. Birds which build distinctive nests are of different species (or sub-species) and are not competing against one another; man is a single species.

Although Dart's material demands a most drastic revision of previously held views of human evolution and hominisation, it does not demand a revision of our views of human instinctual endowment even if, which is still unproven, *Australopithecus africanus* were some day to be established as directly ancestral to *Homo sapiens*. It has long been generally accepted that early man was a carnivorous predator who used hunting implements to kill other species for food; if pre-hominids did do the same, it does not make man any more, or any less, "a killer." This phrase, loaded with ambiguity, is a favourite of Ardrey's. All meat-eaters (scavengers appear to be only a partial exception) are "killers" of other species for their food; among the mammals there is no clear evidence for any species being "killers" of their co-specifics intentionally, other than rats and men.

Ardrey thinks that this new material demands a complete revision of human instinctual endowment, that it shows that man is instinctually a killer with an innate propensity for using weapons against his fellow-man; and, more reasonably, that the notions of Special Creation, or of Original Goodness, are now untenable. The final chapter of *African Genesis* is entitled "Children of Cain" * and argues that man has "an aggressive imperative" and cannot survive without war and the weapons of war. Organised warfare between states is, of course, a very modern human invention, subsequent to the neolithic revolution of about 10,000 years ago when the first nation-states were established; it is a source of considerable ambiguity to use the same term for the short skirmishes between a few people which typify primitive "war" and the wars between nation-states as we have known them in recent millennia.

Besides the information on paleo-anthropology and his deductions therefrom, Ardrey deals with many themes in *African Genesis* which he takes up again in greater detail in *The Territorial Imperative;* he also has one chapter, very richly illustrated, on status, dominance, and deference within animal societies. His de-

---

* This phrase is a typically misapplied cliché. If Ardrey had gone back to his sources (*Genesis:* 4) he would have found that Cain was a vegetarian, not a carnivore, and so, if you will, the descendant of *paranthropus;* Abel was the carnivorous descendant of *Australopithecus africanus;* and Cain killed him because Jehovah preferred meat to vegetables. The mark of Cain was to prevent anyone else killing him; and there is nothing in the Bible to suggest that Cain ever killed a second time.

duction from this material is "that among all animal sources of human behaviour, the instinct for status may in the end prove the most important." To date, this assertion is not backed by any study of human behavior; but it is interesting to note how Ardrey finds ethological justification for all the values of "rugged individualism."

The Territorial Imperative is a much more important and thorough book; Ardrey is justified in his claim that this is the first book since 1920 to deal comprehensively with the concept of territory. He has drawn very widely on the scattered and copious literature. He defines his topic as follows:

> A territory is an area of space, whether of water or earth or air, which an animal or group of animals defends as an exclusive preserve. The word is also used to describe the inward compulsion in animate beings to possess and defend such a space. A territorial species of animals, therefore, is one in which all the males, and sometimes females too, bear an inherent drive to gain and defend an exclusive property.

Under this definition, a majority of the vertebrate species so far studied and some invertebrate species are territorial animals; it is highly likely that some analogue to this instinct is also part of man's instinctual endowment. But territory is used by Ardrey, and by many of the ethologists he quotes, in a highly ambiguous fashion; it is a word of multiple meanings, which are seldom explicitly distinguished.

The word was first introduced into modern studies of animals by H. E. Howard, whose observations were based on British birds. Birds may have four types of territory: (1) the nest or breeding area, which is nearly universal; Ardrey quotes Howard as stating that a male with a mate and no territory is a natural impossibility. Territory (2) is an area surrounding the nest which will be defended against intrusion from male co-specifics. The song and bright plumage of the male are, quite probably, a warning to other males not to trespass; if trespass does occur, it is always successfully repulsed. Territory (2) varies in its extent from species to species. Predators often have territory (3), an exclusive hunting area. Finally a few species, such as blackcock, ruffs, sage grouse, and bower birds have territory (4), a copulating area (the lek of the black-cock) where only those dominant males who have acquired a stamping ground are selected by the females for mates. This rare type of territory is also found among the Uganda Kob, a species of antelope; this was first observed and reported by Helmut K. Buechner; Ardrey visited the rutting areas (which he calls "are-nas") and gives a vivid and fascinating account of them. Social mammals, including most of the anthropoids, have a variation of territory (3) in which the hunting or food-gathering area is shared and defended by more than one adult male and their mates and young.

While territories (1) and (2) are occupied and defended, the occupier can be considered the proprietor, and the territory its property. But this proprietorship differs in many ways from "pri-vate property" as understood in the modern world. It is not alien-able or heritable and must be continuously defended or "earned." The data do not suggest that the territorial instinct is a natural validation of the ownership of transferable property by human beings. The demand for territory (1), a private breeding ground, does seem to be nearly a human universal; even those societies which have "long houses," or other types of extended-family dwell-ings, provide a private breeding area by means of walls or parti-tions. A society which fails to provide adequate breeding areas for the newly mated may well evoke deep feelings.

As far as social mammals are concerned, territory (3), the hunt-ing and food-gathering territory, is almost always shared; rather than an analogue to private property, territory (3) is an analogue to common land, to socialised ownership.

Ardrey introduces two terms of his own to describe the spacing of territories (1) and (2) and the defence of territory (3) re-spectively. When breeding territories are close together, as in the breeding colonies of many seabirds, and the occupants of these ter-ritories spend more energy in mutual disputes, in inward-directed antagonism, rather than in defence of the colony's territories against other co-specifics, he uses the term *noyau*. He has taken this term from J.-J. Petter, who used it to describe the behaviour of one of the nocturnal species of lemur in Madagascar. It is quite a useful term for describing a fairly uncommon type of mammalian, and a fairly common type of avian, behaviour; but it is a metaphor of very doubtful validity when transferred to human beings. Some types of clique could perhaps be so described without stretching the analogy too far. But to write "Italy is a *noyau*. It is not a nation" tells us nothing about Italy, though something about Ardrey's preferences and prejudices.

"Nation" or "biological nation" is the other term which Ardrey has introduced to describe mammalian defence of territory (3).

> The biological nation, as I define it in this work, is a social group containing at least two mature males which holds as an exclusive possession a continuous area of space, which isolates itself from others of its kind through outward antagonism, and which through joint defence of its social territory achieves leadership, cooperation, and a capacity for concerted action. It does not matter too much whether such a nation be composed of twenty-five individuals or two hundred and fifty million.

There is no justification in any ethological writing, as far as I am aware (and Ardrey quotes none) for applying the term "nation" to any animal grouping; and since this is a word in common use with an accepted meaning,* to give it a private significance is treating words as Humpty Dumpty did ("When *I* use a word it means just what I choose it to mean—neither more nor less") and far from the responsible behaviour of a scientist or of a writer dealing with scientific subjects.† The confusion is compounded because on occasion (*e.g.*, p. 214) Ardrey uses "nation" and "society" as synonyms when discussing animals. He also transfers what he has learnt from ethologists about the defence of territory (3) by social animals to some contemporary nation-states without modification. This renders the three final chapters of *The Territorial Imperative* seriously misleading.

When he discusses the contemporary scene, Ardrey reserves the term "biological nation" for those states whose military conduct he

---

* The Shorter Oxford English Dictionary gives the definition: "A distinct race of people, characterised by common descent, language or history usually organised as a separate political state and occupying a definite territory." It quotes as an obsolete meaning "A particular class, kind or race of persons or of animals."

† An analogy could perhaps be drawn between introducing a concept into a context where it does not belong and introducing a skull into a stratum where it does not belong, as happened at Piltdown.

approves of. The United States of America is of course the "biological nation" *par excellence* (he does not explain the appropriateness of the adjective to a nation of immigrants and immigrants' children); but Britain, Finland, Greece, and some other societies of Northern Europe also qualify. Italy, as we have seen, is a *"noyau . . . not a nation."* "France, in the years between the wars had slipped, like Italy, to the status of a *noyau,* the society of inward antagonism which it yet, in all probability, remains." Black Africa has no nations: "none of the new states remotely resembled biological nations"; but white South Africa (pp. 315–17) is most emphatically a "biological nation." The one exception to the apparent generalisation that only white-skinned Protestant Nordics are capable of composing "biological nations" is that the same distinction is accorded to Israel; but the re-territorialisation of the Jews has made the "Jewish personality" disappear (pp. 307–12).

These three final chapters are so full of oversimplifications, questionable statements, omissions and plain inaccuracies that it would take a second comment as long as this to list and analyse them. Ardrey shows only the most superficial knowledge of contemporary events, practically no knowledge of the history of the old world or of contemporary sociology and social anthropology. His categories and preferences are bound to give comfort and provide ammunition for the radical Right, for the Birchites and Empire Loyalists and their analogues elsewhere; there is, however, no evidence to show that Ardrey himself holds or advocates any such political views. His dramatist's employment of ambiguous metaphors and symbols has brought him to these ambiguous conclusions.

Ardrey has done a service to the literate English-reading public by making the novel findings of ethologists and biologists so vividly available. This service would have been far greater if he had confined himself to the animals, and omitted his views on *Homo sapiens.* As it is, *The Territorial Imperative* demands a wrapper: "Handle carefully. Read with critical scepticism."

KENNETH E. BOULDING

Am I a Man or a Mouse—or Both?

Two recent books by Konrad Lorenz and Robert Ardrey have aroused a great deal of discussion and have raised at least by implication some important questions. Lorenz is a very distinguished Austrian ethologist who has made a life-long work out of studying animal behavior. His earlier book, *King Solomon's Ring,* is a classic in the field. I am not professionally equipped to assess his scientific contributions, but to judge from some of the scientific reviews, Lorenz is a pioneer in the field of the study of animal behavior, that is, ethology, but like many pioneers he is now regarded as somewhat old-fashioned by the rising generation striding forward into the field. But whatever may be the scientific merits of Lorenz, the literary merits are unquestionable. He writes with great vigor and charm and opens up new and exciting worlds to the reader. The animal world is never the same again after one has read Lorenz; he opens one's eyes to its richness and complexity.

Ardrey is not a scientist but a playwright and a moralist, though it would be legitimate to describe him as a popularizer of science. He has both read and listened widely. Nevertheless, he almost literally has an axe to grind and enters the courtroom of the mind, as it were, with a brief. His style, while it is readable and has a superficial charm, often seems to me to weaken itself by straining for effect, and does not have the effortless grace of Lorenz. His works,

From *War/Peace Report,* March 1967, pp. 14–17. Reprinted by permission.

furthermore, betray a life-long love affair with himself which gets rather tiresome, and he can be irritating enough to make one want to throw the book across the room. However, he has something to say, and his brief at least deserves to be examined carefully and judged in the light of further evidence.

There are many things common to these two books, which is not surprising, as they both deal with essentially the same subject of animal behavior. Both deal with aggression in animals, although neither of them defines it. Both are concerned with territoriality, that is, the tendency that many animals have either as individuals, as pairs or as groups, to stake out a territory in the environment, mark it with some distinguishing odor or disfigurement, and defend it against intruders of the same species. Where the theme of territoriality is central to Ardrey, to Lorenz it is merely part of a much larger problem of conflict management within a species, having many other aspects. Both the authors are naturally concerned with the processes of evolution, especially of genetic or biologic evolution, and neither of the authors hesitates to make a great leap from animals to man or from genetic evolution into cultural evolution, and to draw conclusions about man from the behavior of animals. It is this last aspect of the work which has aroused most of the controversy and to which I propose to devote most attention, though it should be noted that the strictly ethological material of these works is by no means immune from criticism, for ethology is a young and rapidly advancing science and has still explored only a very imperfect and probably biased sample of its field.

What Can We Learn?

Let me begin then by raising the central question of what we can learn about man and the social system by the study of animals and animal society, before we examine in detail the conclusions which these authors have drawn. There is no doubt, of course, that a man is a physiological organization produced by a growth process which is largely organized by characteristics coded into the total genetic structure of the fertilized egg. The characteristics contained in man's genetic code are accumulated over billions of years and are the end result of a very complex process of mutation and selection. We could in theory postulate an unbroken genetic chain from the primordial amoeba or whatever it was that started life to any individual person existing today. The further back we go in this sequence of genetic structures, presumably the simpler they get in terms of the characteristics they code. Presumably the genetic structure of an amoeba is much simpler than that of a fish, a fish simpler than that of a monkey, a monkey simpler than that of a man.

There are probably no representatives around today of organizations of the identical genetic composition of man's ancestors. Even the amoeba today is probably a little different from the one-celled organism of two billion or more years ago from which we sprang, but nevertheless there are parallels. Some branches of the great tree of evolution have changed less than others. The amoeba today, therefore, is probably a good deal like man's one-celled ancestors, the fish of today may resemble man's fishy ancestors and the monkeys of today have some similarities with man's simian ancestors. This is one conceivable justification for the belief that the study of animal behavior will throw light on human behavior. By studying the behavior of simpler living organisms, we may be able to perceive patterns which may have been present in our ancestors and which may therefore also be present in the complex system of man himself.

We can see immediately, however, how dangerous the method of analogy may be. None of man's direct genetic ancestors are any longer around. Their behavior cannot be studied, though their bones may be. The monkeys of today may have diverged almost as much from their ancestors of two million years ago as man has diverged from his. In jumping from monkeys to man, therefore, we are really making two leaps in the dark, one from the monkey back to man's common ancestor, and again from this ancestor to man. A leap in the dark, of course, may land us on the right side of the pit, but it has to be scrutinized with unusual care to be sure that we have not fallen into serious error. The greatest danger here is from leaping from the simple to the complex, for it is precisely what is not in the simple system that may constitute the essential character of the complex. Hence, even if the simple system is itself embodied in the complex one, this fact only carries us a very little way toward understanding the nature and behavior of the complex.

We could perhaps draw a parallel here from the evolution of

man's artifacts, which follow a course of mutation and selection not unlike that of biological evolution. There is a kind of genetic chain in man's imagination and skill leading from the flint knife to the metal axe to the pneumatic drill to the modern coal-mining machine. Also, shall we say, from the wheelbarrow to the cart to the automobile to the jet plane. The problem with deducing the nature of the artifacts of primitive times from those which are around today is not so difficult, especially as primitive artifacts have left a good many traces. The critical question is how much we could learn about the jet plane from studying the wheelbarrow or even from studying the automobile; if the jet plane is man, the automobile perhaps is the mammal, the wheelbarrow the fish, in terms of relative complexity of system.

Nobody would deny that we could find out something about the jet plane by studying the wheelbarrow. We could find out perhaps about metals and about wheels, but we certainly would not find out about flight. An even better comparison would be between a one-task machine like a loom and the modern computer that is capable of learning and can be programmed to innumerable tasks. Because a loom has a shuttle are we to say a computer must also have a shuttle, or some analog of it? Similarly, if displaced aggression in the goose leads to love, as Lorenz says it does, or if territoriality is a characteristic of the Uganda kob, as Ardrey describes, does this mean either that man's ancestors possessed these qualities and attributes or that man today does? It is clear that a great leap has been made in the dark but it is by no means clear that our feet have landed on firm ground.

The crux of the matter, of course, is the old argument about nature and nurture, heredity and environment, instinct and learning. There is little doubt that the oriole's genes build into the bird itself both the knowledge and the desire to build an oriole nest and that this knowledge comes from the information in the gene rather than information coming into the bird through its senses. It is the great peculiarity of man, however, differentiating him from all the other animals, that what his genes endow him with is an enormous nervous system of some 10 billion components, the informational content of which is derived almost wholly from the environment, that is, from inputs into the organism from outside. The genetic contribution to man's nervous system is virtually complete at birth. Almost everything that happens thereafter is learned. It is this consideration which inspires the modern anthropologist to declare that man has virtually no instincts and that virtually everything he knows has to be learned from his environment, which consists both of the physical world in which he lives and moves and the social world into which he is born. It is this characteristic that differentiates cultural evolution from biological evolution. The time seems to be approaching, indeed, when cultural evolution will dominate biological evolution because man will acquire power to manipulate the gene pool directly. Up to now he has not been able to do this, but even so, in at least the last ten thousand years the cultural evolution has dominated the scene, transmitting information through the learning process and not through the information coded in the genes.

The critical question here is the extent to which the genetic composition of the human body limits and determines what it can learn from its environment. That such limits exist there can be no doubt, for no man has an indefinite capacity for learning. Furthermore, it is clear that genetic defects which, for instance, produce the mongoloid or the idiot, result in a very serious limitation of the potential field of learning, even though there is a good deal of evidence accumulating that this limitation itself is a function of the culture into which the child grows and may be less confining than we now think. We are pretty sure that it is genetic constitution which prevents a dog or a chimpanzee from learning to talk; we are not quite so sure about the dolphin. What does seem to be clear, however, is that for the normal human being the limits on learning imposed by the physiological constitution of the human nervous system are very far out, and that most of the limits come from a dynamic failure of the learning process in experience rather than from any limitations imposed by the physiological nature of the human nervous system, the capacity of which seems very far from having been exhausted. It is, indeed, the existence of large excess capacity in the human nervous system which it seems to me vitiates the arguments of those who seek to find in "instinct" any explanation whatever of human behavior beyond the most elementary and primitive acts of the newly born.

The argument is complicated, however, by the fact that environments themselves can breed. Culture is a body of coded information which is passed on from generation to generation, suffering mutation and selection, just as the coded information in the gene is passed on, except that cultural evolution is much more subject to mutation and proceeds at a much more rapid rate than the evolution of the genetic structure. Consequently, the concept of a cultural instinct is by no means absurd, even though the genes of culture are much less stable and much more subject to mutation than the biological genes. We have not learned aggression, however, from our remote biological ancestors, nor have we learned territoriality from them. Insofar as aggression or territoriality play a part in human culture—and they do—each generation learns them from the previous generation and perhaps in a lesser degree from its own physical environment and random events.

A change in human affairs comes hardly at all from changes in the gene pool and its distribution in mankind, though this cannot be wholly excluded. Genetic changes do take place slowly as previously isolated gene pools intermingle through the breakdown of concepts of caste and race, as aristocracies fail to reproduce themselves, and as peasants multiply, but it would be surprising if these factors accounted for more than a fraction of one per cent of social change and social evolution. It is new inputs of information into a culture that constitute mutation in social evolution and these inputs can affect either the image of the world or the value systems, according to which decisions are made. Human aggression and human territoriality are products of social systems, not of biological systems, and they must be treated as such, even though concepts and analogies which are derived from biological systems may occasionally be helpful. The naive analogizing, therefore, even of Lorenz and especially of Ardrey will not stand up to a moment's serious criticism.

An Ideological Need

In light of the fact that these works have been rejected by the scientific community almost without exception as serious scientific documents, at least in regard to the conclusions which they draw about society, it is important to ask why they have received so much attention and why they seem to meet an ideological need, especially in the United States. This is a question, unfortunately, to which a fairly clear answer can be given out of the analysis of social systems. I say unfortunately, because the answer is a disagreeable one, but I see no way of escaping it. By a very complex series of events the "establishment" of American society, that is, those people who are either important decision-makers or close to them or identified with them have "learned" that the international system is primarily a "threat system" and that threats must be made credible by occasionally carrying them out, even though this involves inflicting appalling suffering upon innocent people.

The war in Vietnam can only be interpreted as an attempt to make the American threat system credible by demonstrating our willingness to be cruel and merciless so that people will believe the threat implicit in our enormous military establishment. To be effective, however, it is not enough that threats should be credible; they also should have to be legitimate, especially in the minds of the threatener himself, for unless he feels that his cruelty is justified he will find it hard to continue in it. The rise of Hitler and of Pearl Harbor in the 1930s and early '40s taught this country that naive idealism did not pay so we decided to throw away the idealism.

On the other hand, idealism of some sort is necessary for justification and legitimation, for no line of policy can be pursued for very long without self-justification. A line of argument like that of Ardrey's, therefore, seems to legitimate our present morality, in regarding the threat system as dominant at all costs, by reference to our biological ancestors. If the names of both antiquity and of science can be drawn upon to legitimate our behavior, the moral uneasiness about napalm and the massacre of the innocent in Vietnam may be assuaged. Dr. Lorenz, I am sure, who is a gentle, humane soul, still, one would judge, living in the afterglow of Franz Josef, would be horrified by this suggestion. Nevertheless, one cannot altogether absolve even Dr. Lorenz (to whom I owe some of the most delightful hours of my reading life), from the sin of using the prestige of one science to jump to unwarranted conclusions in another, and hence to bring the weight of scientific authority behind essentially unproven propositions. In Ardrey's case the need for legitimation is more obvious, and there are real dangers of a pseudo-science used to bolster and legitimate an otherwise untenable moral position. Even Ardrey, however, I am sure, is a decent fellow at heart, and is on the side of man. Nevertheless, the pit that he is leaping over in the dark is very wide and destruction lurks at the bottom, and those who have the interests both of science and mankind at heart at least need to turn on their flashlights.

We have seen in the Nazi movement how appallingly dangerous a pseudo-science can be in the legitimation of an absurd and evil system. I am not suggesting that either Lorenz or Ardrey is a racist theorist like Gobineau or Houston Chamberlain. However, one could imagine their superficially attractive neo-social-Darwinism applied to very ill uses indeed, and the fact that it is scientific humbug does not unfortunately detract from its attractiveness.

RALPH HOLLOWAY

Territory and Aggression in Man:
A Look at Ardrey's *Territorial Imperative*

This book should be subtitled "An Autobiography of Primitive Thought." Ardrey's book proves his main point regarding continuity of behavior in modern man with lower animal forms: what remains a difficult task is to ascertain which ancestors are most responsible for this thought—planarian worms, lemurs, slime-molds, or the brash cock robin. If this appears vindictive, the reader is correct: I would prefer to have my time back. Actually, according to Ardrey's thesis regarding the instinctual basis of human behavior, the question has a sense of fairness in it. Initially, my reaction was that nobody had really understood Ardrey's aim—here was one of the best satires written—but further reading led unerringly to the conclusion that the author is indeed serious.

Nowhere in this book will one find a closely, tightly knit reasoned statement or hypothesis which interrelates a number of scattered variables such as territorial behavior, aggressiveness, amity, enmity, stimulation, security, identity, natural selection, and which could be tested for logical consistency or empirical support. Instead, in dramatic and scattered fashion the author parades forth a plethora of behavioral instincts (some his own invention), under the protective wrapper of "the new biology" (which alas, is denied

Reprinted with permission from the *Political Science Quarterly,* December 1967, Vol. LXXXII, No. 4, pp. 630–32. New material added by author, 1968.

to our children's education), and does little more than assert that anyone in disagreement with his view of man and his instincts is ignorant, a clinger to religion, a throwback to an older generation of non-informed biologists, a sycophant trying to rationalize his own instincts. In short, Ardrey has almost constructed a religion, very much along Freudian lines, where dissent or skepticism is explained by the theory itself. Perhaps this is fine drama—it is hardly science. When Ardrey says that this is a "personal inquiry" he is not exaggerating. Unfortunately, the "personal" aspects enter into the argument—we are constantly reminded about his personal acquaintances, drinking buddies, and the recent budding generation of baboon watchers, all brought to the reader's attention as authoritative—the possibility that many of this list of heroes very likely might disagree with Ardrey is never mentioned. In short, this is one of Ardrey's tactics. We learn of Ardrey's competence and professional background—he once lectured in anthropology in one of the booths at the Chicago World's Fair in the 1930's.

The methodology needs explanation. Ardrey starts by making a general assertion as if it were heretical, e.g., that man's behavior is a product of evolution. He expands this into a non-sequitur that man carries around some particular behavioral pattern from his ancestry. Next, Ardrey recounts the animal studies (it may be slime-molds, birds, or penguins) to prove that behavior, e.g., territorial defense, has an instinctual, innate basis. Next, one is warned that if he dissents and doesn't see the instinctual basis of human international behavior in these examples, he is guilty of not believing in evolution, and a sort of "see there, I told you so," mentality takes over—Ardrey feels he has proven his point. His strategy is to repeat this tactic again and again, going from the slime to the sublime until the brainwashing is hopefully communal. Nowhere does one find a single whit of evidence provided for human instincts: that is unnecessary according to Ardrey's methodology. We simply jump to collective farms, National Character, or International relationships to prove the innate basis of individual men's behavior. Associated with these tactics is the ever-occurring assertion that he is breaking new ground—that nowhere in his extensive notes has he ever found this approach used before. The phrase "Social Darwinism" never appears in this book. Too bad, for that is essentially the message of the book. Ardrey is uninformed if he thinks that there have never been attempts to reduce human group behavior to a few animal instincts. He is wrong if he believes that International bodies have never before been seen as organisms. Ardrey accepts group selection theory as proven, even though most biologists know that this is an area of considerable debate. There is misinformation about the ubiquity of primate territoriality, and many of the recent advances in the eufunctions of spacing behavior particularly in terms of disease resistance and adaptation are omitted.

It is worthwhile to go more deeply into this matter of tactics whereby one is branded anti-evolutionistic if he views the discontinuities between man and other animals of signal importance. Nowhere has this been better phrased than in Konrad Lorenz's article, "Ritualized Fighting," in *The Natural History of Aggression.** Indeed, many parts of Ardrey's book rely on Lorenz's formulations, but in more dramatic and less careful ways. Lorenz notes:

> There cannot be any doubt, in the opinion of any biologically-minded scientist, that intraspecific aggression is, in Man, just as much of a spontaneous instinctive drive as in most other higher vertebrates. The beginning synthesis between the findings of ethology and psychoanalysis does not leave any doubt, either, that what . . . Freud called the "death drive" is nothing else but the miscarrying of this instinct which, in itself, is as indispensable for survival as any other.

Now, what about dissenters?

> However, it comes very hard to people not versed in biological thought to concede that Man, with a capital M, still does possess instincts in common with animals. That particular kind of pride which proverbially comes before a fall prevents men from understanding the workings of their own instincts, including that of aggression. As it is causal insight alone which can ever give us the power to influence chains of events and to direct them to our own ends, it is highly dangerous to assume the ostrich attitude in respect to the nature of human instincts. (p. 49)

* J. D. Carthy and F. J. Ebling (eds.), *The Natural History of Aggression.* New York: Academic Press, 1964.

Man, like any other animal, has evolved a repertoire of behavioral patterns under the exacting influence of natural selection. The notion of species-specific behavior, its ontogenesis and structural underpinnings need not require a cathection upon some list of instincts to explain human behavior. One does not have to search very far in the literature to find many "biologically-minded scientists" who do not feel that man's aggression is best compared with the "spontaneous instinctive drive as in most other higher vertebrates." One does not have far to go in the literature to discern a general displeasure with the proposition that any higher vertebrates have instincts. Names such as Lehrman, Schneirla, or Berkowitz do not appear in Ardrey's book, and the whole hoary question of innate patterns is assumed already solved.

This leads directly to another maddening shortcoming of this general holier-than-thou approach of the "true" biologically-minded scientist. One of the outstanding successes of the ethologist school has been the investigation and delineation of critical sign-stimuli, the cue functions of the environmental surround which figure in an adaptive sense in the animal's behavior, and which act to release certain sequences of motor action in the animal's interest, providing that the internal conditions are appropriate, whether it be in terms of self- or species preservation.

What are the critical sign stimuli for the human, which act to release stereotypical adaptive responses? What are the invariances of the cue functions in the human environment which help to release specific motor patterns built up through evolution by natural selection? Red feathers, blue gew gaws, green turf, butyric acid, white eye lids, the exposed neck, flashing white tails, etc., etc., have been identified for numerous animals. What are the critical sign stimuli which make up the human "Umwelt"? The question is not about human aggressive responses to stimuli. The sordid history of man attests well to the fantastic plurality of "stimuli" that can be cooked up to elicit aggression. How natural are they? Have the gentiles undergone a special process of evolution and natural selection so that they respond instinctively to some critical sign stimulus of Jewishness, and vice versa? To reduce the question to absurdity, would any "biologically-minded scientist" aver that each human symbol cluster that elicits aggressive responses was gained through natural selection just as the stickleback reacts to red, or certain bower birds to blue? Until the specific sign stimuli can be identified (as for one possible example, the smiling face and the human infant's reaction to it), the analogies to lower animals' species-specific patterns represent outrageous intellectual slighting, not ground-breaking. Skepticism about human instincts is not any attack on the animal nature of man, or an arrogant suggestion that man does not act according to natural and man-made laws. Such skepticism need not blind anyone to the possibility of innate dispositions in humankind to define certain environmental contexts as inimical to their interests, and to act aggressively toward these clusters. The object is not, as some social scientists have tended to do, to rid man of his biological heritage, or to deny that his psychobiological makeup is species-specific. Innate predispositions are not the same thing as instincts, a concept continually being amended to include more outside variables integrated with learning and internal physiological state.

Perhaps egoism and self-esteem are innate properties of the species man, which during ontogenetic development can go in different but limited directions depending on the cultural milieu in which various peoples thrive or cope. Hostility and aggression toward sources frustrating the attainment of particular cognitive definitions of the self can be biologically based and species-specific without recourse to the suggestions of Lorenz and Ardrey that such responses can best be understood by studying the birds, bees, and baboons. Human aggression is no less real, or without biological basis because it is acted out in extraordinary various ways, or that it responds to an almost infinite variety of physical and symbolic stimuli. The variety itself implicates the overriding importance of learning in different cultural contexts, the types of frustrations particular subcultures are most prone to suffer, and the vast mass of literature in the psychological (both experimental and social) and sociological journals is replete with numerous instances of cultural manipulation of aggression. The biological literature is no less prepared to offer Ardrey numerous examples of the importance of learning and the nature of cue functions in nonhuman animal aggression. Almost all of the examples used by Ardrey, and those from the major works of ethological research show a fairly clear-cut locking-in between discrete stimuli or environmental cues, action patterns, and adaptation to selected coterminous features of the environment. The peculiarly locking-in aspects for man have been replaced by plasticity welded into a species-specific pattern of ego structuring and maturation, the whole imbedded in a wide variety of symbolic environments. Animals other than man are interesting objects of study, and one cannot disclaim that the results of such have heuristic merit. For man, however, we need a species-specific theory which will not only account for aggression, but the total psychobiological matrix which has also been under natural selection, and has evolved during at least two million years of evolution. Human sentiment structures are varied and deep. Tears, laughter, sympathy, empathy, altruism, sacrifice, love, cooperation, prolonged deferment of gratification, each is a part of the human specificity. Their integration presupposes an evolutionary development far more complicated than the relatively simple key-lock framework of lower animals' behavior and evolution. To this reader it seems somewhat stupefying to reduce the reactions felt by many Americans after the bombing of Pearl Harbor to a set of simple territorial patterns of behavior. The question of "how many wars have been fought over women and how many over land (territory)" seems no more refined than popular drama requires.

There are some good points to this book. It is well-written—Ardrey can write—and the reader will appreciate the dramatist's skill, and will learn something about the behaviors of different animals (often fascinating), without having to read the dry, original scientific reports. That is, if he is willing to trust the selectiveness of Ardrey's perception and accuracy of reportage. The type is large, his wife's illustrations succinct and dramatic, and the book reads quickly—a distinct advantage for the reader. People with various prejudices for and against Italians, Jews, Black South Africans, free enterprise, and collective farms, will be treated to the end products of Ardrey's thought processes. The Italians are organized like the Lemurs. Black South Africans now prospering under the largesse of Apartheid policies will (85%) rise up in indignant wrath and defense of their White benefactors should any liberation attempts be made on the part of their brothers in the rest of Africa. In short, this book is an apology and rationalization for Imperialism, Pax

Americana, Laissez Faire, Social Darwinism, and that greatest of all evolutionary developments, Capitalism. Of course, there is a drawback which Ardrey takes pain to elaborate upon. Those intruded upon gain a certain energy from the fact that the territory is theirs, so intruders must take into account the likely intensity of reaction to their intrusion. (This energy gain is based on numerous animal studies in which the defender usually drives the intruder back into its own territory—never mind what the nature of the stimuli might be for the intruder.) This framework will surely interest those who have studied the history of the Third Reich. One thing Ardrey does not explain is why, when a Nation (organism?) has ample territory, abundance of food, resources, stimulation, security, it nevertheless wants more and more. Territorial instincts, energy gains and losses, slime molds, noyaus, bower birds, identity, stimulation, amity-enmity-hazard, are hardly necessary, and one fails to see how they offer any richer understanding than simple *greed* and *stupidity*.

In the final chapter, the Three Faces of Janus, one has the distinct impression that at last Ardrey has raised the really important issues, that somewhere in all this anthropomorphizing and animalizing of man's behavior, there are truths, and that Ardrey is on to something very important. Perhaps his next book will do it. This one fails and in a maddening, glib way.

It is only fitting to close this review with a quote from Ardrey: "Men, unlike mockingbirds, have the capacity for systematic self-delusion."

JOHN HURRELL CROOK

The Nature and Function of Territorial Aggression

Ethology and Mass Culture

Within the last few years the young science of ethology has become
"popular" with consequences that its more reserved practitioners
have yet to comprehend. Television interviews, articles in magazines, comment in the press and books of mass circulation all
thrust this rather reticent science increasingly before the public
gaze. In addition, when some of its earlier tenets are presented as
explanations for human ills in areas seemingly untouched by psychology and social science, it is not surprising that the clamour becomes a marketable product.

Mr. Robert Ardrey, in his introduction to *The Territorial Imperative,* eloquently describes his personal discovery of the huge body
of attentive readers his book *African Genesis* had disclosed. Mass
literacy provides a market for mass products and indeed a new
genre of publication on the problems of animal behavior and
their relevance to the "human situation" has come into being;
a genre distinguishable in many ways from popular scientific writing of the type presented, for example, by the Pelican books on
scientific subjects. In the latter an authority presents a carefully
weighted digest of contemporary research and theory for public information and discussion. The new product, burnished and fur-
nished with all the artifice skilled authorship can employ, seeks the
simple statement, the dramatic story, and, above all, an essentially

sensational account of human troubles that in simple explanation relieves the anxiety born of our massive concern with war, aggression, and sex in a disordered world. A good talking point sells better than serious argument.

It would be dangerous, however, for behaviour scientists to think that such works were merely *kitsch*, mass products for a consumer society, for they are informed by extensive reading of the authoritative texts. Furthermore, the viewpoints presented are plausible, entertaining, and appear to instruct. They also reflect, albeit darkly, the contemporary trend towards biological explanation in both psychology and social anthropology largely the result of two main developments. First, the recent conceptual revisions of motivation theory in ethology have allowed a closer relationship with comparative psychology, so long dominated in America by a theoretical framework derived from behaviourism. Techniques of operant conditioning become tools in motivation research by ethologists, and psychologists pay a new respect to ethological experimentation in field and laboratory. Naturally, unresolved conflicts remain, but enough has been achieved for R. A. Hinde (1966) to subtitle his recent important textbook *Animal Behaviour*, with the phrase *A Synthesis of Ethology and Comparative Psychology*. Second, the study of the relationship between behaviour and ecology and the evolution of animal social organization, for long the field of ethology alone, has attracted the attention of certain social anthropologists (e.g. Fox, 1967) looking for a new derivational approach explaining the origins of human behaviour and social structure in terms of those of our nonhuman forebears.

The question that disturbs the practising ethologist is whether the new genre adequately presents the difficulties inherent in the new orientations of behavioural biology or whether it is a glib or one-sided approach which could bring the whole endeavour into disrepute. As M. V. C. Jeffreys (1962) describes in *Personal Values in the Modern World* it is extremely difficult for the individual subjected to a mass culture to discover the basis for views that affect ethical values—even more so when complex doctrines of social and maybe political relevance are purveyed in popular form and become rapidly the stock subjects for after-dinner conversation and assertion. We shall return to this problem in our last paragraphs. Our first concern is with the adequacy of certain of the popular accounts of ethological theory recently published. Do they really inform as much as they may entertain? Our task is to discuss Mr. Ardrey's account of territorial behaviour in man and animals, a task that leads us also to consider some views expressed in Konrad Lorenz's popular book *On Aggression* (1966), which in certain respects bears the same theme.

Instinct, Territory, and Social Engineering

Anyone who has listened to the film script of *Khartoum* will recognise in Robert Ardrey a dramatist of calibre. In *The Territorial Imperative* the same gifts of authorship are displayed prominently. He has a feel for the beauty of natural environment and the ability to describe the excitement of observing animals at close quarters, be it in the savannahs of Africa or in the plastic dishes of the wormrunner's laboratory, which must be the envy of his less-endowed fellow enthusiasts. He has also read in some depth the detailed studies relevant to his theme. He portrays too with vivid pen the conflicts, joys, disappointments, and the often narrow-minded conformity of practising scientists—a picture of a community of men often far from flattering. For the general reader there is much here to relish and enjoy.

Ardrey is concerned basically with the cause of war and man's unpleasantness to man. His explanation centres upon an account of territorial behaviour. Man, Ardrey tells us, is a species of animal whose natural properties include an instinct of territorial aggression. Territoriality is conceived as an innate character of the human species as a consequence of evolutionary inheritance and, more generally, treated as a genetically determined form of animal behaviour. We find him repeatedly referring to an "instinct" or "force" "called territory" (pp. 59, 62, 166). Territoriality expresses an innate drive to gain and defend property, but, in that animals recognise the rights of ownership and withdraw when threatened by an owner, the behavior reveals individual restraint which is interpreted by Ardrey as a form of natural morality. The functions of ownership are said to be the provision of nest site (in birds), a territorial periphery at which stimulative interaction with companions may occur, and identity in that an individual becomes part of an interacting community. These three points, derived in part from the work of well-known naturalists, are stressed again in the last chapter, although here the order of importance is reversed. The basic primordial psychological necessities to life are now identity, stimulation, and security, all of which the instinctive drive to gain and preserve a territory provides. The fact that many animals do not appear to be territorial is evidently of scant relevance because it is those that show this similarity to man that are the focus of interest.

Ardrey distinguishes between two types of society—the *noyau*—a term lifted from the French text of a work by J. J. Petter (1962) on the lemurs of Madagascar—and the *nation*. The *noyau* is a society of "inward antagonism" held together, Ardrey claims, by the mutual animosity of its members. In species after species, Ardrey reminds us, natural selection appears to have promoted social mechanisms that seem to function for no other reason than to alleviate boredom through the promoting of antagonism and excitement. Why this should be so he leaves unexplained (p. 162), but considers the *noyau* an "evolutionary step towards societies characterised by mutual aid" (p. 167), one, indeed, that provides a primitive security of mutual hate. The other type of society, the biological *nation,* is a social group which must contain at least two adult males and which is separated from other groups by antagonism. In a *nation* joint defence of territory promotes the emergence of ingroup leadership and co-operation. Examples of *noyaux* include herring gull colonies, song sparrow neighbourhoods, the small and solitary groups of *Lepilemur* in Madagascar forests, and the "family" groups of gibbons and *Callicebus* monkeys. Among *nations* may evidently be included baboons, even though territorial behaviour is usually marked by avoidance on the fringes of home ranges rather than aggression, and those diurnal societies of lemurs that live with *Lepilemur* in Madagascar forests. Ardrey leaves the question as to why Petter's six nocturnal species of lemur appear to form *noyaux* while the nine diurnal ones are evidently *nations* unanswered, in spite of the strong ecological clues suggested by Petter himself. Ardrey's distinction between *noyaux* and *nations* is difficult to maintain. His **noyaux** species show very diverse types of social structure from pairs, to colonies, to family parties, to groups;

and the reason why a pair of song sparrows, herring gulls, or gibbons collaborating in rearing young and defending their borders should be distinguished in any fundamental way from groups of baboons doing essentially the same thing is unclear. Certainly the "inner antagonism" of baboon troops is considerable, even though overt aggression is reduced through the social role-playing of animals learnt in relation to their individual dominance, age, and sexual statuses. Ardrey's categories indeed overlap so disastrously that the distinction largely disappears on close examination. This is not to say, of course, that major contrasts in social groups cannot be described by using well-defined natural criteria.

The difficulty is magnified when suddenly we read that Italy is a *noyau,* France (in 1939 without de Gaulle as alpha male) also, but Germany, Britain, Japan, and the U.S.A. evidently not; nor, we may infer, is the Soviet Union. These are the nations. Greece was a *nation* because the Greeks with notable courage threw out Mussolini's soldiers in 1940. Mussolini thought his soldiers belonged to a *nation* but he was wrong. The Jews finally became a *nation* once the hazards of border defence imposed territory upon them, thereby eliciting those instincts they had forgotten for so long.

Ardrey asks how human territorial defence and war arose when man's most immediate ancestors were apparently nonaggressive apes resembling chimpanzees or gorillas. He provides a more or less orthodox interpretation from the authorities, noting the likely effect of increasing aridity in Africa in the relevant time period and the consequent development of carnivorous habits in protohominids. Armed with weapons and searching for limited protein resources supplied by the animals of the plain, men soon began to compete, formed territories, and this foreshadowed the development of the nation-state.

Modern man thus brings with him basic needs for identity, security, and stimulation, all of which are satisfied by territorial behaviour, through which that greatest stimulant, war, has come upon us. Ardrey's philosophy of real estate thus gains biological approval and the only trouble is that, nowadays, the war-game is too hazardous to play. In a chapter called the "Amity-Enmity Complex" Ardrey predicts that the removal of external hazard should result in the increase of enmity within groups. Above all, the removal of war necessitates a substitute, a ritualisation of aggression. The space race, he suggests, is not so much covert aggression but rather ritualised aggression—a game in which our tensions may be resolved without combat. Ardrey then takes from V. C. Wynne-Edwards the concept of "conventional competition," originally coined in a quite different and thoroughly rigorous context, and suggests that through "conventional competitions" identity and stimulation may be provided without the dangers of destructive conflict. The "natural morality" whereby intruders understand that aggression leads to stronger territorial response has not yet been acquired by men, possibly because his carnivorous propensities emerged late. We must learn to know ourselves and devise conventions. Whether morality without territory is for man a possibility remains for Ardrey the final problem.

Although imbedded in numerous digressions Ardrey's argument comes through the noise clearly enough. His book, published in 1967, resembles in certain details the ideas on human aggression published by Konrad Lorenz in *Das Sogenannte Böse* in 1963, translated into English in 1966. Lorenz, the "father" of ethology in its classical period, is justly considered one of the most distinguished of the older comparative ethologists and he has made major contributions to motivation theory, the study of parent-offspring relations and early learning, behavioural evolution, and the use of behavioural characters in taxonomy. He shares with Ardrey a profound concern with the human predicament and, in his book, seeks to utilise ethological concepts, largely of his own original formulation, in explanation of aggression in man and animals. The book, addressed to the general public, resembles Ardrey's in its style of popular presentation and in its selectivity of argument. Like Ardrey, Lorenz adopts a highly personal approach, writes in the first person and, as in his earlier *King Solomon's Ring*, reveals the joy and delight that any contemplative naturalist has in the study of complex animal behaviour. Lorenz considers aggressive behaviour in man and animals to be the expression of an innate drive; an appetite seeking consummation in its expression upon release by an appropriate stimulus presentation. He provides a chapter on motivational studies concerning the "spontaneity" of innate drives, which he uses as evidence for his particular approach.

Aggression is of survival value to its practitioners because it ensures the dispersal of individuals and hence the optimum utilisation of resources. Competition ensures that only the fittest individuals breed. Fighting within groups promotes the formation of hierarchies which allow for the emergence of leadership. Aggressiveness is not, however, directed inappropriately to any member of a species, nor is it biologically advantageous for it to lead to the death of one antagonist and the possible exhaustion of the other. Natural selection has led to the development of postures which signal the submission of one of two opponents thereby reducing the attack drive of the other. Encounters become ritualised into threatening matches—intruders withdraw and owners retain their territories, a tiring opponent signals submission and the fight ceases. Sometimes complex relationships between individuals become based upon such rituals and involve the formation of strong affectional ties. Indeed, strong personal ties appear characteristic of societies within which marked intraspecific aggression occurs. Lorenz thinks that aggressiveness lies at the root of personal affection. Man differs from many other animals in that he lacks major morphological weapons and, in Lorenz's view, has thus never evolved the means of diverting disadvantageous aggressiveness through innate ritual. Man now lives in a society in which there is little acceptable opportunity for the useful or harmless release of his aggressive drive. Furthermore, with the advent of nuclear weapons, man holds the tool for his own extinction in his hands while he is yet unsure of the restraints he can impose on the impulse to attack. Lorenz, like Ardrey, suggests that competitive games provide the outlet for the collective fury of the *nations*. Through ritualisation and sublimation, aggression may be tamed enough to make life tolerable.

Certain assertions occur in both books. First, that man, in common with many other animals, has an innate territorial or aggressive drive seeking consummation in periodic performance. Second, a superficial comparison of animal societies reveals a variety of territorial and social dispersion patterns to which simple survival values are attributed in terms of optimum utilisation of commodities, selective elimination of the least fit, security and stimulation for the survivers. Third, man is defective in his control of his aggression by reason of his recent evolution without concomitant development of innate ritualised restraints. In both books the possibility that the leopard may change his spots through learning is dismissed. The instinct, rather, must be diverted into conventional substitutes for war. The case for social engineering rather than education is complete.

Is the account in these texts a reasonable basis for the inference from animals to man? To find out we must evaluate the key aspects of the story. First, we may pinpoint the main questions. 1. What is the evidence for an innate aggressive drive involving the defence of territory? Is such behaviour really the compulsive, spontaneous, unalterable force it is supposed to be? Or are aggressive animals modifiable, educable? 2. Do biologists really conceive of the survival value of territory in terms of security, stimulation, and identity? Upon what theoretical contributions have these ideas been based? 3. What is the role of territory in man's primate relatives and what may be inferred from this regarding the evolution of his social organization? 4. Is the Lorenz-Ardrey explanation an adequate account of recent ethological thinking in relation to the problems of human relationship?

Motivation and Territoriality

Ardrey repeatedly speaks of a force or instinct called "territory." The meaning of this term requires elucidation. A solitary animal cannot be territorial, for, to show defence of an area, at least one neighbour is needed. The term "territory" cannot, therefore, refer to an intrinsic aspect of the motivation of an individual but, rather, it refers to a relationship between two or more animals with respect to a location. Territory is a "group characteristic" arising out of the cohabitation of individuals in a given locality and which, as a result of their interaction, come to show a particular pattern of dispersion.

Traditionally, ethologists have been concerned with the fixed action patterns common to all individuals of a species population and which are mostly as stable in their manifestation as morphological traits. In many cases there are good reasons for considering such patterns to be more or less directly under genetic influence and their physiological control may be reasonably described as "innate." Lorenz's own work has contributed greatly to the understanding of such movements, the relative stereotyping of which permits their use in the systematics. Similar arguments may perhaps be applied to many of the movements expressive of emotion in primates including man. Species characteristic behaviour attributes such as temperamental traits and other more complicated features cannot, however, always be treated as innate characters. Common conditions of early rearing and parent-child relations throughout a population are now known to account for many regularities. Highly specific modes of learning may account for the elaboration of simple reflex patterns, as in the case of recent studies of bird song. Behaviour observably beneficial to individuals cannot therefore always be attributed, without extensive investigation, directly to the operation of natural selection of genes over many generations. Other processes may be at work. This is a particularly significant viewpoint when "group characteristics" such as "territory" or "dominance" are under consideration. The physical and social environment of a population may impose direct constraints on social structure. A salmonid fish, the ayu, shows territoriality in shallow brooks but moves in shoals in deep pools (Chapman, 1966). Certain rodents may be highly territorial in some environments at certain population concentrations but fail to show such behaviour under different conditions (Anderson, 1961). Populations of vervet monkeys have been found to be territorial in one habitat but to move in groups of contrasting size and behaviour in undefended home ranges in another (Gartlan, 1966). Ecological and social conditions are thus important in determining whether a population does or does not exhibit territorial behaviour. Its inevitability as a species character cannot simply be assumed.

Nevertheless, it is clear that in species which, under given conditions, reveal a population dispersion based on territoriality there must be some behavioural property that induces the members so to distribute themselves. In an important review, Tinbergen (1957) points out that when we are considering the defence of a geographically fixed site or area, territory is the result of two tendencies shown by the owner; first, site attachment and, second, hostility to that class of animals the members of which comprise the rivals or competitors. These two tendencies can occur independently of one another. Thus certain birds make use of regular roosting sites without defending them; and partridges, after pair formation, attempt to prevent the close approach of conspecifics, although this occurs without reference to a particular site. Furthermore, the functions of these two tendencies are commonly different. Tinbergen remarks that Howard's important studies of territorial behaviour (1920) tended to hinder the development of this distinction by focusing attention on their combined effects. "Simply because birds happen to be 'landed proprietors' (Selous, 1933) or, in other words, combine site attachment with hostility, there is a natural disinclination to consider the two aspects separately." Again, in considering territorial maintenance, both attack and escape are involved, and many cases of territorial dispersion result essentially from mutual avoidance rather than from combat. While all these factors combine to produce territorial behaviour, any analysis of its motivational control must consider each facet of the system separately. Several interrelated mechanisms are likely to be at work and susceptible to differential modification under changing conditions of population pressure or environment.

It is clear, however, that the most important element in the complex is the willingness of an individual to fight to maintain ownership when conditions require it to do so. The question is whether an innate drive to aggression of the sort described by Lorenz and assumed by Ardrey accounts for the observed phenomenon.

Lorenz's account of the proximate determination of aggressive behaviour is based upon a formulation of motivation theory largely developed by him in the classical ethology of the 1930's. According to his famous "hydraulic model" of instinctive behavior (see Lorenz, 1950) the performance of fixed action patterns, such as are shown in sexual behavior or feeding, depends upon the accumulation of energy specific to these activities in centres in the conceptual nervous system. Release of this energy occurs when appropriate stimuli are provided, but in the absence of stimulation the energy must sooner or later find an outlet in relation to an inappropriate stimulus or even "in vacuum." Lorenz has commonly used the apparent spontaneity of behavior under minimal stimulation as support for this view. However, the occurrence of aggressive behavior seems rarely to fit such an account even descriptively. Lorenz's ideas were in large measure based upon Wallace Craig's distinction (1918) between the appetitive and consummatory phases of cyclic drives. According to Lorenz's account the action-specific energy appears first as appetitive behaviour and finds outlet in the performance of the consummatory act. In considering aggression Lorenz ignores, however, Craig's (1918, 1928) further and more important distinction between "appetites" and "aversions." Aversive behavior is a response to undesirable or harmful stimulation and persists until the individual flees or until the stimulation is removed. Aggression, which Craig described as an "aversion," occurs in the social context only on the appearance of an offending individual and continues until one or other of the mutual offenders goes away. According to this account, aggressive behaviour is nonrhythmic and lacks an appetitive phase. (See Chapter 5 in Marler and Hamilton, 1966.) There is no theoretical requirement for aggressive behaviour to well up spontaneously without prior stimulation; and this appears to accord well with descriptive data. Studies which have revealed persistence in attacking on reduction in stimulation appear commonly to implicate a learning process whereby the repeated performance of aggression has secured beneficial reward and the response has generalised to a wide range of stimuli. Unusual persistence may also be due to changes in physiological conditions imposed by hunger, for example, or the recent performance of other aggressive acts. There is in fact no uncontroversial evidence that in the absence of stimulation, aggressiveness must find a spontaneous outlet. Lorenz's attempt to justify his explanation of the causes of aggression with descriptions of rhythmic behavior in other contexts is largely irrelevant and fails to convince. In any case, the whole structure of motivation theory in ethology has undergone a major conceptual revision in recent years and even if aggression could be classified descriptively as an "appetite," the simple Lorenz-Ardrey account of its causation would have to be severely modernized. As Hinde (1967) remarked in a critical review: "Since Lorenz claims that his facts are verified and makes many generalisations with a voice of authority, while ignoring the bulk of the experimental literature on his subject, it is as well to reflect on them."

In animal societies, individuals do not fight because they have territories; they have territories because, among other things, they fight. The territorial context is not the only one in which aggression occurs. Individuals of many species, but by no means all, maintain a space around their bodies within which they repel approaching individuals. Individual distance infringements both in wild flocks of certain birds and in caged groups are thus a common cause of aggressive encounters. Marler (1956b) has shown that at sources of food chaffinch males usually either attack or withdraw if a companion approaches within about 20 cms. Females may approach more closely before they are attacked, but if they are experimentally coloured to look like males then they are repulsed at the same distances as other males. The weaver bird *Quelea quelea,* an extremely social species, tolerates approach to about 4 cms., and in caged groups some individuals rapidly come to win encounters more frequently than others so that individual distances are maintained as much by avoidance of attack by relatively subordinate individuals as by actual aggression (Crook, 1961). Repeated encounters give rise to hierarchies, the so-called "peck order" first described from flocks of chicken. Such dominance hierarchies are also found in many mammals living in social groups and, as in baboons, may become very complex with individuals playing elaborate roles resulting from their relative dominance, sex, and age statuses. Locations for sleeping, mating, nesting, or for a whole complex of activities can become an external reference for dominance. The relative dominance of Steller jays at feeding stations placed in winter at various distances from the nesting area of the previous season varied inversely with the distance (Brown, 1963). In great tits, robins, and many other species, interaction occurs primarily at the periphery of a territory within which intruders invariably flee. External reference for inter-male dominance may consist in the temporary location of a male's "family," as in wild geese and among male hamadryas and gelada baboons. Crowding and hormonal states may effect the type of aggressive reference individuals show. In certain fish, birds, and rodents, high population densities produce a shift from the holding of territories to the maintenance of individual dominance. Chaffinches, which show individual distance maintenance in winter flocks, show an increase in the area of intolerance as the gonads enlarge in spring; this enlargement rapidly acquiring topographical reference and leading to the establishment of territories (Marler, 1956a).

Territoriality is thus a special case of spatial defence not easily separable from the maintenance of personal space. It appears that the intolerance of individuals of certain species to the approach of conspecifics may increase under the influence of reproductive hormones, leading to an increase in individual distance. Much experimental work has shown that testosterone administration lowers the threshold for aggressive response, the hormonal effect being mediated via particular areas of the brain. Other hormones are now known to effect aggression. The ranking positions of starlings and queleas in hierarchies can be altered by the administration of luteinising hormone (L. H.)—experimentals improving their status. In *Quelea* the status ranking of individual birds in small groups may differ according to whether the hierarchy is calculated from encounters due to individual distance infringements on perches or based on the results of competitions for nesting material. Individual distance is maintained by L. H.-mediated aggression while testosterone level affects competitiveness for reproductively valent commodities (Crook and Butterfield, 1968). The relative subordination of female *Quelea* appears due to the inhibitory effects of oestrogen. Aggression is thus not an unitary phenomenon but the expression of the effect of the interaction of a number of factors both intrinsic and extrinsic to the performer. As our structural account of the process becomes more complete, the need to discuss it in terms of "instinct" will disappear (Bolles, 1967).

Increased hunger tends to provoke an increase in fighting through food competition. Many such encounters can be attributed to increased crowding at food sources and a high frequency of infringement of personal space. Some authors have, however, attributed such increases in aggressive encounters to frustration—meaning an interference preventing the completion of an on-going goal response. Certainly there is a great deal of psychological evidence supporting this contention for man (Dollard et al., 1939), but experimental studies with animals have not yet clarified the question. Marler (1957) describes a caged male chaffinch of unstable rank in a hierarchy that developed the habit of making infrequent visits to the food source, remaining there longer than normal and fighting vigorously all others that approached him there. After the completion of the experiment this bird continued to show threat and to attack others at considerable distances whenever it became hungry. Although detailed studies remain to be done, it does not appear difficult to relate, at least in principle, the work on frustration and aggression in man to that on fighting in lower organisms. The complex programming of behaviour through the acquisition of cultural norms in both human and nonhuman primates leads to the inception of much inhibition or delay into ongoing behaviour. Whereas aggression in more primitive animals is elicited by a variety of relatively precise stimuli in given social contexts, the more complex interplay of motives within the elaborate societies of higher animals gives rise to greater problems of explication. At present the use of mentalistic terms such as "frustration" suffice to indicate behavioural contexts in which the threshold of aggressive tendencies is reduced. Continuing research will provide the precise details of the environmental and physiological circumstances attending this fact. Frustration was once considered to be the sole cause of hostility. There is no need now to adopt that view. The alternative, however, is not a nativistic explanation of the type presented in the books under discussion but a closer investigation of the precise conditions under which aggression is elicited in higher mammals.

In higher mammals and in man, as well as in more lowly creatures, the hereditary component of aggression consists in the tendency to react with attack or hostility to certain classes of stimulation. There is, however, as we have seen, no effective evidence for a genetically determined appetite for aggressive behaviour. The social organisation of advanced birds and mammals is, furthermore, known to depend upon the adoption of appropriate roles by young animals subject to learning in "socialisation." Ample work with nonprimate and primate mammals testifies to the importance of various types of learning and other nongenetic factors in the determination of individual temperament and behaviour (e.g. Thomson, 1965; Harlow and Harlow, 1965; and others). It is to be expected, therefore, that the tendency to show aggression may be modified by contrasting socialisation procedures. Freudian analysis has shown that in man, contrasts in toilet training during the "anal period" of maturation produce differing effects with regard to children's compliance or resistance to parental demand. Overpunitive methods tend to produce a fixation of defiant characteristics, including petulancy, pedantry, and overassertiveness involving aggressive elements. Conversely, guidance without punishment yields a more compliant character. The work of Robert Sears and others (e.g. Sears, Maccoby, and Levin, 1957) has shown that aggressive children are likely to come from homes where the expression of aggression is not regulated by family rules but rather is heavily punished. By the age of twelve, however, such children show less aggression than those from permissive homes with neither rules nor punishments. The least aggressive children come from homes which confront them from infancy with strong rules to prevent aggression but in which bad behaviour is controlled in a nonpunitive manner. In such homes praise and affection are balanced against the withdrawal of love when the child behaves badly. It appears that such treatment is effective in eliciting a strong conscience. The child's personality is developed through the necessity to consider his behaviour and decide upon his subsequent attitudes. Much depends upon the nature of parental "permissiveness" and the sort of rules used in family control of aggression. Current research has yet to describe fully these relationships and much work remains to be done.

There is no doubt that Ardrey is right to emphasise the fact that human beings like animals show assertion and aggression of many kinds in relation to the ownership of objects and property and also in relation to ethnic or national territory. Attitudes towards ingroups, out-groups, foreigners, other races, and the newspaper accounts of the doings of other governments and nations must nevertheless be determined in large measure by the cultural concomitants of socialisation experienced in childhood and adolescence. To ignore or dismiss important research on these effects is to abandon the most relevant evidence on the subject.

The Functions of Territory

The problems presented by territorial behaviour in nature remain many and mostly unresolved. Certainly the subject has not received the attention it deserves although current research into both avian and mammalian social organization is rapidly increasing the information available for analysis. The subject has been reviewed several times; the studies by Nice in 1941, Hinde in 1956, Tinbergen in 1957, and Carpenter in 1958 give a comprehensive account of the history of the concept and state of knowledge up until those years. Recent work has tended to see territoriality as part of a wider conception framed, as it were, within the social system of a species itself considered in relation to population dynamics (Wynne-Edwards, 1962; Crook, 1965; Lack, 1966). Ardrey himself provides many good accounts of the earlier investigations and summarises many of the views current until about 1962.

Animals, particularly birds, have been recognised as holding territories at least since the days of Aristotle. Carpenter (1958) describes the history of the concept from Willughby's notes on the nightingale in 1678 to the modern definition of the subject by Altum in 1868, Moffat in 1903, and Elliot Howard in 1907–14 and 1920. The descriptive data showed that territoriality involved the defence of an area more or less well-defined spatially and within which intruders normally fled when challenged, the most aggressive encounters occurring on the periphery of the territory bordering that of another individual. In its territory a bird makes itself conspicuous by vocal or visual display as also do, for example, the males of groups of certain lemurs, the vervet monkey, and the howler monkey, which live in territorial areas. Much of the aggression in territorial defence consists of threatening display or ritualised fighting whereby spacing is achieved with little damage done to the protagonists. Real fighting is, however, not always avoided. In early work the prime functions of territory were considered to be the maintenance of an area ensuring a sufficient food supply for the defender and his family and provision of a topographical focus for mating and nesting. Territory was also considered to be a mechanism limiting the number of pairs of birds in an area by spacing them. Fighting was thought to ensure that the strong rather than the weak reproduced.

The main body of information on territory has come from ornithology. In particular, a great diversity of territorial arrangements has become apparent. In his 1956 paper Hinde classified bird territories into four main types. The first consists of a large breeding area within which nesting, courtship and mating, and most food seeking usually occur; as in certain warblers (*Sylviidae*) and the robin, for example. The second type is a large breeding area but one which does not furnish most of the food, as, for example, in the nightjar, reed warbler, and the Euplectine weaver birds. In the third type, the territory is confined to a small area around the nest as in many bird colonies. Colonial polygamous species may build several nests in a territory. Feeding obviously occurs elsewhere and the spacing effect occurs only within the confines of the colony itself. In the last type the defended area, of small extent, is used solely for pairing or for mating. In gulls, pairing territories exist early in the breeding season separately from those locations used later for nesting. In "arena" birds males occupy small sites often placed closely together and to which females come. The males show elaborate displays and complex procedures exist whereby females choose a mate, the most remarkable system so far described in detail being that of the ruff. In addition, work on the birds of paradise and bower birds in Australasia and the manakins in Central America suggests that the tropical forests hide much that will prove remarkable. After mating, the females of "arena" birds go elsewhere for nesting and rear their young alone. In addition to normal territoriality, birds of certain species defend areas around their mates, their families, their young or a number of young irrespective of parentage, and, as we have seen, themselves. Defence of an area by a group is not common among birds but a number of examples are known. Among the *Crotophaginae* the ani lives in groups of 15 to 25 birds and defends an area around a communal nest in which several females lay (Davis, 1940). The Australian magpie (*Cracticidae*) holds group territories throughout the year and fights in teams, cock with cock and hen with hen (Carrick, 1963). In a number of other species, communalism involving the participation of a number of adults and juveniles in the rearing of young in a territory also occurs.

Among mammals, the family home or nest may be the focus of territorial behaviour, as in many rodents. In other cases, areas may be defended by relatively large groups that may spend some or all of their time there. The vicuna, a species of South American llama, has a system in which a male defends an area against other males and keeps his herd within bounds (Koford, 1957). Red deer move within circumscribed areas (Lowe, 1966), and prides of lions may attack other lions trespassing within their range (Schenkel, 1966). Adult male seals hold territories on beaches where a population hauls out for breeding, and the male Ugandan kob, studied by Buechner, whose report is well described by Ardrey, defends a small territory in an arena. The male kob's behaviour there resembles that of blackcock on a lek. The wildebeest in the Ngoro-ngoro crater near Serengeti apparently are territorial but, on the plains nearby, they defend mobile harem groups during long migrations. As with birds, some mammals are "distance" species and resent close approach, whereas others allow close contact.

In a survey of mammalian territories, Burt (1943) made an important distinction between areas that are actually defended and the area over which a group ranges. In many species, actual territorial defence does not occur and the home ranges of groups overlap markedly. Usually such ranges contain a "core area" in which the group centres most of its activities. Such "home range" systems intergrade with territorial ones, as in cases where groups avoid close contact rather than showing aggression. There is thus a gradient between tightly packed territorial groups and groups wandering in more or less undefended ranges often sharing the use of certain environmental commodities such as good feeding grounds or water holes. An important survey of a variety of such systems has recently been published under the editorship of Peter Jewell and Caroline Loizos (1966).

The very diversity of these mammalian and avian dispersion types suggests that any simple statement about the function of territorialism in general is almost bound to be inadequate. Among the many functions attributed to territory holding have been the promotion of dominance, the selective breeding of the strong, the reduction or regulation of sexual fighting, the enforcement of monogamy, the protection of nests and young from predators, the regulation of group size, the preservation of food supplies, the dispersion of populations, the localisation of waste disposal, and the limitation of the spread of diseases. The condensation of this range of possibilities into abstract principles such as identity, security, and stimulation not only appears premature but neglects the diversity of the phenomena; in different species territories may certainly have functions of widely differing kinds.

Although there is a considerable range both in the referents to which territorial behaviour may be shown and in the types of dispersion produced by it, early work suggested that all forms of territorial aggression, in common with other types of agonistic relationship such as dominance or individual distance behaviour, were due basically to the same motivational source, (Hinde, 1956). Nevertheless, while all forms of fighting are essentially similar, it is clear that the threshold for the elicitation of aggressive behaviour is dependent upon a complex of physiological conditions which may vary independently and change seasonally. This threshold may be expressed as the distance from a territorially valent object towards which approach will elicit attack. Thus some species of bird become aggressive at greater distances from the nest than others. The sensitivity of individuals to the relationship between defended object and the distance at which aggression occurs appears subject to natural selection and—in that characteristic mean sizes of territory have been described for certain species—may be due to factors based on genetic inheritance. If fighting in territorial defence gives reproductive advantages to breeding male birds, for example, it can be predicted that the genetic basis for the trait will become relatively fixed and transmitted from generation to generation.

The fundamental survival values of aggressive behaviour in social life can be conceived only in relation to intraspecific competition. In addition, however, the holding of space appears to reduce direct competition for a commodity and to allow the development of social competition promoting the evolution of ritualised ceremony. Lockie (1956) pointed out that birds which maintain individual distances in winter flocks keep to an interindividual dispersion that reduces actual combat for food. The more dominant animals defeat subordinates in spatial threat during competition for a food object, but the latter, which remain undamaged, can continue to search. Actual combat could damage the subordinate severely and weaken the stronger bird. Nevertheless, fighting for food does occur when starvation is sufficient to override distance maintenance. The effect of a range of individual dominance values in flocks is thus likely to produce differential starvation during food shortage—the more dominant birds being more likely to survive.

Intraspecific competition is most meaningfully discussed in the context of population dynamics. Most bird species in temperate zones show an annual cycle of numbers with marked winter mortality. Following an unusually severe winter, losses are replaced by spring breeding and numbers increase until breeding individuals are forced more closely together in their chosen habitat. There will come a point at which certain commodities essential for life or reproduction, such as nesting sites, appropriate cover, or food, come into short supply. Clearly the type of commodity most likely to fall into shortage will depend greatly on the ecological niche occupied by a species. The successful defence of such commodities will tend to ensure the perpetuation of an individual's genes through successful reproduction and hence the selection of the traits that gave it advantage. Territorial defence is likely to arise in many species but, in that they tend to experience different types of competitive contingency, the sorts of territoriality displayed will be quite diverse over a wide range of cases.

An explanation of a territorial system may not, however, rely only on the concept of the natural selection of genetic factors. While in some species territory size is markedly stable, in others considerable variation is found. Certain swamp-dwelling weavers breed in large territories in small bushes fringing the swamp, but they may also utilise a large tree islanded in the flood wherein they breed in extremely small territories crowded together and forming a colony. The baya weaver of India commonly breeds in large palm trees in colonies, but in homogenous scrubland relatively isolated nests have been recorded. Here the territory size is highly labile, the individual adapting itself to the apparently optimum circumstances in any given locality. Species that otherwise appear to show stable territory sizes are probably affected to some extent in a similar way. For example several British woodland birds breed at greater densities near housing estates, where their winter survival is higher than in natural woodlands, where it is comparatively low. On Mandarte Island, Canada, a population of song sparrows divided up the habitat into similarly sized territories for several years. Then, suddenly, they increased numbers by half as much again indicating that the territory size was not strictly controlling the number of birds present but was rather an expression of it (Tompa, 1964). A similar increase in the numbers of great tits breeding in a wood near Oxford suggests the same could be true for this species. In all these cases then the dispersion of a species population was largely controlled by ecological aspects and population density. Territories, however, appear to be of limited compressibility and hence provide a species with certain environmental qualities without which its members cannot reproduce.

Unfortunately, relatively little experimental work has been done on the territories of wild animals and hence the relative importance of the different determinants of territorial dispersion in any given case remains to be determined adequately. It seems, however, clear that the information required for an adequate account of a given dispersion pattern must come from at least three sources. The first concerns the hereditary traits of the species governing its tendency to maintain the defence of certain commodities and the distances (thresholds of response to intrusion) from these at which aggression will occur. How far such responsiveness is actually inherited or acquired during some process of imprinting in relation to habitat and parental behaviour requires experimental analysis. The second group of factors concerns the relative availability of commodities essential for survival and reproduction. The third set concerns the density of the population and the type of social community in which the population exists. We have already argued that territoriality cannot be conceived as a species property, like leg length or plumage pattern; rather it is a group characteristic expressing the effects of the interaction of individuals with one another and the environment. Territory is but a single aspect of the social system shown by a species. An understanding of the system as a whole is more likely to inform us regarding territory than will the particular study of territory to the neglect of other social behaviours.

In recent survey of avian social systems in relation to ecology,

Crook (1965) examined correlations between some six types of nonbreeding social-dispersion pattern, four types of breeding-season pattern, and a number of ecological characteristics including habitat and food type, food dispersion, and nest sites of 115 avian taxonomic families in which little variation between species in social organisation had been reported. Seventy-nine showed patterns of dispersion involving the holding of sizeable pair territories for breeding. Of these, territory holding characterised nonbreeding dispersion in some forty families. The remaining thirty-nine families showed gregarious flocking outside the breeding season. Twenty-four families showed colonial breeding involving the holding of small territories in densely occupied sites and flocking behaviour in the nonbreeding period. No families, however, showed a pattern involving out of breeding season territoriality with breeding season flocking. The most persistently territorial birds occurred in some twenty-eight primarily insectivorous families, two carnivorous ones, four fish eating, two nectar feeding, and a few more or less omnivorous ones. Almost all these birds must hunt or search for their food and their success depends on cryptic approach, speed, and skill. The relatively solitary nature of these species is therefore considered an adaptation to this mode of food exploitation for which gregarious flocking would tend to be of little assistance. This is, however, not the whole story. When the territorial breeders which flock in "winter" are considered, an association between territory holding and cryptic nest siting in locations not otherwise naturally protected from the approach of predators is found. Protection of nests and their contents thus emerges as an important function of territorial behaviour. The flocking behaviour in the nonbreeding season is related to the utility of rapid congregation made possible at dispersed food sources and to protection against predators. In certain species such as the kingfisher, the linear shape of the habitat along the river banks, for example, appears to correlate with the holding of sizeable territories. The nest site in holes seems sufficiently protective to allow colony formation should this be advantageous. However, an increase in population density in a restricted breeding site would rapidly deplete food resources in the vicinity and necessitate search at a distance. It would be advantageous for members of a species in such a habitat to disperse themselves more "in order" to work less hard in food finding when rearing young. Territory size in such cases may be related to the food content of the territorial area.

Colony formation commonly develops in correlation with evidence that the chosen sites are in some way protective and prevent the intrusion of predators. Dense breeding is also associated with a large surrounding area from which the colony inhabitants may draw sustenance for their young in common. Within colonies the actual spacing of nests may be related to the incidence of predator intrusion. Tinbergen (1953) showed that the herring gull colonies to which predators had gained access had nests more widely dispersed than usual. Among the species of Euplectine weavers those with nests in the most protected places in swamps tend to nest territorially in colonies but those building nests hidden in homogenous grassland have much larger territories dispersed in "neighbourhoods." In this case the discovery of one nest by a predator would not lead easily to the discovery of another.

The maintenance of territories within dense colonies is evidently related not only to the defence of a nest site but more particularly perhaps to the prevention of interference from rival males or females in the pairing and mating procedure of the owners. In weaver colonies, males may sometimes attempt copulations with neighbouring females in the absence of the territory owner, and females may attempt to occupy already occupied nests and have then to be driven out by the owning pair. In weavers, too, a great deal of nest robbing for nest-building materials occurs. In some species with short breeding seasons, males rarely leave their territories except to obtain materials and food in brief sallies. The development of true communal life involving co-operation between members of a group is rare in birds, and limited research suggests it occurs when parents experience difficulty in rearing broods and the participation of juveniles or other "helpers" becomes of selective advantage both to parents and, in their turn, to their helpers. Complex social interactions involving ritualised ceremonies reducing the incidence of intragroup aggression have evolved in some of these groups. Certainly intragroup aggression tends to be markedly reduced in such groups which have sometimes been referred to as "sisterhoods." Some of these groups appear to be "clans"—closely related individuals of two or more generations living together. Such species may breed at considerable population densities and then, as in the well-studied case of the Australian magpie (*Gymnorhina tibicen*), group territoriality appears, the function of which appears related to food supply (Carrick, 1963).

The complex group territories of certain mammals associate both with the defence of females by a male and with the holding of a relatively well-defined area (i.e. the vicuna) within which the food supply is located. In the "arena" breeders such as the kob, territory holding is related to competition between males for the sexual attention of females, and the holding of space prevents or greatly reduces the likelihood of interference with mating once it starts. Among seals and sea lions, males hold territories that contain their "harems."

While the diversity of cases is considerable and each requires detailed individual analysis, enough has been said to suggest that among the main functions of territory holding are: the maintenance of dispersion, so that individual hunting techniques may be performed without interference; the maintenance of an area providing a food supply requisite for rearing young or maintaining group existence; the reduction of crowding of cryptic nests so as to reduce the likelihood of their discovery by predators; and the prevention of interference with nesting, courtship, mating, and sometimes the rearing of young. We need not quibble with Ardrey over his use of the blanket term "security" to cover all these cases. We should, however, stress that the diversity of functions that territory holding performs is a consequence of adaptive radiation of species into a wide variety of ecological niches. The nature of competition imposed by the adaptations of a species to a given habitat defines the type of territorial behaviour seen.

Ardrey is right to point out that many territories occur in neighbourhoods or colonies and that equally suitable areas may remain unoccupied. He discusses this in terms of the stimulation evoked by the defence of territorial peripheries but he does not treat its probable function. Darling's (1938) original suggestion referred to the possibility that the social stimulation of colonial life helped to synchronise breeding, thereby reducing the length of the breeding period which in turn decreased the period of heavy predation on young. His data did not, however, prove the point unequivocally, and it remains a fascinating hypothesis. The role of behavioural interaction in promoting breeding synchronisation has, however, been accepted by several recent authors with particular reference to colonial birds. Synchronisation may function in at least two ways. First, it may ensure that as many birds as possible start breeding early in a short breeding season and this increases the likelihood of their rearing young in the annual period of optimum food supply. Second, the mass departure of young may reduce the effects of predation. In theory at least, if the young birds were leaving at staggered intervals a greater number would fall foul of the waiting carnivores. Should these hypotheses be tested in further studies such as those by Patterson (1965) and generally confirmed, the survival value of social stimulation will be seen as a consequence of environmental adaptation rather than as providing excitement of value in itself, as Ardrey seems to suggest.

One of the effects of holding a sizeable area of land for breeding is certainly to space out the individuals of a population. V. C. Wynne-Edwards (1962) has suggested that not only is the prime function of territory to produce dispersal but that dispersion itself functions to control population size (see also Moffat, 1903). This hypothesis forms part of a broader theory which holds that social organisation is essentially a mechanism for providing "conventional competition" whereby numbers are regulated by homeostatic dispersal in relation to food resources. Populations are thereby believed to maintain optimum numbers in relation to resources. Competition is said to be conventional in that its putative function is to measure the density of the population present and relate the finding to food supplies. If the indicated numbers are likely to overexploit the actual supply an exodus of the surplus population follows. Territorial competition is treated as a convention having these supposed advantageous effects. It is true that dispersal may result from territorial behaviour but the suggestion that this is a primary survival value is far from proven. Territorial behaviour could have this effect even if the functions for which it was evolved were quite different. In any case our comparative study of the range of territory types shows that only some of them could function in the way Wynne-Edwards's theory requires and none of them need necessarily do so.

Wynne-Edwards's hypothesis regarding the significance of social structure has received much criticism and appears unlikely to prove acceptable in its entirety (Crook, 1965; Lack, 1966; and others). The evidence from field studies relating population dispersion to the natural control of numbers and territorial behaviour is furthermore highly inconclusive. Lack (1966) has recently surveyed the findings of several of the more detailed ornithological reports on the relation between territoriality and population control. For example, each pair of wood pigeons defends an area around its nest and the resultant spacing probably assists the concealment of nests from predators. The birds, however, feed in flocks; the territory cannot therefore conserve a food supply and there is no reason to think it regulates numbers. In other species, population is known to be regulated by actual food shortage rather than by any factors producing dispersion. Again, as we have already remarked, both the song sparrow on Mandarte Island and great tits at Oxford showed numbers of breeding birds that in certain years greatly exceeded the usual population of the study area so that the average territory size seems to have little to do with the control of numbers. In some species, however, such as the red grouse and ptarmigan in Scotland and the population of skylarks studied at Ravenglas, breeding density is related to the holding of territories, and unsuccessful birds are pushed into peripheral habitats and fail to reproduce (e.g. Jenkins, Watson, and Miller, 1963; Watson, 1965; Delius, 1965). Older work on great tits in Holland had also indicated that in a particular habitat territorial behaviour set an upper limit to numbers (Kluijver and Tinbergen, 1953).

It seems, in fact, certain that in contrasting habitat conditions different factors will play the crucial role of key constraints imposing density-dependent mortality (see Cody, 1966; Blank, Southwood, and Cross, 1967; Southwood, 1967). In environments subject to severe winter mortality involving food shortage, the numbers of birds present may rarely reach such proportions that territorial behaviour limits their settlement for breeding. In richly endowed habitats, however, or in particularly stable ones, territorial behaviour may become the prime constraint controlling breeding density. The relative frequency of such cases remains to be determined. Their effective demonstration, however, would not necessarily establish Wynne-Edwards's contention. Territorial competition may be "real" rather than "conventional" in that without the maintenance of space for uninterrupted mating, for example, breeding might not be able to occur at all. Exclusion of some individuals from breeding would then be an effect of competitive social behaviour of a functional value to the successful individuals of the species for reasons unconnected with dispersal. The overall social system is best conceived as an open arrangement controlled by inputs from factors both intrinsic and extrinsic to the structure itself rather than a biotic adaptation especially evolved for population control.

Finally, we should again emphasise that social systems are characteristics of groups. Discussion of their "evolution" poses a number of semantic problems akin to those involved in the treatment of the evolution of ecological communities (Williams, 1966). Social systems develop historically through interactive effects of population size, social behaviour, and environment. Their control is not a "property" of the species in question but rather lies in the relations its members have established with one another and with the features of their habitat. Evolution by the natural selection of the genetic endowment of the population forms only a part of this historical process. If these arguments are found to be sound then Wynne-Edwards's technical use of the term "convention" is of doubtful explanatory value. Its adoption by Ardrey without an adequate examination of Wynne-Edwards's theory adds nothing to current usage. Football matches and the space race may well be "conventions" but the link between them and biological theory is not established.

Primates, Man, and Territory

Perhaps the most striking feature of those nonhuman primates the behaviour of which is of most relevance to man is precisely their lack of easily defined territorial behaviour. There have been several recent surveys of this material (e.g. Hall, 1965; Washburn, Jay and, Lancaster, 1965; Crook and Gartlan, 1966; Rowell, 1967) and space allows only brief discussion here. Comparative studies of forest fringe, and savannah *Cercopithecus* and *Macaca* monkeys, the baboons of the genera *Papio* and *Theropithecus,* the chimpanzee and gorilla do not provide evidence of rigorously defended territories. On the other hand, populations of several forest primates in Madagascar, Africa, and South America do defend group territories by means of elaborate vocal and visual displays, border skirmishing and olfactory marking in some cases. These species are, however, of less relevance to man than the savannah monkeys and the great apes.

Several kinds of social organisation in the African grasslands and savannah have been reported. All are complex and consist either of troops containing several males and rather more females with attendant juveniles, or of single males with "harems" of females, again with their young. In the latter case groups of nonreproductive and usually subadult males move separately from the reproductive units. The multimale troop is well known from the research of K. R. L. Hall, S. L. Washburn, I. DeVore, and Thelma Rowell on *Papio ursinus, P. cynocephalus,* and *P. anubis* and from Altmann's and Southwick's studies on the rhesus monkey on Cayo Santiago Island and in India. In addition, detailed studies have been made on the Japanese macaque. The one-male reproductive unit has been reported from *Papio hamadryas,* the patas monkey, and the gelada baboon. In the former the units tend to comprise subunits of large troops which may coalesce to form herds. In the patas they move separately in large home ranges, whereas in the gelada they congregate in large herds over good grazing but tend to scatter and forage separately in the dry season of poor food availability. In *Papio ursinus,* the macaques, and the patas the social units forage within large home ranges which tend to overlap to varying extents. Dispersion is maintained mostly by the withdrawal of the intruders. "Ritualised" border encounters do not occur but, in certain unusually structured environments such as temple precincts in India, rhesus troops coming suddenly upon one another may fight, in which case individuals will inflict severe injury upon one another. In the gelada even the maintenance of home ranges is uncertain. Certainly gelada herds comprise any number of reproductive units and all-male groups each of which is quite free to enter or leave a congregation and to travel separately over several miles. While populations utilise core areas in particularly appropriate parts of their habitat, there seems no behavioural factor preventing their wandering off and joining any other feeding congregation at considerable distances from their usual foraging area. No evidence of avoidance of any kind has been seen.

Gorillas forage within large home ranges that overlap extensively and there is no clear evidence of marked avoidance, although a preference for small group life is evident. Chimpanzees live in "open groups" with considerable interchange of membership and all appear to utilise a common range of sizeable extent (Reynolds, 1965).

All these social groupings are extensively structured owing to complex relations between individuals dependent upon relative dominance, age, sex, the adoption of particular roles, and the formation of friendships. Compared with most nonprimate societies, life for these animals is a particularly rich social experience.

The adaptive significance of these different types of society has received some recent attention, and they can be related quite clearly to different environmental contingencies—the nature and availability of sleeping sites, the abundance and seasonal dispersion of food supplies—and to predation pressures. Precise details, however, remain to be worked out. The process whereby this adaptation of society to environment occurs is clearly complex and appears to depend upon the establishment and maintenance of learnt traditions of a protocultural kind gradually acquired by the phenotypic adaptations of individuals to their home locality and social group repetitively over many generations. Social structure is furthermore apt to differ in subtle or pronounced ways in different localities, thereby emphasising the importance of the direct effect of contrasts in environment. Although innate behaviour patterns play important roles in communication of affect within these groups there appears to be no case for suggesting that "instinct" plays a major role in the moulding of social structure as such. This is probably also the case in other advanced nonprimate mammalian societies, few of which have yet been studied in any detail.

Both Rowell (1966) and Crook (1967) have pointed out that where social structures of a primate species appear relatively specific the ethologist, traditionally a student of innate behaviour patterns, could be misled into making incorrect assumptions concerning the origins of the systems observed. Rowell's detailed studies in field and laboratory have amply demonstrated the importance of social learning in the structuring of groups. Learning is a continuous process and the individual's behaviour is markedly adaptable in relation to changes in natural reinforcement contingencies. Hall (1963) has stressed the importance of observational learning in monkey groups; the experience of one animal is witnessed by others and the information obtained utilised by them on later occasions. Social structures appear to diverge in contrasting or changing ecological conditions owing to shifts in reinforcement contingencies controlled by such factors as the frequency of food finding, hours needed for satiation, spacing of individuals in relation to food dispersion, size of food object, frequency of food antagonism, and time available for playful interaction and social grooming. Life for these animals may be conceived in terms of sets of complex natural learning "schedules," each providing various types of reward. In particular, the time needed for foraging, the patterns of spacing best suited for search, and the rate of movement required for optimum reward will effectively ration the time available in the day for social activities. Crook and Aldrich-Blake (1968) recently related the rather stereotyped behaviour of geladas at a site in Ethiopia to the long hours they had to spend feeding. Doguera baboons in woods nearby obtained food in larger units and spent less time foraging and more time in social interaction. Their more flexible, reflective behaviour in relation to the presence of the observers might be meaningfully related to these contrasts.

It has been argued that the one-male groups of geladas and certain other primates are sociological adaptations to arid environments (e.g. Crook and Gartlan, 1966). One large male is adequate for the fertilisation of several females and exploits a low percentage of the food available to the nomadic group. The reproductively more important sex then tends to get the most food. Large troops with many adult males are typical of richer environments with both more food and more predators. In arid country individual males and females appear to contribute more to the next generation by living in one-male groups than they would in larger social units that would tend to overexploit the resources of the ground over which they ranged. Probably increasingly arid environments impose splits in troops so that small parties wander separately. Indeed, there is evidence from Japanese macaques and African baboons to support this view. Competition between reproductive males for females in small parties would then tend to produce the separation of subordinate and juvenile males into their own parties, leaving single males in reproductive units. The adaptation to environment in this case thus appears essentially phenotypic. Such changes would appear, however, to initiate new patterns of social and sexual selection such that individuals of differing temperament from those in the parent society may gain reproductive advantages. Concomitant shifts in the genetic basis of individual behaviour may occur and have the effect of stabilising the patterns of interindividual interaction and hence the social structure as a whole.

As Ardrey says, the reappearance of aggressive territory holding in man contrasts strongly with the relatively peaceable affairs of other higher primates. The advent of carnivorous habits, use of weapons, and competition between groups for limited sources of animal protection are indeed the most likely original causes. It seems that the emergence of the new territoriality involved shifts in social traditions in relation to ranging and an acquired lowering of the threshold for aggression towards out-groups as a result of repetitive experiences of hunger and ultimately an intellectual appreciation of its cause. Certainly our modern appreciation of the important role of learning and tradition in the maintenance of non-human primate societies would lead us to emphasise this kind of historical change rather than the possible development of a terri-torial instinct of the type Ardrey requires.

This is not to deny, however, the probability that changes in human social organisation and the adoption by man of carnivorous feeding habits may not have affected his aggressive reactivity through the selection of certain inherited traits rather than others. Certainly the necessity for increased control of individual behaviour in relation to hunting and role playing in co-operative social life will have entailed the marked development of the ability to delay responding, to interiorise and reflect on alternative causes of action, and to cope with motivational frustration. Aggression itself would have become increasingly complex in manifestation and often separated in time from the events that lowered the threshold for its expression. The hunter's pleasure in killing prey may also have arisen at this time and the "cruelty" inflicted on the "game" animals thus became available for translocation into a social agonistic context.

The development of ownership of tools, homesteads, and domestic animals would greatly have increased the opportunities for conflict within communities, these things becoming in effect extensions of a person's "individual distance." Complex patterns of conventional behaviour (in the usual sense of the word) would arise, giving way in due course to codified laws concerning property and its exchange. International conduct may be conceived as an extension of this principle to a community and political level.

Early in his book Ardrey remarks that "there will remain always the chance that what we observe in man is a kind of mirror held up to nature; our culture and our learning reflect the natural way without in a biological sense being beholden to it" (p. 103). The likelihood that the motivational control of territorial behaviour in man is at a different level from that of fishes and birds suggests that human resemblances to the lower animals might be largely through analogy rather than homology. Indeed this is certainly the impression given by a careful reading of the several papers comparing man and animals at the 1963 symposium on "The Natural History of Aggression," in London (Carthy and Ebling, 1964). Ardrey fails to recognise that the great advances in learning ability and intelligence in the higher mammals mean that historical change through "cultural" processes is possible among them too and the concept need not be reserved for man alone. Man is indeed an animal—but we should not forget his primate status and the behavioural complexity of his relatives. The idea that "the territorial nature of man is genetic and ineradicable" would appear unnecessarily parsimonious.

Conclusions

By adopting a limited Lorenzian view of the nature of aggression Ardrey ignores most of the experimental ethological literature on the subject. Instead of resulting from an innate and ineradicable force demanding repetitive expression, aggressive behaviour occurs normally as a response to particular aversive stimuli and ceases upon their removal. The prevalence of aggression in modern man may thus be attributed to aversive features in the complex overcrowded, overcompetitive, overstratified social world in which he lives rather than to some unsatisfied vital urge. In man, also, aggression is commonly associated with frustrations born of the delay in responding imposed largely by his learning to play social roles in a community. There is every reason to suppose that individual sensitivity to stimuli likely to evoke aggression is determined during socialisation. The manifestation of aggression in human society is thus largely a cultural attribute.

Ardrey's account of the function of territoriality in terms of identity, security, and stimulation is derived from ethological research reports concerned largely with the adaptive significance of behaviour. He provides little detailed discussion on the evolutionary significance of social behaviour in relation to the adaptations of members of a population to their physical and social environment. In this paper this problem is treated at length to clarify the arguments presented in the sources. In discussing man Ardrey gives his three terms a motivational significance in which they represent needs satisfied by the holding of territory. Reflection brings to mind, however, many individuals, who in their maturity found identity, security, and excitement in activities far removed from real estate of any kind. If an instinct is present in a species it should be apparent in the individual members.

Man's nearest relatives among primates are singularly lacking in simple territorial behaviour. Man's recovery of this attribute may be seen as a continuation of trends already present in protocultural social organisations found in primates and originally influenced by acquired carnivorous feeding and competition for sources of protein. There is no need to explain the behaviour in excessively parsimonious terms based on a misleading and outdated account of aggressive behaviour in lower organisms. The relevant hypotheses lie nearer home.

The behaviour of crowds watching "conventionally" competitive sports often indicates the arousal of aggressive attitudes rather than their happy sublimation. Further, the behaviour of players cannot always be recommended. The wanton destruction of train interiors by British football team supporters on the way to an "away" fixture certainly reveals a release of social tensions in what would appear to be highly convivial surroundings. Indeed, the holding of major sporting events is often manageable only when effective rules of crowd control are operative. As an example of social engineering such conventions alone seem to achieve little in enhancing human conduct. Man's aggressive potential is hardly likely to be controlled solely by attempts at redirection or sublimation. The solution must lie rather in detailed research into those aspects of human experience which influence aggressive reactivity. In particular the problem concerns those patterns of socialisation and education that give rise to hostile feelings towards the stranger and the out-group. The development of attitudes remains an area as yet poorly explored by psychologists, but with an increasing grasp of experimental techniques there seems no reason to abandon hope for the future. Social psychologists are well aware of these problems and strive to find solutions. That their efforts so far may appear academic and slightly naïve is related to the novelty of the research, the complexity of the subject matter, and the youth of this branch of science. The biological basis of human life and its evolutionary history are of great relevance to this enquiry but only when a proper understanding of the advanced level of social organisation and its control in higher primates is taken into account. The promulgation of one-sided and misleadingly simplified doctrine is of no assistance to those concerned and could lead them to neglect those highly relevant contributions that modern ethological theory and experimental method can legitimately supply.

The merit of *The Territorial Imperative* is to have brought an awareness of a major research problem to the attention of many who may not have considered it seriously before. The book nevertheless leaves an unfortunate impression. Apart from its faulty statement of current ethological theory, the view of life—the *Weltanschauung*—portrayed is unhappily pessimistic and for a wrongly conceived reason. Sir Julian Huxley, in a treatment of the relevance of biology to man, once argued strongly against "nothing but-ism" as an unhealthy attitude of unreflective science. Was man indeed "nothing but" a creature of overpowering destructive impulse, hope for the future would be dark. These decades present the advanced technological nations with problems of menacing proportions. Men everywhere are potential victims of an unparalleled background anxiety magnified and reflected at every turn by mass media of communication. The image of man, already demoted from his place near the angels through the popularisation of Darwinian and Freudian ideas, is all too vulnerable to further erosion. The *Zeitgeist* extols the mechanism, and we may perhaps see ourselves as no more than that; but the mechanism is wonderfully complex, its properties poorly understood, and as subjects we remain uniquely self-aware. Although the phenomenon of man cannot be explained by simplistic argument pandering only to the pessimism of an age, the image that most of the people acquire is apt to shape the values of a community. Indeed, a parallel is apparent in the recent past when ideas derived from a misunderstanding of "Social Darwinism" played their part in the history of European fascist politics. Who knows whence a "New Right" may gather a cloak of respectability to condone, perhaps in some new "Report from Iron Mountain," the defence of racial garrisons in the *noyaux* of the near future? The new genre of popular biological exposition neglects the humanity of man. We would do well to meditate upon the reasons.

REFERENCES

Anderson, P. K. (1961). Density, social structure and non-social environment in house-mouse populations and the implications for regulation of numbers. Trans. N.Y. Acad. Sci. Ser. II, 23, (5): 447–451.

Ardrey, R. (1967). The territorial imperative. A personal inquiry into the animal origins of property and nations. London.

Blank, T. H., T. R. E. Southwood, and D. G. Cross. (1967). The ecology of the partridge. 1. Outline of population processes with particular reference to chick mortality and nest density. J. Anim. Ecol. 36: 549–556.

Bolles, R. C. (1967). Theory of motivation. New York.

Brown, J. C. (1963). Aggressiveness, dominance and social organisation in the Steller jay. Condor 65: 460–484.

Burt, W. H. (1943). Territoriality and home range concepts as applied to mammals. J. Mammal. 24: 346–352.

Carpenter, C. R. 1958. Territoriality. *In* Behaviour and evolution. A. Roe and G. G. Simpson (eds.). New Haven.

Carrick, R. (1963). Ecological significance of territory in the Australian magpie, *Gymnorhyna tibicen*. Proc. 13th Int. Orn. Congr. 740–753.

Carthy, J. D. and F. J. Ebling (eds.). (1964). The natural history of aggression. London.

Chapman, D. W. (1966). Food and space as regulations of salmonid populations in streams. Amer. Nat. 100: 345–356.

Cody, M. J. (1966). A general theory of clutch size. Evolution 20: 174–184.

Craig, W. (1918). Appetites and aversions as constituents of instincts. Biol. Bull. 34: 91–107.

Craig, W. (1928). Why do animals fight? Int. J. Ethics. 31: 246–278.

Crook, J. H. (1961). The basis of flock organisation in birds. In Current problems in animal behaviour. W. H. Thorpe and O. L. Zangwill (eds.). Cambridge.

Crook, J. H. (1965). The adaptive significance of avian social organisations. Symp. zool. Soc. Lond. 14: 181–218.

Crook, J. H. (1967). Evolutionary change in primate societies. Sci. J. 3. 6: 66–72.

Crook, J. H. and P. Aldrich-Blake. (1968). Ecological and behavioural contrasts between sympatric ground-dwelling primates in Ethiopia. Folia Primat. In press.

Crook, J. H. and P. A. Butterfield. (1968). Effects of testosterone propionate and luteinising hormone on agonistic and nest building behaviour of captive *Quelea quelea*. Anim. Behav. In press.

Crook, J. H. and J. S. Gartlan. (1966). Evolution of primate societies. Nature. Lond. 210: 1200–1203.

Darling, F. F. (1938). Bird flocks and the breeding cycle. A contribution to the study of avian sociality. Cambridge.

Davis, D. E. (1940). Social nesting habits of the smooth-billed ani. Auk. 57: 179–218.

Delius, J. D. (1965). A population study of skylarks, *Alauda arvensis*. Ibis 107: 465–492.

Dollard, J. et al. (1939). Frustration and aggression. New Haven.

Fox, R. (1967). In the beginning: aspects of hominid behavioural evolution. Man. 2: 415–433.

Gartlan, J. S. (1966). Ecology and behaviour of the vervet monkey. Lolui Island. Lake Victoria. Uganda. Ph.D. Thesis. Bristol Univ. Library.

Hall, K. R. L. (1963). Observational learning in monkeys and apes. Brit. J. Psychol. 54: 201–226.

Hall, K. R. L. (1965). Social organisation of the old world monkeys and apes. Symp. zool. Soc. Lond. 14: 265–290.

Harlow, H. F. and M. K. Harlow. (1965). The affectional systems. *In* Behaviour of non-human primates. Vol. 2. A. M. Schrier, H. F. Harlow, F. Stollnitz (eds.). New York.

Hinde, R. A. (1956). The biological significance of the territories of birds. Ibis 98: 340–369.

Hinde, R. A. (1966). Animal behaviour. A synthesis of ethology and comparative psychology. New York.

Hinde, R. A. (1967). The nature of aggression. New Society. 2nd March.

Howard, H. E. (1907–14). The British warblers, a history, with problems of their lives. 6 vols. Cambridge.

Howard, H. E. (1920). Territory in bird life. London.

Jeffreys, M. V. C. (1962). Personal values in the modern world. London.

Jenkens, D., A. Watson, and G. R. Miller. (1963). Population studies on red grouse, *Lagopus lagopus scoticus.* J. Anim. Ecol. 32: 317–376.

Jewell, P. A. and C. Loizos (eds.). (1966). Play, exploration and territory in mammals. Symp. zool. Soc. Lond. 18.

Kluijver, H. N. and L. Tinbergen. (1953). Territory and the regulation of density in titmice. Arch. Nethl. Zool. 10: 266–287.

Koford, C. B. (1957). The vicuña and the puna. Ecological Monographs 27: 153–219.

Lack, D. (1966). Population studies of birds. Oxford.

Lockie, J. D. (1956). Winter fighting in feeding flocks of rooks, jackdaws and carrion crows. Bird Study 3: 180–190.

Lorenz, K. (1950). The comparative method in studying innate behaviour patterns. Symp. Soc. Exp. Biol. 4: 221–268.

Lorenz, K. (1963). Das Sogenannte Böse. Vienna.

Lowe, U. P. W. (1966). Observations on the dispersal of red deer on rhum. Symp. zool. Soc. Lond. 18: 211–228.

Marler, P. R. (1956a). Territory and individual distance in the chaffinch (*Fringilla coelebs*) Ibis 98: 496–501.

Marler, P. R. (1956b). Studies of fighting in chaffinches. (3) Proximity as a cause of aggression. Brit. J. Anim. Behav. 4: 23–30.

Marler, P. R. (1957). Studies of fighting in chaffinches (4). Appetitive and consummatory behavior. Brit. J. Anim. Behav. 5: 29–37.

Marler, P. R. and W. J. Hamilton. (1966). Mechanisms of animal behavior. New York.

Moffat, C. B. (1903). The spring rivalry of birds, some views on the limits to multiplication. Irish Nat. 12: 152–66.

Nice, M. M. (1941). The role of territory in bird-life. Amer. Midl. Nat. 26: 441–487.

Patterson, I. J. (1965). Timing and spacing of broods in the black headed gull. *Larus ridibundus*. Ibis 107: 433–459.

Petter, J. J. (1962). Recherches sur l'écologie et l'éthologie des Lemuriens malgaches. Mém. du Mus. Nat. de l'Hist. Naturelle. Sér. A, 27. Fasc. 1. Paris.

Reynolds, V. (1965). Some behavioural comparisons between the chimpanzee and the mountain gorilla in the wild. Amer. Anthropologist. 67: 691–706.

Rowell, T. E. (1966). Forest living baboons in Uganda. J. Zool., Lond. 149: 344–364.

Rowell, T. E. (1967). Variability in the social organisation of primates. *In* Primate ethology. D. Morris (ed.). London.

Schenkel, R. (1966). Play, exploration and territoriality in the wild lion. Symp. zool. Soc. Lond. 18: 11–22.

Sears, R. R., E. E. Maccoby, and H. Levin. (1957). Patterns of child rearing. New York.

Selous, E. (1933). Evolution of habit in birds. London.

Southwood, T. R. E. (1967). The interpretation of population change. J. Anim. Ecol. 36: 519–530.

Thomson, W. R. (1965). The behaviour of offspring. Sci. J. August: 45–50.

Tinbergen, N. (1953). The herring gull's world. Collins. London.

Tinbergen, N. (1957). The functions of territory. Bird Study 4: 14–27.

Tompa, F. S. (1964). Factors determining the numbers of song sparrows *Melospiza melodia* (Wilson) on Mandarte Island. B. C. Canada. Acta. zool. Fenn. 109: 1–68.

Washburn, S. L., P. C. Jay, and J. B. Lancaster. (1965). Field studies of old world monkeys and apes. Science 150: 1541–1547.

Watson, A. (1965). A population study of ptarmigan (*Lagopus mutus*) in Scotland. J. Anim. Ecol. 34: 135–172.

Williams, G. C. (1966). Adaptation and natural selection. A critique of some current evolutionary thought. Princeton.

Wynne-Edwards, V. C. (1962). Animal dispersion in relation to social behaviour. Edinburgh.

OMER C. STEWART

Lorenz/Margolin on the Ute

My long association and interest in the Ute Indians * compel me
to call attention to the completely false picture of these people
which has appeared in the popular book, *On Aggression,* by Konrad Lorenz. On pages 244–45, Lorenz writes:

> Sydney Margolin, in Denver, Colorado, made very exact psycho-
> analytical and psycho-sociological studies on Prairie Indians, par-
> ticularly the Utes, and showed that these people suffer greatly
> from an excess of aggression drive which, under the ordered con-
> ditions of present-day North American Indian reservations, they
> are unable to discharge. It is Margolin's opinion that during the
> comparatively few centuries when Prairie Indians led a wild life
> consisting almost entirely of war and raids, there must have been
> an extreme selection pressure at work, breeding extreme aggres-
> siveness. That this produced changes in the hereditary pattern in
> such a short time is quite possible. Domestic animals can be

* My study of the Ute began in 1930 and has continued to the present time. My
research has been concerned with their ancient ethnology, their history, and their
adjustment to modern life. I have had a special interest in their religion and have
been a participant observer in the ceremonies of the Ute Sun Dance and the Native
American Church (Peyote religion). From 1959 to 1964, I was co-director of an
interdisciplinary project, with psychologists and sociologists, financed by a grant from
the National Institute of Mental Health, of the U.S. Dept. of Health, Education, and
Welfare (Project No. 3M–9556), which included collecting and analyzing all available records of the past history of the Ute of Colorado, as well as making an ex-
haustive study of their present values and behavior. Our first major publication, by
Richard Jessor *et al.,* is in press.

221

changed just as quickly by purposeful selection. Margolin's assumption is supported by the fact that Ute Indians now growing up
under completely different educational influences suffer in exactly
the same way as the older members of their tribe who grew up
under the educational system of their own culture; moreover, the
pathological symptoms under discussion are seen only in those
Prairie Indians whose tribes were subjected to the selection process described.

Ute Indians suffer more frequently from neurosis than any other
human group, and again and again Margolin found that the
cause of the trouble was undischarged aggression. Many of these
Indians feel and describe themselves as ill, and when asked what
is the matter with them they can only say, "I am a Ute!" Violence toward people not of their tribe, and even manslaughter, belong to the order of the day, but attacks on members of the tribe
are extremely rare, for they are prevented by a taboo the severity
of which it is easy to understand, considering the early history of
the Utes: a tribe constantly at war with neighboring Indians and,
later on, with the white man, must avoid at all costs fights between its own members. Anyone killing a member of the tribe
is compelled by strict tradition to commit suicide. This commandment was obeyed even by a Ute policeman who had shot a member of his tribe in self-defense while trying to arrest him. The of-
fender, while under the influence of drink, had staubed his father
in the femoral artery, causing him to bleed to death. When the
policeman was ordered by his sergeant to arrest the man for
manslaughter—it was obviously not murder—he protested, saying that the man would want to die since he was bound by tradition to commit suicide and would do so by resisting arrest and
forcing the policeman to shoot him. He, the policeman, would
then have to commit suicide himself. The more than short-
sighted sergeant stuck to his order, and the tragedy took place
exactly as predicted. This and other of Margolin's records read
like Greek tragedies: an inexorable fate forces crime upon people and then compels them to expiate voluntarily their involuntarily acquired guilt.

It is objectively convincing, indeed it is proof of the correctness
of Margolin's interpretation of the behavior of Ute Indians, that
these people are particularly susceptible to accidents. It has been
proved that accident-proneness may result from repressed aggression, and in these Utes the rate of motor accidents exceeds that

of any other car-driving human group. Anybody who has ever driven a fast car when really angry knows—in so far as he is capable of self-observation in this condition—what strong inclination there is to self-destructive behavior in a situation like this. Here even the expression "death wish" seems apt.

Since Lorenz gives no bibliography on Margolin and Margolin seems not to have published his work on the Ute, I take it Lorenz's information about the Ute came from Margolin in private conversation or lecture. Margolin has lectured on the Ute, and having heard two of his lectures, I believe he would subscribe to the views attributed to him by Lorenz.

It is always disconcerting when two people, both studying the same subject at the same time, come up with entirely different conclusions, and to be one of them. One would expect some difference, of course, stemming from a psychoanalytical, Freudian approach, on the one hand, and an objective, historical-anthropological approach such as I use, on the other.* However, I disagree with Margolin's facts, as well as his conclusions, and I object to the looseness of his language regarding anthropological facts. For instance, the Ute Indians are not Prairie Indians, but are Mountain and Great Basin Indians.

Furthermore, Plains and Prairie Indian ethnohistory does not reveal that those people "led a wild life consisting almost entirely of war and raids." They had war and they did raid, but their history was not of such war and raiding to make them unique among social groups. The Ute Indians were early horsemen and hunted buffalo on the High Plains. While there, they were prepared to fight or run, and they always returned to the Rocky Mountains and maintained their homes there. In early historic times, they were often referred to as the "Swiss" Indians.

The implication that the Ute were a violent people, addicted to war, is not borne out by historic facts. With the early Spanish settlers, the Utes were primarily friendly traders; later, they had amicable relations with Americans. In 1776, the Utes guided Escalante

* See my paper, "Need To Popularize Basic Concepts." I realize that anthropology today is being fertilized by many disciplines, including psychoanalysis, and although this is certainly beneficial, anthropologists should not lose sight of basic anthropological concepts.

through their territory; in 1806, they guided Pike. They were col-
laborators with the American trappers following the Louisiana
Purchase and the explorations of Lewis and Clark. During the
Civil War, they served as paid scouts and allies of the U.S. Army
in wars against plains tribes and the Navaho, yet immediately after
these skirmishes, they made visits to the same tribes and welcomed
return visits. The Utes collaborated with the U.S. government in
nearly every way and became aggressive only under extreme provocation, such as when betrayed by Agent Meeker and threatened by
an unwarranted armed invasion of their reservation in 1879.

The Utes not only were not addicted to unusual "violence toward people not of their tribe," but they did not have a rule that
"anyone killing a member of the tribe is compelled by strict tradition to commit suicide." I have known personally four Utes who
killed fellow Utes; none committed suicide. One, living on the
Southern Ute Reservation in 1964, was convicted of murdering his
uncle who was a policeman. He had served time in a Federal
Prison and was home on parole. A similar case was a Ute who had
killed his wife. Suicides and attempted suicides among the Ute
have not been murderers of fellow tribesmen.

Like most other American Indians, the Ute have been victims of
alcohol and under its influence have committed many criminal acts
and have been careless with their own lives and the lives of others.
But this has been true of the tribes of the Atlantic Coast states, the
Chippewa of the Great Lakes, the Northwest Coast fishing Indians, etc. All of these Indians, like the Utes, are known far and wide
for their accidents while under the influence of alcohol. The problem of the American Indians' excessive use of alcohol is a very real
problem, but is it not unique to one tribe, the Ute, and there appears to be no justification to make a separate explanation of Ute
or Prairie Indian alcoholism as resulting from repressed aggression.
Ute accident rate is high because excessive use of alcohol is high.

Interested in what others closely associated with the Ute thought
of Margolin's description of the Ute as reported in Lorenz's book, I
duplicated the passages quoted at the beginning of this paper and
sent them to three people who have had many close associations
with the Ute: Elbert J. Floyd, former extension agent and superin-

tendent to the Ute, now living near the Ute Reservation in retirement from the Bureau of Indian Affairs and closely associated with the Ute since 1919; John R. (Bob) White, employed by the Ute Indians as "information officer," from 1954 to 1961, then hired as assistant to the superintendent of the Consolidated Ute Agency, Colorado, until 1963, since then associated with other tribes; and Arthur L. Warner, M.D., M.P.H. Medical Director, San Juan Basin Health Unit, 1958–1965. I asked them to read the passage and then sign the following statement with me, if they cared to do so:

> The undersigned have read pages 244–245 of the book, *On Aggression*. "It is erroneous to say that Utes have killed or seek to kill non-Utes while avoiding attacks on fellow Utes. Utes have murdered members of their own tribe as frequently as they have killed non-whites in the last century. Utes who have committed suicides were not Ute murderers. In excessive use of alcohol the Ute are like other Indians. Ute accident rate does not exceed that of other heavy drinking groups."

All three signed this statement. In addition, Dr. Warner wrote: "I have studied vital statistics and social behavior of the Utes, and I am thoroughly acquainted with their patterns of injury, suicide, and death." Mr. Floyd wrote, in part, "I am personally familiar with a case where a Ute Mountain Ute policeman shot and killed a fellow Ute while attempting an arrest; however, the policeman did not commit suicide." Mr. White added, "The high rate of Indian auto accidents has been a matter of concern of tribal governments, the Bureau, and the Public Health Service for some time. But this situation is by no means confined to the Utes. It applies to almost every Indian tribe. The statement on page 245 that 'anyone killing a member of the tribe is compelled by strict tradition to commit suicide' certainly came as news to me. The Ute Mountain suicide rate was a matter of some concern at one time, and still may be, but I cannot recall any suicide linked to a previous killing."

Margolin's statements of fact which are subject to testing concerning the Ute Indians are simply not correct. Others are questionable. Has Margolin the statistics to substantiate the claim that "Ute Indians suffer more frequently from neurosis than any other human group"? As a group, the Ute Indians seem to differ slightly from other people in a number of ways. These differences are not great, or sensational, or sweeping. They are, however, based on painstakingly collected facts, established by psychologists and sociologists, as well as anthropologists, using carefully prepared interview guides, selected samples, and statistical analysis. These are contained in the reports of the Tri-ethnic project published or in press under the names of Richard Jessor, Robert Hanson, and Theodore Graves.

Finally, the peyote religion of the Ute is a significant refutation of the Lorenz-Margolin thesis. The Ute appear to have been receptive to peyote as early as 1900, according to Mooney, who reported their participation in the peyote religion with the Jicarilla Apache. Their interest grew by means of visits to Taos and Oklahoma until the cult was firmly established, especially on the Ute Mountain Ute Reservation in south-western Colorado, where it flourished from 1916 on. The peyote religion is a syncretistic cult, incorporating ancient Indian and modern Christian elements. The Christian theology of love, charity, and forgiveness has been added to the ancient Indian ritual and aboriginal desire to acquire personal power through individual visions. Peyotism has taught a program of accommodation for over 50 years and the peyote religion has succeeded in giving Indians pride in their native culture while adjusting to the dominant civilization of the whites.

ANNOTATED BIBLIOGRAPHY

Aberle, David F. and Stewart, Omer C. 1967. *Navaho and Ute Peyotism: A Chronological and Distributional Study.*
University of Colorado Studies—Series in Anthropology: No. 6, 129 pages.
This study documents the long-standing intimate relationship which has existed between Ute and Navajo Indians, in spite of the wars between them before 1870. The Navaho learned peyotism from the Ute during years of mutual participation in ceremonies, often directed by peyote priests from other tribes.

Bolton, Herbert E., ed. 1950: Pageant in the Wilderness, *Utah Historical Quarterly,* XVIII.
Translation of the journal of Father Escalante, who led a small expedition for months in 1776 through the Ute Indian country in what is now the states of Colorado and Utah. His observations

leave no doubt that the Ute then had primarily a Great Basin culture, notwithstanding the fact that the easternmost groups had horses and hunted from time to time upon the High Plains immediately east of the Rocky Mountains.

Rockwell, Wilson. 1956. *The Utes: a Forgotten People.* Denver, The Sage Press. Historical account of the friendly relationship between Ute Indians and white Americans.

Slotkin, J. S. 1956. *The Peyote Religion: a Study in Indian-White Relations.* Glencoe, Illinois: The Free Press.

In a brilliant analytic study of the theology and history of peyotism, Slotkin found: "The peyote religion was nativistic but not militant. Culturally, it permitted the Indians to achieve a cultural organization in which they took pride. Socially, it provided a supernatural means of accommodation to the existing domination-subordination relation."

Stewart, Omer C. 1942. *Culture Elements Distribution: XVIII, Ute, Southern Paiute.* University of California—Anthropological records. 6:231–380.

A recording, in chart form and notes, of the basic elements of Ute and Southern Paiute culture traits, as remembered by many of the oldest members of these tribes in 1937 and 1938, in both Utah and Colorado.

—— 1948. *Ute Peyotism.* University of Colorado Studies—Series in Anthropology, No. 1, 42 pages.

A description of the peyote ceremony of the Ute, based on participation in the religious cult on Unitah Reservation, Utah, and the Ute Mountain Ute Reservation, Colorado. About 90 per cent of the Ute Mountain Ute are active peyotists. Peyotism is a minority religion on the other Ute reservations.

—— 1952. "Southern Ute Indians Adjustment to Modern Living," *Acculturation in the Americas: Selected papers from the XXIXth International Congress of Americanists (New York, 1949).* University of Chicago Press, pp. 80–88.

This is a preliminary report of reasearch in Colorado, initiated in 1948, and continuing.

—— 1964. "Questions Regarding American Indian Criminality," *Human Organization,* vol. 23, No. 1, Spring, 1964, pp. 61–66.

Nation-wide comparative study of Indian difficulties with the law, which usually involved an excessive use of alcohol.

—— 1964. "The Need To Popularize Basic Concepts," *Current Anthropology,* vol. 5, no. 5, pp. 431, 442.

Anthropologists should return frequently to teach the concept that culture is entirely invented by man and is transmitted by learning.

—— 1966. "Ute Indians: Before and After White Contact." *Utah Historical Quarterly*, vol. 34, No. 1, (Winter 1966) pp. 38–61.

A short analysis of Ute culture which reveals its basic Great Basin character. This paper contains also a review of the long record of friendly relations betweeen the Ute and the U.S. government.

HERMANN HELMUTH

Cannibalism in Paleoanthropology and Ethnology *

A series of finds of human bones aroused interest both because of their great age and their significance concerning our phylogeny, and also because of the generally accepted fact, or at least assumption, that these bones were the remains of cannibalistic feasts. The splitting of the long bones for the extraction of the marrow, exarticulations, injuries to the skull and especially the opening of the skull base are seen as clues. The finds of human bones and bony remains which were scattered in firesites or kitchen-middens are highly convincing evidence for the occurrence of cannibalism. These bones and skulls, as well as parts of the postcranial skeleton, show clear evidence of the application of force by men, and they indicate that the biological inhibition of killing an individual of the same species disappeared a very long time ago.

What evoked even more interest than the evidence of cannibalistic practices was the attempt to speculate about the thoughts which gave impetus to this action among prehistoric men. What ideas, what religious or cultural modes of thought were implied in cannibalistic practices? Is it possible for us to suppose that they had be-

Translated and revised by the author from "Kannibalismus in Paläanthropologie und Ethnologie." First published in the *Ethnographisch-Archäologische Zeitschrift*, 9, 1968, p. 101–19, edited by Dr. phil. habil. H. Grünert, VEB Deutscher Verlag der Wissenschaften, 108 Berlin, Johannes-Dieckmann-Str. 10.

liefs about life and death, that they had views on the state of being dead and, alternately, on the state of being alive? Or is the eating of fellow beings simply to be attributed to bad nutritional conditions, i.e., hunger or starvation? What knowledge can we gain from these finds with respect to the interrelationships of men? Through an assessment of the recovered material we are able to bring to light some of the ideas and motives of the *Homo erectus* and Neanderthal forms. However, the mental state, spiritual beliefs and capability levels of these early forms of man, as well as their ability to abstract and to reflect, cannot be discovered by any examination of the skull's capacity, its shape or its inner form. This is best illustrated by Elliot Smith's (1926) examination of endocranial casts and brain organization. The comparative study of the endocranial cast of the forged Piltdown skull-cap and the Pithecanthropus I calotte was taken to reveal that the organization of the brain—and hence, intelligence—of Piltdown man were more primitive than those of Pithecanthropus. The inadequacy of this method requires the undertaking of an attempt to examine the psychic and sociocultural level of man by means of cultural objects and remains, thus shedding light on an aspect of man's past. To acquire some ideas of the spiritual world of fossil human forms, we must take into account the psychic-biological environment to which the thoughts of men refer. By examination of cultural products, chiefly stone, and, later, bone and antler tools, it is possible to say that the Pithecanthropus and Sinanthropus forms (about 300,000 years ago), and the Neanderthaler (about 100,000–30,000 years ago) lived the life of hunters and gatherers. The abundance and diversity of the flora and fauna of early glaciation periods differed from the ecological conditions of present-day hunters and gatherers. It should be recognized that the passage of time, in itself, may alter ideas. The 30,000–50,000 years which have passed since the disappearance of Neanderthal men must be considered in the light of changes in modes of thinking and in customs which served as the technical means, created by man of that period, and enabling him to actively control and participate in his environment. It is also necessary to note that the number of individuals living together in any group was probably small. This, together with the degree of technical development at that time, could well have resulted in a feeling of helplessness in the natural environment, unknown in our modern technological society. Because the physical world of diluvial man was so inherently different from our present ecology, we can also expect his ideas to have been different. Should we wish to find a modern-day analogy to the world of early man, then the environment of economically weak and illiterate peoples serves as a better model than that of Western civilized man.

An attempt will be made to offer out of our evolutionary past several possible examples of cannibalism based on an examination of burned and split human bones. Further, present modes of thought, both in their diversity and their variability, related to the custom of anthropophagy, may be illustrated.

First, a few examples from the distant past of this "typically human behaviour" (Weinert)—the killing and devouring of one's own kind—will be given. In this connection, a discussion of the evidence of intrahuman killing has recently been published by Roper. Opinions concerning intentional or accidental killing, self-induced injuries or even breakage and damage after death varied widely. It seems that intentional killing is by far more difficult to prove than supposed anthropophagy.

If the question of an intrahuman killing can be positively answered, then an explanation for the disappearance of the original "instinct" not to kill members of the same species must be sought. With the exception of the lion (Schaller) this kind of behavior is peculiar to man; a simple gene mutation (i.e., gene loss), however, as suggested by Weinert, seems hardly acceptable. Traditional norms or customs which became preponderant could more likely have repressed the old mammalian "instinct." In this sense, it might well be understood as a peculiarly human characteristic.

The South African Australopithecine finds—collections and fragments of the bones of these hominid forms as well as the remains of animal bones—were ascribed to the activity of the Australopithecines themselves (Dart). Also implicated in these killings were the more recently discovered forms of *Homo habilis* as well as hyenas (Washburn).

This question certainly cannot be settled, and the great age, manner of fossilization and preservation in limestone breccia can lead to only relatively vague assumptions.

Just as vague are the interpretations of cannibalism in the case of the thigh bone of the first *Pithecanthropus erectus* find. According to Dubois, the traces of gnawing might also have resulted from crocodile teeth. On the other hand the assertions of Weidenreich with regard to the manner of death of *Sinanthropus pekinensis* from Choukoutien go far beyond mere assumptions. In the case of this generally accepted and hitherto earliest known act of anthropophagy, firesites contained human bones which had been broken and split by other humans.

A similar case of a cannibalistic meal of large proportion is to be found amongst the Neanderthalers of Krapina described by Gorganovic-Kramberger. Here, too, fragments of human skulls and long bones were discovered hacked and burned beside remnants of animal bones in and around a firesite. Skerlj holds the opinion that the finds from Choukoutien and Krapina, which are supposed to prove cannibalistic acts, in fact point to the existence of another hominid species which lived contemporaneously with Neanderthal man—though fossil remains of the former have not yet been found. His critical remarks can be refuted today. There can be no doubt that the tools from Choukoutien as well as the burned and split bones in the firesite belong to Sinanthropus. Today, the number of species in the systematics of the Hominidae has been greatly reduced. The Pithecanthropus and Sinanthropus forms are fused together under the species name of *Homo erectus*. Therefore, the assumption that Pithecanthropus killed and devoured Sinanthropus implies cannibalism. In the same manner, the objections of Skerlj to cannibalism among Neanderthal man can be rejected.

Remains of a cannibalistic meal appear to be evident among the early Neanderthalers from Weimar-Ehringsdorf (Virchow; Weidenreich; Behm-Blancke, 1959/60), and also the finds of La Quina are further proof of the cannibalistic customs of the Neanderthalers (Weinert; Gieseler 1952). The base of the skull of most of the eleven skulls from N'gandong (von Koenigswald) had been opened, probably for the extraction of the brain. The impression of unusual circumstances in the case of the finds of N'gandong is further strengthened by the fact that only two tibiae were found among the skulls although the rich accompanying fauna had "yielded many complete skulls and jaws, even larger joined pieces of the backbone" of other animals (von Koenigswald). The Neanderthal skull from Monte Circeo shows an opening in the skull base, together with an injury on the left side near the orbit which reaches up to the wall of the temporal bone. Since the skull was found alone in the rear part of the cave and surrounded by a circle of stones, this too could suggest a cannibalistic rite, probably part of the death ceremony. Whether the skull simply represents the remains of a meal or was brought into the cave for ritual purposes, it is impossible to say. Theories have also been developed with regard to the cause of death in many other paleoanthropological finds; for example, that of the Old Man of La Chapelle, the youth from Le Moustier, the finds from La Ferrassie, Mount Carmel, and Teshik-Tash. They all suggest that the death of these Neanderthalers was the work of man. Yet, nothing definite can be said about them and no conclusive evidence that cannibalism was practiced at these places is available. More detailed and accurate assertions concerning the manner and purpose of death have been made by Gieseler (1952), Mollison, Grimm and Ullrich, Behm-Blancke (1956) in the case of more recent skeletal finds belonging to *Homo sapiens.* Traces of cuts on the cervical vertebrae, implying decapitation (Hohlestein skulls, South Germany), openings in the base of the skull (Stetten I), and openings of the skull (Ofnet finds), together with the mutilation of the corpse in the case of a skeleton from Doebritz, Thuringia, are clearly ascertained. Circumstances in the case of numerous finds from Bad Frankenhausen (Middle Germany) likewise seem to attest to cannibalistic practices (Behm-Blancke 1956; 1958). The skeletal finds from Neuessing (Gieseler 1953) revealed evidence of injuries and mutilations chiefly of the extremities in the area of the joints. The effects of fire were also obvious.

With regard to the area now known as Great Britain, Brothwell doubts that cannibalism was ever practiced there, since the hitherto most convincing find of Maiden Castle (Dorset) calls for other interpretations than cannibalism. Remains of human bones which were also found in the kitchen-middens of North America among the Hopi (Turner and Morris) and the Iroquois sites (Tuck), on the coast of Cayenne, Brazil (Boehm) and Sumatra (Wastl) testify not only to the antiquity but also the wide distribution of anthropophagy. Additional paleoanthropological and later examples of cannibalism could be cited; yet the cases listed here may suffice since it is of these that we are most certain.

By cannibalism, or anthropophagy, as used in the following section, is understood the custom of eating human flesh, associated with certain ideas. It is common knowledge that everywhere in times of starvation, even in Western Europe, human meat has been eaten, but these extreme cases shall be excluded from a consideration of "cannibalism" defind as a custom or habit.

Among the examples given for anthrophagy and associated ideas and modes of thought, those which will be mentioned first relate to the custom of "patrophagy" and/or endocannibalism (Steinmetz), i.e., the ritual of eating members of one's own tribe. Herodotus (3.38) relates the contrast between the burial rites of the Greeks and those of an Indian tribe, the Kallatians. Since their custom was to eat the dead, people of this Indian tribe regarded as barbaric the burning of the dead which for the Greeks was a normal, unremarkable practice. According to Herodotus, both the Massagets and the Issedons, who lived to the east of the Caspian Sea, indulged in patrophagy. Herodotus' observations were somewhat confirmed later by a report by Mueller on the occurrence of cannibalism in recent times in the Swat Valley in Eastern Afghanistan. Unfortunately his report gives no account of the nature of the cannibalism and what ideas motivated men to such behavior. According to Tylor, the Slavs also engaged in patrophagy. All these reports deserve special attention insofar as they, as the earliest sources of information on cannibalism, refer especially to endocannibalism.

Several aboriginal tribes of Australia were famous for their custom of eating their dead (Thurnwald 1926). Among the aborigines of southeastern Australia, the Dieri, an old man who was a relative of the deceased, cut all the fat from the face, belly, arms and legs of the latter, then handed it round to eat. Among other Australian tribes, the flesh too, was devoured. The fat is regarded as the seat of extraordinary powers which may be acquired by eating. In addition, there is also the desire to absorb the personality and soul of the dead for oneself and the tribe in general. The wish to remain together with the dead, and both physically and spiritually unite with him, also motivates this act. If a youth from the tribe of the Turrbal died during the ceremonial combats after the initiation ceremonies, it was the custom to eat his body. Offered as a reason for this was the fact that the youth was known and loved, and thus it was believed that, regardless of where his soul might be roaming, his flesh would not be allowed to rot.

Even in such a narrowly circumscribed area, we encounter different ideas of the background to patrophagy. Together with the view that one incorporates into oneself valuable qualities, the feeling of belonging together, the idea of helping to preserve the way of life, the means of transmission of the soul, and participation of the dead man in the life of the tribe, also play a role. Thus friendship with the dead man, respect and love also bear a relation to the consumption of human flesh by other humans.

In South America endocannibalism was common in a different way than in Australia. In the belief that the soul resided in the bones, the Amahuaca, Tucana, Jumano, Waika, Surara, Pakidai and other tribes (Steward, Zerries, Dole, Becher) used to mix the ashes of the dead with their drinks, in order to preserve for the tribe the life located in the bones and to ensure that the life separated from the body secured a new abode which it could not have found otherwise. Among the Chiribichi, the fat which ran from the body when it was roasted was collected and drunk with *chicha*. In this way, the dead man was kept within the tribe, his life remained preserved in his fellow tribesmen.

Much more widespread than this so-called endocannibalism was exocannibalism—cannibalism practiced on other tribes. This form of anthropophagy was also not alien to the aborigines of Australia. The southeastern tribes of the Theddora and the Ngarigo consumed muscles from the arms and legs, the skin, and the flesh from the sides of the body. The meal was accompanied by expressions of contempt and scorn (Thurnwald 1926). Thus the act of eating may be seen as a way of mocking and showing contempt for the dead man.

Likewise Thurnwald (1908) observed cannibalism on the Island of Nissan (a Solomon Island) and in the Carolines. In order to eat human flesh, a network of obligations of different chieftains was developed in accordance with different rules. One participant in the ritual offered the victim, usually a widow (previously fattened for this purpose); a second person killed her; and a third was allowed to eat her. By continually changing the roles, it was possible to preserve this custom for a long time. Here, according to Thurnwald, revenge and a general lust appeared to be the main motivation for the enjoyment of eating human flesh. It was not motivated by any lack of animal flesh. In addition, the eating of human flesh is supposed to confer strength and power, and, in the case of female flesh, to heighten sexual potency. Thus here a general potency is seen to reside in human flesh. Originally this assumption could have been extended to the transmission of the powers of the dead person. In this instance, certain parts of the body are seen as the repository of special qualities.

Among the Klemantan of Indonesia, anthropophagy can be traced to another belief. When all other means of curing a sick boy had failed, the relatives were wont to kill his sister. Then the boy was given the flesh of his sister to eat. In this way an attempt was made to appease the evil spirit which had brought about the disease. In order for the sick person to obtain the best advantage from the victim, it was necessary for him to eat the flesh of the latter.

In Africa, exocannibalism was widespread among such tribes as the Fan or Fang, in Central Africa, and the Ovimbundu, in Angola. Czekanowski cites anthropophagy among the tribes of Momvu, Central Africa, who "have the reputation of being passionate anthropophagists who supposedly don't even refuse a corpse." As followers of the same custom, he names the Baluba, Bakondja, Basongo, Mabudu and other tribes of Central Africa. Koch, who was sent into the area around the Victoria and Nyanza lakes to help in the campaign against sleeping sickness, reports that it was not possible for his party to carry out autopsies since the natives believed that they wanted to eat the corpses, and "it is a fact that at the moment there is still a secret sect which digs up corpses and eats them. . . ." "They believe that whoever eats the flesh of corpses becomes possessed of sinister, magic powers and is capable of changing himself into wild animals." (Koch p. 465). One can suppose that among these tribes the belief in the metamorphosis of the dead man into his totem animal and thus in the transmigration of souls, results in the consumption of the flesh of corpses so that the eater can change himself into an animal by devouring the flesh of the dead man. The direct way to a transformation, i.e., death, is of course to be avoided and thus the objective is gained in a round-about manner by eating a human being who is already capable of assuming the form of an animal. Here we are confronted with a special form of anthropophagy which can be neither characterized as exo-, nor as endocannibalism. At least during the period in which observations were carried out, both members of the same tribe and those of other tribes were eaten after their death, though they were not killed.

With reference to the cannibalism of the Ovimbundu or Um-bundu, Childs reports that the Ovimbundu were not ordinarily cannibals, and that except on definite and unusual occasions, the common people never ate human flesh. Yet no king was ever allowed to rule or to be crowned unless he had eaten human flesh. For this purpose, it was the custom to kill a fattened slave and to eat his flesh mixed with that of animals. This custom has a direct connection with an old tradition, according to which the legendary king of the Ovimbundu, Wamba Kalunga, who had a special predilection for human flesh, stole and ate small children, and even dug up the dead in order to devour them. The continuation of this custom, first instituted by a great king, was enshrined in the belief in the power of repetition, that that which once was the essence of kingship must continually be reproduced, and can be understood as the motive of royal cannibalism among the Ovimbundu.

Some African tribes which indulged in cannibalism were, like us, of the opinion that the consumption of human flesh was a cruel and horrible thing. But since the office of the king demanded cruelty, and feelings of humanity contradicted the state of kingship, the king was forced to endure an extreme degree of horror in order to harden himself.

Cannibalism is also encountered in Africa in its funereal form. Burial ceremonies then become the occasion for the consumption of the flesh of sacrificed slaves or enemies. Among the Jaga it was the custom to decapitate the victims over the grave so that the blood would drip down on to the grave and quench the thirst of the dead person. The sacrificial victims were killed as food for the dead. Some of the flesh was buried in the grave, some was also eaten. Thus, in order to transport oneself from the world of the living to the world of the dead, it was necessary to eat the same food as the dead. The eating of human flesh at funerals, especially that of important personalities, was "not a funereal custom of the living but a rite and necessity of the dead which must be shared by the living' (Volhardt). This case of anthropophagy is connected with a communion or identification with the dead person.

Whether or not the Azande tribes of Central Africa also indulged in cannibalism, as various explorers (among others, Schweinfurth, Czekanowski) have reported, is a question which now has been answered by Evans-Pritchard in the affirmative. It is, however, regarded as a rare phenomenon. Prisoners of war, criminals and other persons who had been expelled from the tribe were eaten because of hunger for human flesh. Evans-Pritchard surmises that cannibalism was taken over from other originally cannibalistic tribes and given this peculiar form.

As is well known, the term "cannibal" comes from the name, Caribe. Cannibalism was however not restricted to these Indians but was also found among the Tupí-Guaraní, the Tupinamba, Colombian tribes, and among the Arawaks and Botokuds (Steward). Although especially in South America, cannibalism led to excesses, in the course of which mass slaughters and the eating of several hundred persons supposedly occurred, a lack of animal protein cannot be considered as the reason for these excesses, except perhaps in the case of the Saé and Guayupé. In the case of the South American Indians, also, ideas of a religious ethical nature lie at the basis of cannibalistic practices. Among the Sumo, bodies of slain enemies were chopped up and eaten in order to insult the enemy even though he was already dead, and to ensure his being deprived completely of any power to do harm. The Sumo also wanted to prevent the dead man from taking revenge on his murderer. The Mesoamerican Chorotega and Nicarao were cannibalistic, as were the tribes of the Quimbaja, Arma, Picara, Putima, Pijao and Pozo, in the Cauca Valley in the northwest of South America. Though nothing is known about the reasons for anthropophagy among the former, the world of ideas of the latter has been passed on. In the case of anthropophagy practiced in the Cauca Valley, only the warrior was given the right to devour an enemy warrior. The heart and the blood were eaten raw immediately after death to ensure the absorption of the strength of the dead man. The belief that the powers of the dead were transmitted through the eating of flesh or special parts of the body resulted not only in the practice of cannibalism, but also in sacrificial offerings to the gods in order that they too would share in the strength. Reports exist of cannibalism among a number of other tribes in the Cauca Valley, but the motives behind this are no longer known. Among the Tupinamba the belief in a transmission of life and strength also appears to have been prevalent. Withered old women would eat the flesh and fat of dead men, presumably in order to preserve their health and vitality and to take life into themselves. The small children were given blood to drink, while their mothers rubbed the blood of the dead man on their breasts. Amongst the Guaraní, the children dipped their hands into the still warm blood in order to become audacious and courageous and also to avenge the killing and devouring of their relatives by the opposing side.

Among the Parintintin there was another reason for anthropophagy. The eyes, the tongue, the muscles of the arms and legs of their dead enemies were eaten to prevent them from being able to see, speak, walk and shoot again; in this way they would be unable to take any revenge on their murderers. Here the fear of reprisal was the factor which led to the destruction of the organs necessary for revenge and, in this way, ensured forever that the dead would be no danger. Among the Caribs' neighbors, the Arawaks, the motivation behind cannibalism was certainly the desire to avenge themselves on their hereditary enemies. The desire to show contempt, to mock and to carry out vengeance was probably also the reason why cannibalism became the custom among the Omagua, a tribe of the Tupí-Guaraní. After prisoners of the Omagua had lived free for a long time, and had even been allowed to marry women of this tribe, they were ritually slaughtered and eaten. In order that not even one piece of human flesh remained in the body, participants in the ritual were afterwards forced to vomit the flesh.

Among the Cubeo tribe, a fertility cult was connected with anthropophagy. At the end of the meal, the wife of the chief used to eat the penis of the slain man in order to increase her fertility.

The Amniapä and the Guaratägaja killed and ate their own tribesmen who had been found guilty of crimes.

The Chebero had a preference for such organs as the liver, heart and intestines, for it was felt that great magical powers resided in them.

The coincidence of endo- and exocannibalism, especially in South America, raises a question whether one form could have developed out of the other, and which form of cannibalistic behavior might be regarded as the original. This problem was already recognized by Steinmetz in 1896. In the light of anthropological knowledge of that day, there was the conviction that endocannibalism was to be regarded as the earliest form. This was justified by (1) the belief that original man lacked a fine esthetic sense, and (2) by the necessity of recourse to richly abundant flesh in times of food scarcity. In recent times, Behm-Blancke (1958; 1959/60) and Becher have concerned themselves with this question. They are in agreement, although for different reasons, that patrophagy, as a form of endocannibalism, must be regarded as the origin of all cannibalistic customs. Dole's assertion that the origin of anthropophagy was to be found in exocannibalism was opposed by Becher who claimed that exocannibalism had been practiced by planters and farmers of the South American cultural area, but the primitive hunters and gatherers (Surara and Pakidai) practiced endocannibalism. For Becher it appeared easier to imagine that hate and contempt could arise from love and respect than the other way round. Behm-Blancke regards patrophagy and cannibalism of fellow tribesmen killed in battle as the original form of cannibalism; from this developed such exocannibalistic practices as burial cannibalism, fertility cannibalism and magical cannibalism.

The hypothesis brought forward by Becher will later be investigated by means of larger statistical material. The question can be posed as follows: Is endocannibalism connected with the social structure of gatherers and hunters and similar lower social organizations, or is there a correlation between exocannibalism and a plantation-type economy, tilling of the land and a higher, more or less sedentary way of life in settlements similar to villages? In order to answer this question Indian groups from the South American continent were examined; the sources of information there were especially favorable, and both types of cannibalism occurred along with different forms of agriculture and social organization. To keep these factors as comparable as possible, no attempt has been made to examine the cultures of other continents. Due to the age and uncertainty possibly connected with the terms, endo- and exocannibalism, as used by Steinmetz, his work was not applied. According to the *Handbook of South American Indians* (Steward) sixteen tribes or sub-tribes in South America practice or practiced *endo*cannibalism. In the case of a further three tribes (Uraba, Arapium, Araukans) only uncertain or incomplete information was available and was therefore excluded from any further statistics. The number of tribes of South American Indians which practiced *exo*cannibalism is much higher; thirty-eight groups have been reported. Comparison of those tribes which practice endo- and exocannibalism and their economic and organizational forms resulted in the following table (data on social organization and economy were taken, in the main, from the *Handbook of South American Indians,* and to a much lesser extent, from the *World Ethnographic Sample* [Murdock]).

TABLE I

	Endocannibalism	Exocannibalism
1) Tribes with:		
(a) hunting-gathering economy agriculture missing or unimportant	14	6
(b) Plantation and farming as basic form of subsistence economy (maize, manioc)	2	32
$chi^2 = 50.46 \quad p > 0.1\%$		
2) Tribes with:		
(a) minimal social differentiation, band, nomadic or semi-nomadic organization	13	4
(b) sessile, village-like social organization	3	34
$chi^2 = 44.13 \quad p > 0.1\%$		

To provide a more detailed picture, the tribes comprised in the chart and their social and economic characteristics have been mapped separately in Table 1a.

TABLE IA

Tribes with Exocannibalism	Subsistence Economy	Agriculture or Horticulture	Settlement Pattern and Social Organization
Cenufana	C, R	D	V
Nutibara	C, R	D	V
Caramanta	C, R	D	V
Buritica	C, R	D	V
Ancerma	C, R	D	V
Antiochia	C, R	D	V
Catio	C, R	D	V
Abibe	C, R	D	V
Arma	C, R	D	V
Quimbaya	C, R		V
Pijao	C, R		V
Pozo	C, R		V
Amani	C, R		V
Maracapana	C	CD	V
Cumanagoto	C, R	D	V
Palenque	C, R	D	V
Guaraní	R, C	D	V
Tupinamba	R, C	D	V
Yuruna	R, C	D	V
Shipaya	R, C	D	V
Mundurucú	R, C	CD	FS
Parintintin	C, R	D	V
Apiaca	R, C	D	FS
Amniapä	C, R	D	V
Guaratägaja	C, R	D	V
Canichana		Important, not predominant	V
Ruanagua	C	Important, not predominant	H ?
Cashibo	C	Important, not predominant	H
Chébero	R	D	V
Encabellado	R	CD	V
Cubeo	R	D	V
Caribs	R	D	V
Arawaks	R	D	V
Chiriguano	C	D	V
Chorotega	C	D	V
Nicarao	C	D	V

TABLE IA (cont'd)

Tribes with Endoconnibalism	Subsistence Economy	Agriculture or Horticulture	Settlement pattern and Social Organization
Guayupé	R	CD	Sedentary
Saé	R	D	Sedentary
Mayoruna	Hunting, gathering	Present, unimportant	Seminomadic
Conibo	R	Not predominant	Bands
Capanahua	C	Present, not predominant	Bands
Remo	C	Present, not predominant	Bands
Amahuaca	C	Present, not predominant	Scattered
Setebo	C	Present, not predominant	Bands
Yuminahua	R	Present, not predominant	Scattered
Zapa	R	Present, not predominant	Bands, Scattered
Roamaina	R	Present, not predominant	Scattered
Sirionó	Hunting, gathering	Present, unimportant	Seminomadic
Waica	Hunting, gathering	Present, unimportant	Bands
Guaharibo	Hunting, gathering	Present, unimportant	Scattered
Tapuya	Hunting, gathering	Present, unimportant	Sedentary
Tarairiu	Hunting, gathering	Present, unimportant	Scattered

Explanation of Signs

C	Planting of cereals (e.g., maize)
R	Planting of tubers (e.g., manioc)
V	Village organization
FS	Fortified Settlements
H	Hamlet
D	Dominant, basic type of subsistence
CD	Basic subsistence augmented by additional means

The differences in the frequency distributions of tribes with different forms of organization and economy were tested for their significance according to the chi² method, and were shown not to be dependent on chance. On the contrary, one can assume with a degree of certainty (there is a statistical probability of >0.1 per cent) that the tribes of South America which practice endocannibalism are in general on a different level of economic and social organization than those which practice exocannibalism. The statistics also show that there is a close connection between the degree of economy and organization. This unity was an a priori assumption and does not offer any additional argument to support the hypothesis described above. Without entering into a detailed discussion of the ideas expressed by L. H. Morgan, it can be stated that just as hunting and gathering communities are more ancient and "primitive" than planting and farming economies, endocannibalism is older than and primary to exocannibalism. On the basis of this conclusion one can agree with Becher's theory. At least for this part of the New World, this implies a greater age of friendly, amicable feelings connected with the consumption of human flesh than hostile or magical feelings.

In South America especially, head hunting and the hunt for human trophies were closely associated with the custom of anthropophagy. Although the real object of examination is anthropophagy, a quick glance at the head hunting of the Jívaro and the Munduruku would seem to be justified. A "tsantsa" brought luck to its owner; for one reason, because the treated head contained magical powers as a result of the preparation itself, and for another, because the ancestors assured the owner of a shrunken head their support and good will since their desire for revenge had been fulfilled. Head trophies were also of great value and importance among the Guaraní and Omagua. Contempt and mockery led to the custom among the Araukans of making drinking cups from the skulls of slain enemies. For the same reason, the Huanca as well as the Incas and the Quechua used to stuff their slain and devoured enemies and make drums from the skin or flutes from the bones. These few words suffice in regard to human trophies in the South American cultural area.

Compared with South America, North America had little incidence of cannibalism. Here, according to Driver, only the Pawnees and Iroquois practiced cannibalism. The reason seems to have been a desire for revenge. New evidence comes from the Hopi, where at the site of Polacca Wash the slain, dismembered, mutilated and burnt bones of thirty Hopi Indians were found—according to Turner and Morris, "The most convincing evidence of cannibalism in all Southwestern archaeology." Information given by Steinmetz on endocannibalism among several North American tribes is not confirmed by more recent material (Swanton, Driver) and thus is not taken into account.

Cannibalism was widely distributed in the Polynesian area. On the Fiji Islands, concepts relating to "Mana" led to the desire to share in this magical power by devouring parts of a man or even the man himself. The result of the idea of transmission of "Mana" was the eating preferably of chieftains and other important men, as these understandably contained the greatest amount of "Mana." No doubt the same ideas were to be encountered in other areas of Polynesia, yet Williamson mentions that on Paumatu, murderers were killed and eaten; in other words, that cannibalism represented a punitive act. This judicial form of cannibalism cannot be easily fitted into the old scheme of endo- and exocannibalism and therefore the underlying psychological factors should be preferred as the criterion. On the Marquesas Islands, the fear of the return of the soul of the dead man and of revenge on his murderers became the reason for anthropophagy. The prevention of posthumous revenge has already been cited as the reason for cannibalism among South American Indians.

Likewise, the Marind-anim in New Guinea practiced cannibalism for purely secular reasons. The myth of fire being first brought to man is re-enacted as authentically as possible in the Rapa ceremony. The men, who belong to the secret order of the Rapa, have the task of igniting the fire each year anew. Since, according to their myth, fire originated from an act of copulation, the ceremony consists of a coital act with a girl, who is then thrown in a fire which others, in the meantime, had started by using long red sticks. The victim is eaten and the bones, painted red, are stored away in a hut. The repetition of the myth, the belief in it, the power and the desire to continue the tradition of tribal life, led, in this case, to anthropophagy.

Some of the most illustrative and in our view horrible cases of

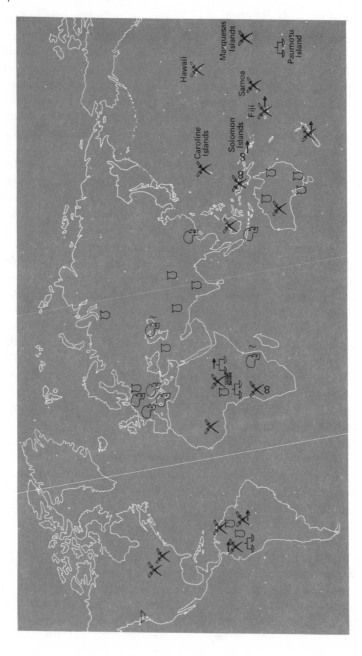

exo- and endocannibalism in New Guinea have been described by Berndt (1962). Here in the Eastern Highlands cannibalism was only one among several "avenues through which aggression" could "be expressed legitimately" (Berndt 1962, p. 269). However it was also practiced as a customary way of disposing of the dead (Berndt, 1962, p. 269) and the bodies of men and women, enemies, kin or affines were eaten. The reasons for this custom are given as: a) deficiency in protein, b) disposal of a corpse, c) the belief that human blood, bones etc. would magically increase garden fertility, d) the preference of the dead to be eaten, but not necessarily "to absorb the 'power' or strength of the deceased" (Berndt 1962, p. 271). In this relatively restricted geographical region, examples of almost every type of cannibalism have been described, such as endo-, exo-, ritual, fertility, funerary cannibalism. The motives ranged from a desire to be aggressive, to ridicule, to revenge, to prevent revenge, to simple physiological appetite, to cure or heal diseases, to respect the wishes of the dead, and sentiment.

If in New Zealand a chieftain was killed during a war between two tribes, hostilities ceased for the moment. The body of the chieftain was chopped up, roasted by his opponents, partly sacrificed to the gods, and partly eaten by the celebrants. If the gods accepted the sacrifice, the war was continued; if not, the war ended. The reasons for this are to be found in the wish for revenge and rage, but equally also in ideas on taboo. The strength, the courage, and the taboo powers of the enemy are transmitted by the eating of the flesh. According to Frazer, cannibalistic tribes also wanted to arouse fear and horror among noncannibalistic tribes and to terrorize them.

On the North Bougainville Islands, it was the custom at the birth

ILLUSTRATION 1: Distribution of Anthropophagy and its motives.

Paleoanthropological finds, indicating or suggesting anthropophagy.
Endocannibalism, motivated by love and affection.
Juridicial cannibalism.
Exocannibalism motivated by hate and scorn.
Exocannibalism for the purpose of transmittance of power.
Cannibalism, motivated by the idea of continuity.
Magical-ceremonial cannibalism.
Funerary cannibalism.
(Not all European finds are included, for lack of space.)

of a child to kill a man, eat him, and bury his head. Riesenfeld sees a connection between this fact and the following myth: according to legend, two brothers competed with one another—one was killed and devoured. The victorious brother became the founder of the tribe and its culture. This act of founding is repeated as a ritual on the birth of a child. If the newborn child is to grow into the order of tribal life, from the very beginning the correct path must be taken.

This brings to a close the exposition of ideas which either lead to cannibalism or are associated with it. However, it must be added that by no means all tribes could be mentioned which practice this custom or who, at the time of their discovery or of close contact, still possessed legends in which anthropophagy appeared. The intention here is simply to give an indication of the varieties of ideas associated with this custom. Even though the belief of the transmission of qualities was undoubtedly the most widespread, completely different concepts, often between neighboring tribes, also played a role. Mockery, contempt, revenge, fury and hate, fear of the return and revenge of the dead man, punishment for a crime, as well as feelings of friendship and belonging together, resulted in anthropophagy. Also, the attempt to preserve a continuity, an already existent order, lay behind the eating of human flesh.

The most frequent causes of anthropophagy as well as the most verified finds which point to cannibalism are shown in their geographical distribution on the accompanying map. Where there was agreement between Steinmetz's views on the reasons for cannibalism and more recent literature, his data were also recorded on the map. It can be seen from the diagram that—if time is not taken into account as a factor and only space is considered—a variety of possibilities for interpreting fossil finds exist. Since the following ideas are closely related, the finds of N'gangdong for example could be interpreted as the result of hate and contempt or of a belief in cultural continuity, or even in terms of a transmission of powers and qualities. In the case of the Sinanthropus finds, ideas such as love and respect would be more likely to be responsible since these motives have been proved in neighboring Indian areas. As various motives are to be found in the African world, the possibility of interpretation no longer seems to exist.

The map also makes evident that an attempt might be made to

establish an order of sequence for the beginning of anthropophagy and to trace its development not only with regard to South America but to other continents and cultural areas. Due to the absence of adequately precise information such as that provided by the *Handbook of South American Indians* this problem was not pursued in the case of Africa or Australia.

The examples of anthropophagy with which we have become acquainted from finds of early man are separated from each other by both considerable periods of time and great distances. Even though to our modern way of thinking the enjoyment of human flesh arouses a deeply rooted disgust, cannibals can present a variety of ideas which can make any disgust incomprehensible, and indeed, in many cases, the fine taste of human flesh is underlined. In light of these finds, it is probable that the relativity of human customs and moral laws (as Herodotus understood them), and the influence of ideas and modes of thought on human behavior must be very ancient.

The assumption is certainly well justified that tools from the Paleolithic or a later period were made for the same purpose as similar items found among today's nonliterate peoples on a lower level of technological development. What the Eskimos call a harpoon, a pointed tip with a bored hole, an eye or hook to connect it to the part from which it is to be released, is to be considered as a harpoon even though it may have been found in Mesolithic strata. In both cases, the principles of construction are the same, according to which we can confidently assume the same function. The same is true, as Underwood showed, of those objects which were thought to have magical functions and have been termed "batons de commandement." The same methods of construction characterize the so-called "baton de commandement" as those which are unmistakably evident in the case of the spear-throwers of the Eskimos and the implements of the Aurignacian and Magdalenian. But the case is different in regard to cannibalism. Here we cannot assume that the same phenomena imply identical causes or intended effects. Due to the variety and the differences in the manner of thinking, we cannot, as was originally thought, simply transfer ideas formed among present nonliterate peoples from one area to those of Paleolithic or Mesolithic times; any such attempt is bound to remain on the level of vague surmise. By reference to the very manifold and different modes of thought which lie behind anthropophagy, it was attempted to show that a principle of uniformitarianism, as borrowed from geology (Lyell), can only be applied with great caution to the form of human worlds of thought.

The variety and the contrast of modes of thought justify a further inference with regard to the psyche of early human forms. The broken and gnawed bones of Sinanthropus, the Neanderthalers and diluvial man were seen as evidence for hostile human actions carried out by and among men of the same kind (Freeman). The ideas sketched in the ethnological part of this article and the feelings associated with them are incapable of supporting this assumption. The belief in a transmission of qualities, fear of revenge, punishment for crimes, repetition of a myth, as well as a certain love and a feeling of belonging together, or complete indifference on the part of the subject toward pain and the essence of the object eaten, are not connected with aggressive feelings. The assumption of aggressive feelings or aggressive behavior of man towards his fellow man is not justified without certain conditions since this assumption too represents nothing else but an application of ideas deduced from a present situation to a past one. With the same justification, one might argue that an Indian or an Australian practicing patrophagy could imply a long history of friendly, loving feelings and affection. A comparison of the modes of thought and motives of humans from different and recent cultures makes it possible to reject previously accepted views as too dogmatic. Likewise, a categorization and a comparison of the varieties of human behavior and thought are required for the study of psychic-ethological paleoanthropology, similar, say, to the significance of primatology to physical paleoanthropology.

REFERENCES

Becher, H., 1967: Die endokannibalistischen Riten als früheste Erscheinungsform der Anthropophagie. In: Z. Ethnol. 92, p. 248–53.
Behm-Blancke, G., 1956: Bronze- und hallstattzeitliche Kulthöhlen im Gips-Gebirge bei Bad Frankenhausen. In: Ausgrabungen u. Funde 1, p. 176–77.

——., 1958: Höhlen, Heiligtümer, Kannibalen. Archäologische Forschungen im Kyffhäuser. Leipzig.

——., 1959/60: Die altsteinzeitlichen Rastplätze im Travertingebiet von Taubach, Weimer, Ehringsdorf (Der Kannibalismus in Ehringsdorf). In: Alt-Thüringen 4, p. 131–42.

Berndt, R. M., 1962: *Excess and Restraint.* University of Chicago Press, Chicago.

Boehm, F., 1932: Formen und Motive der Anthropophagie. In: Imago 18, H. 2.

Brothwell, D. A., 1961: "Cannibalism in Early Britain." In: *Antiquity* 35, p. 304–7.

Childs, G. M., 1949: *Umbundu Kinship and Character.* Oxford.

Czekanowski, J., 1924: Wissenschaftliche Ergebnisse der Deutschen Zentral-Afrika-Expedition 1907–1928. Bd. VI/2. Leipzig.

Dart, R. A., 1957: The Osteodontokeratic Culture of Australopithecus prometheus. Transvaal Mus. Memoir No. 10. Pretoria.

Dole, G. 1962: "Endocannibalism among the Amahuaca Indians." *Transactions New York Acad. Sci.* Series 2, vol. 24, no. 5, p. 567–73.

Driver, H. E., 1961: *Indians of North America.* Chicago.

Eckert, G., 1939: Die Kopfjagd im Caucatal. In: Z. Ethnol. 71, p. 305–18.

Evans-Pritchard, E. E., 1960: "Zande Cannibalism." In: *J. Royal Anthropol. Inst.* 90, p. 238–58.

Frazer, G. J., 1939: *The Native Races of Australasia.* London.

Freeman, D., 1964: "Human Aggression in Anthropological Perspective." In: *Natural History of Aggression.* Institute of Biology Symposia No. 13. London and New York.

Garn, S., and W. D. Block, 1970: "The Limited Nutritional Value of Cannibalism." *Amer. Anthropologist* 72, p. 106.

Gieseler, W., 1951: Die süddeutschen Kopfbestattungen und ihre zeitliche Einreihung. In: Aus der Heimat 59, H. 12.

——., 1952: Schädelverletzungen, Kannibalismus und Bestattungen im europäischen Paläolithikum. In: Aus der Heimat 59, H. 12.

——., 1953: Das jungpaläolithische Skelett von Neuessing. In: Aus der Heimat 61, H. 7/8.

Gorganovic-Kramberger, K., 1906: Der diluviale Mensch von Krapina in Kroatien. Ein Beitrag zur Paläoanthropologie. Wiesbaden.

Grimm, H. und H. Ullrich, 1965: Ein jungpaläolithischer Schädel und Skelettreste aus Döbritz, Kr. Pößneck. In: Alt-Thüringen 7, p. 50–89.

Herodotos von Halikarnassos, 1964: Das Geschichtswerk. Übertr. v. T. Braun. 4. Aufl. Leipzig.

MARSHALL D. SAHLINS

African Nemesis: An Off-Broadway Review

Foreword

Robert Ardrey, the author of *African Genesis,* is a playwright. But
he's a thinking man's playwright. He has conducted, as he puts it,
a personal investigation into the animal origins and animal nature
of man. The investigation focuses on the social behavior of subhu-
man primates and other vertebrates—most notably, birds—and on
the South African "man-ape" (Australopithecine) materials uncov-
ered by Raymond Dart and his co-workers. Ardrey claims to have
discovered not merely the true underlying nature of man, but a
large "unwitting combine" of influential scientists who refuse to
acknowledge the evidences of this true nature. The true nature is
made up of certain "cultural instincts" developed in the course of
animal evolution and genetically transmitted in the human line.
Most of the instincts are bad, and they are responsible for great troubles of the modern world. The combine, intellectually committed to
the "romantic fallacy" that man is basically noble, unique among
animals, and governed not so much by his animal nature as by his
cultural circumstances, will not see this. So Ardrey has taken it upon
himself to present the case to the public. He makes out his discovery to be a revolutionary doctrine, and with great flourish and

From *The Kroeber Anthropological Society Papers,* No. 30, Spring 1964, pp. 83–100.
Reprinted by permission.

considerable flair lets fly many barbs in the general direction of the "phalanx of modern thought" and the bastions of "scientific orthodoxy."

However different the subject, the book then belongs in the popular Kon Tiki genre. It's agin the interests. It portrays a theory that sounds sensible, but which, for fuddy-duddy reasons, the professors-that-be generally ignore. Right away, Ardrey is an underdog. And to add to the appeal: simply by reading the book approvingly anyone can demonstrate that he is the intellectual equal—indeed, the superior of the so-called scholars.

Obviously, it becomes difficult to enter the lists against Ardrey. Who wants to be accused of being a counter-revolutionary? Who *is* a counter-revolutionary? What an improbable position for an anthropological critic. To admit to intellectual conservatism is contrary to the spirit of any science, and not the least so to anthropology. In this context of conspiratorial allegation, how can an anthropologist convey the impression that the theory seems to him unsound? Well, if Ardrey, a dramatist, can pen a book about anthropology, an anthropologist can write his review in play form. That is what I have done.

The play speaks for itself. *Insofar as it speaks well it is because I have woven into it many of Ardrey's felicitous phrases.* It is only necessary to mention that the bracketed page numbers refer to some of Ardrey's more unusual statements, and the dénouement of the drama is not Ardrey's book but my hope. So now your humble patience pray, gently to hear, kindly to judge:

Cast of Characters

ROBERT ARDENT: Former dramatist. Now leader of a revolutionary movement to reveal the true animal nature of man.

EVE ARDENT: His wife.

RAYMOND BLUNT: Anatomist-paleontologist. Discoverer of Australopithecus, the nearest ancestor of man.

DR. L. FAUCET: Noted anthropologist. Discoverer of the early hominid Zinjanthropus—under hazardous conditions due to the menace of prides of black-maned lions.

MARY FAUCET: His wife, the real discoverer of Zinjanthropus.

ANYONE: Almost everyone.

KUNG: A Bushman shaman. (Only we know his real name.)

MR. SHAPIRO: A Mr. Shapiro.

Any resemblance between the characters of this play and persons living or dead is purely incidental.

PROLOGUE

Ardent and Eve on opposite ends of stage front.

ARDENT. Give order that these bodies
  High on a stage be placed to view;
  And let me speak to the yet unknowing world
  How these things came about. So shall you hear
  Of carnal, bloody, and unnatural acts;
  Of accidental judgments, casual slaughters;
  Of deaths put on by cunning and forced cause;

EVE (*an interjected aside*). And, in this upshot, purposes mistook
  Fall'n on the inventors' heads—

ARDENT. All this can I truly deliver.

ACT I

A cave near Johannesburg, late afternoon. A table and chair rear center with typewriter on table. A pile of firewood front center, about eight feet in front of table. Cave mouth, R; cave recess, L. Ardent, standing on table, addressing Blunt, the Faucets, Eve and Anyone. Mary Faucet carrying large rifle.

ARDENT (*dramatically*). A specter is haunting Europe—the million-year-old specter of a killer ape whose home was this very cave, the specter of man's carnivorous ancestor . . . his own murderous specter. All the powers of orthodox science, all the orthodox producers and consumers of the romantic fallacy, have entered into a holy alliance to exorcise this specter: Marx and Freud, Rousseau and Jefferson, the frightened anthropologists and their namby committed publics, the whole troop of howling monkeys that is man won't look in the goddam river of time to see reflected there their own hideous visage. (*Mocking*) Oh what a piece of work is man, they say: how noble in reason, in form and moving how express and admirable, in action how like an angel! The beauty of the world! The paragon of animals! (*Hardens*) Well, that is what he is, the paragon of animals: base to the core in instinct, in form and moving how like the beast of prey, in national action the consummate primate defending to a fool's death all the territory he can grab from others, the beauty of the mushroom cloud! Blunt, Faucet, Anyone—what is to be done? Murder will out, you thought, Blunt. Well you were wrong. So you cheerfully went up to the Livingstone conference to lay before the northern scientists the fossilized evidence from this cave. You put out in plain boxes the stupendous remnants of hominid carnage strewn here by our brutal Australopithecine father. Well, they ignored you! They took refuge behind the laughing hyena—hyenas did it, they said (*laughs bitterly*). And you, Faucet, you and Mary fighting off black-maned lions to dig in Tanganyika, to dig up the truth. I tell you this: they won't listen! Your specialist voices in obscure specialist journals have no echoes—even when you can get your stuff published. And they censor you. And they drown you in the milksop tears of the orthodox romantic prejudice. (*Exhorts*) I tell you this: you need drama! You need someone to put it all together, to forge a knife of prose that will rip the reactionary academics from groin to gorge. You need me! And we together will make our revolutionary truth known. Comrades, we are privy to a revolution in knowledge about man, about what he really is. South African workers in the caverns of man's origins, unite! Man has nothing to lose but the chains of his romantic illusion. Let us make him free with the truth. Let us break through the counter-revolutionary phalanx with a manifesto! And let us write it here—write here, right now! (*Anticlimax*) I have a publisher lined up—and catch this title, African Nemesis. (*Comes down from the table.*)

ANYONE. Is Marx an enemy of the revolution? A counter-revolutionary?

ARDENT. Private property is an animal instinct, a territorial compulsion put into the genes of man a hundred million years before he was born. (*Contempt*) But to the romantics, man is a noble fellow. Circumstances, they say, brought him to this end. A unique fellow, they say, with a soul, or a will, or a culture. I say . . . when Blunt found that bashed-in Australopithecine jaw, it said, said across millions of years of bloody history: man is a jabberwocky, a walkie-talkie, talking to disguise the fact that his talk means nothing. Man is an animal with the soul of a murderous, proprietary, status-seeking, in-group loving predator! Ah, we have found the jaws that bite. Next to this, all else is talk. The instincts must burst through. They are the true legacy of a man. He owns them. They own him.

ANYONE. I'm with you. Marx, fancy that. The history of all hitherto existing society is the animal history of animal struggles. Fancy that.

ARDENT (*motions Eve to table. She sits before typewriter. She types through scene, especially when Ardent speaks*). Light the fire for Eve to type by. Eve, you catch the spirit of the thing. I'll fix it up later.

FAUCET (*lighting fire, laughs good-humoredly*). Good job for the revolution that only man can make fire. (*Ardent glares at him and he stops laughing.*)

ANYONE. Can I put out the fire when we're done?

BLUNT. No me, me—

FAUCET. I made it, and I—

ARDENT. Stop this Freudian romanticism. We'll all do it, all four of us. We'll take different sides. But let's go back to the *real* beginning, the animal beginning, the hundreds-of-million-years old vertebrate beginning. Territory first, love of possession. Fish have it, birds have it, monkeys in the trees have it (Cole Porter 1938:2). It's in the genetic structure. The instinct to possess, the drive to gain, maintain and defend the exclusive right to a piece of territory. Man's cultural instinct for *Lebensraum*. Small hope for any United Nations that won't recognize that. It's the basic condition of war, of crime, of the fact that humans have a general reluctance to love their neighbors. Every man his own. Every tribe, every nation in territorial strife. An umbilical bondage to a piece of ground that decrees xenophobic hatred of the others of his kind. Got that, Eve? (*Listens.*) What's that? A scuffling in front of the cave. (*Sounds alarm.*) Counter-revolutionary scientific orthodox spies! Quiet everyone!

BLUNT. Ardent, I think you're getting a little paranoid.

ARDENT. In a world of man anything else would be insanity. Don't you ever have the feeling, Blunt, that paranoids are after you?

BLUNT. Don't worry, Ardent. I wrote up the report on this cave—no one could possibly find it.

FAUCET (*moves toward front of cave, R., startled, runs L. across stage and exit L., screaming in terror*). It's a pride of black maned lions! Run for your lives!
Mary Faucet advances boldly to cave mouth and fires high-powered rifle twice.

ARDENT (*emerging from behind table*). Get them, Mary old girl?

MARY. Got five lionesses and two cubs. I missed the male, though . . . he ran like hell.

ARDENT. It's hot in here. (*Removes shirt. Begins to pace around fire, with tempo of pacing gradually increasing through scene.*) *Faucet returns from stage left, dragging with him Kung, stone chisel and crude paint brushes in hand.*

FAUCET. Here's your counter-revolutionary, Ardent. He was painting a gazelle(schaft) back there on the walls of the cave. Human all right, but is it art?

ARDENT (*to Kung*). What are you doing here?

KUNG. Hunting.

ARDENT. The hell you are, you're painting an animal back there.

KUNG. Someone has to do the hunting.

BLUNT. He means he's searching out game by imitative magic.

ARDENT. Why don't you hunt like a man?

KUNG. I enjoy it . . . the arrow in the running beast, the red blood, the veldt. It *is* hunting. Besides I'm not very good at stalking. So I do the hunting. People give me some of the game sometimes.

ARDENT. Bushman, aren't you? You do this for band belong-you, people belong-you? Make-um magic?

KUNG. Sometimes for my band. But now I'm hunting for all the bands around here. Boys' initiation ceremony coming up. All the boys of all the bands and their people are coming in next

week. We need a lot of game in our land to feed everyone.
Big time. Good time.

ANYONE. What's your name, Bushman?

No answer.

ARDENT. C'mon, tell us name belong-you.

No answer.

BLUNT. He probably thinks you're going to take his name. He won't
tell it to you. You might do something with his name, and he'll
suffer.

ARDENT (*circling fire faster*). Leave him alone. A harmless people,
and they suffer from it. . . Let's go on with the manifesto.
Where were we? . . . territory, property . . . yes and next . . .
Dominance! (*Excited again.*) The status-seeker. Man's un-
quenchable thirst for rank. An end in itself too; make no mistake on that. A drive, a need, a compulsion to dominate that
continues on whether it's useful or useless. A basic desire for
center stage. Try—

FAUCET. But—

ARDENT (*ignores interruption*)—to build an equalitarian society of
men. Ha! Catch a falling star. How romantic. How delightful.
Ha! Bushmàn, you got-em leader?

KUNG. We mostly listen to Tomu. We like him: a good man. Talks
well. Generous to a fault. It's sometimes up to me, though. I
mean if Tomu doesn't act right, we shamans see that he does.
We know his real name, see. But no doubt you're right. Tomu
must want badly to be the leader. Else why should he be so
good?

*Faucet begins to follow Ardent around fire. After a while he
takes off his shirt and carries it. Pen, matches, cigarettes and
other things periodically drop out of his shirt pocket. He reaches
for them but often misses as he scurries to keep up with Ardent.
Mary Faucet falls in after Faucet, picks up what he drops. Thus
the two of them are stooping every once and a while as the
dance goes on around the fire.*

FAUCET. But listen, this rugged individualism I can understand.
Yet there is some cooperation, you know.

ARDENT. Man is truly a social species, although when I say man here I don't embrace women (Linton 1932; after J. Miller 1698). Baboons too, and lots of lesser mammals. Necessary for survival, protection. Society is the animal's best friend, his defense, so sometimes he plays down his personal desires for the group. It's a kind of primal morality, a development of a double standard. Amity of the in-group, enmity toward the other groups. But listen to me, and don't get me wrong: it's a love born of hate, hate and fear of the outside. It multiplies hate by the factor of society. And in the end, the moral order depends on territory, and so it depends on hostility. Its consummate human product: Xenophobic nationalism. Christ, take a look at what's going on in Africa. Christ, we're in the midst of natural man exercising his natural social hate. Aux arbres Citoyens!

BLUNT (*excited, begins to follow Faucets in dance around fire. Takes off shirt from heat. Faucets stooping at more frequent intervals.*) Why don't you embrace women?

ARDENT. Complete anarchists. Men are the social animals. The male of the primate species is the defender of the horde, of its territory, of its fallen. Even dominance, the sheer struggle of it, breeds order. Man breeds social order, women only children. A specialized child-bearer. And take sex, who is really preoccupied with it? Who, the aggressor? What does order mean to women alongside child-bearing and the competitive struggle to latch on to the best-fixed male? You know why so many women are in psychoanalysis? Because we've been fool enough to give women social roles, votes, masculine jobs. They haven't the instincts for it [p. 165]. Can't clean up the mess that's inside.

Anyone takes off shirt and joins procession around fire, which moves into high gear. Only Kung stands aside, wide-eyed. Eve's typewriter beat becomes rhythmical: tap-tap-tap-tap, tap-tap-tap-tap, bell-carriage slide; tap-tap-tap-tap, tap-tap-tap-tap, bell-carriage slide.

BLUNT. The finishing touch, Ardent. Australopithecus. My cave here. My murderous, small predatory carnivore. My ancestor . . . our ancestor.

ARDENT. Yes, yes, the finishing touch, the jewel in man's crown of instincts: murder. All the primates are vegetarians. But what happened to man's line? Came out of the trees, stood up, lost his ripping canines and found his destiny: weapons. Weapons for defense, weapons for meat, weapons for survival. Cain! We are Cain's children, born with weapons in our hands. Oh, not in Asia and not in innocence is man born. In Africa his genesis, and he is nasty, brutish, and short. Man is a predator with a natural instinct to kill with a weapon [p. 316]. No conditioning force has eradicated it, or can. All human history has had one supreme objective: the perfection of the weapon. United Nations, Ha! We are cursed with an irrational, self-destroying, inexorable pursuit of death for death's sake.

FAUCET. But look, Ardent. Zinjanthropus, you know, the one I . . . uh, Mary and I found. No small carnivore predator. Hunted some smaller animals, maybe. Comes after Blunt's old thing. And he probably made those tools, those pebble tools that started the whole Stone Age sequence. How do you fit that in, I mean.

ARDENT (*sneer*). Abel. A freak. A side-branch. Backward, inoffensive, lumbering ape-man. Chewing structure of a vegetarian ape. He lived at the bottom of a well, on treacle, and he was very ill. Obviously then he couldn't have been man's ancestor. Slain by Cain, who took his tools away from him [p. 282]. Simple. And that's it . . . we've got it, the whole of it. (*Stops pacing around fire, whole procession brought up. Ardent is facing fire and audience. Others, save Kung, ranged on either side of him. The typewriter rhythm continues. Ardent shrieks:*) African Nemesis!

ARDENT	CHORUS OF ALL
Man-is-evil	Man-is-evil
Mammalian-boll-weevil	Mammalian-boll-weevil
Was arboreal	Was arboreal
Became predatorial	Became predatorial
And carnivorial	And carnivorial
Also territorial	Also territorial
Status seeker	Status seeker

Property keeper	Property keeper
Instinct lies deeper	Instinct lies deeper
Here to stay	Here to stay
Won't go away	Won't go away
No matter what you say	No matter what you say
No matter what you say	No matter what you say

Ardent climbs on table. Firelight flickers on face. Spreads arms. Typewriter stops.

ARDENT (*frenzied*). Comrades, what to us is this quintessence of evil? Let this be our watchword: Man delights not me—no, nor women neither! To the publisher! (*He rips the sheets out of typewriter. Leaps with a yell toward cave mouth and exit R., grabbing Kung on way. The rest follow running, yelling, save Eve, left alone, sitting at table.*)

EVE (*with compassion*). Oh Ardent, you were a playwright once— but now what lenten entertainment the players shall receive from you. . . . And how do they expect *me* to put out the fire?

Curtain

ACT II. SCENE 1

The sitting room of a flat in London. Table and chairs R. Door rear center. Members of revolutionary band sitting around. Mary still packs rifle. Ardent in dominant position, sitting on table with feet on a chair.

ARDENT. I'll never understand why the South African government deported us.

KUNG. Maybe the prime minister was jealous.

ARDENT. London's the place for our movement anyhow: the workshop of Marx, the sanctuary of Freud. Most of all, the very bastille of the romantic fallacy, the British Museum: ivory tower of the world, guardian of the fortress of man's ignorance of man. It's the drilling ground of those snob north-of-the-equator anthropologists who turned their backs on Blunt at the Livingstone conference. . . . (*An idea.*) And we're going to storm it tonight! The manifesto wasn't enough, by God. We need evidence. Evidence, evidence, evidence. That's their anthropological currency and we're going to pay 'em in it. But it won't be easy, because I happen to know they've taken it out of the Museum Library, hidden it from romantic eyes. Look, if people really knew how gibbons lived, how long do you think they'd beat their heads against the stone wall of love, how long could they cherish the hopeless hope that things can somehow turn out for humanity? For an hour today I combed through the Museum Library. Get this: not a single copy of Carpenter's monograph on the gibbon [pp. 36–37]. God knows what else they've sequestered. But I have a good idea where. Old Nose Washtree's office! Third floor of the museum. Come, my guerrilla band. To the Bastille! . . . (*They rise, except Kung.*) You too, Bushman. You're one of . . . us now. And Christ, Mary, leave that blunderbuss here. Those were stone lions in front of the museum, take my word.

MARY. Oh, all right. But may I at least take my pistol?

Curtain

ACT II. SCENE 2

Nose Washtree's office, one hour later. A room lined with books, floor to ceiling. A door to hall R. Large desk with swivel chair L. Curtain opens to empty stage. Door yields under pressure and enter revolutionary band, led by Mary Faucet, waving pistol and motioning for quiet. She turns on light and closes door.

MARY. We're safe now. I'll stand guard. (*Posts self at door.*)

ANYONE. Look at all these books. Wha' does he do with them?

ARDENT (*rapidly crosses to desk, stands in front of it*). All right, everyone. Revolutionary discipline. We have to work fast. Eve, you take that bookcase there (*at R., nearest door*). Faucet, you the next one, then Anyone, then Blunt, and I'll take care of this corner (*largest space. Kung, conspicuously left out, finally gravitates to one of the shelves. Ardent now ranges before books, reading shelf labels.*) European Paleolithic . . . North African Mesolithic . . . A huge compost heap of scientific orthodoxies. I hardly need impress upon you the revolutionary importance of this mission, and now you see its difficulty. The evidence of man's nature must lie hidden as a few slim needles in this great romantic haystack. What are all these shelves? South American *ethnology?* . . . *African ethnology?* . . . *ethnology of the Pacific?*

FAUCET. Ethnology is the study of peoples, the various conditions of mankind, primitive cultures, that sort of thing—hundreds of them, Ardent.

ARDENT. Paleozoic ethnology they never dreamed of. (*Sits at desk with feet on it.*) More things in heaven and earth, oh academics—

EVE. Look, I drew the *sanctum sanctorum* . . . (*puzzled*) so far it is from his desk too. (*Reads titles.*) Das Jean-Jacques Rousseau Problem, The Social Contract (*takes out Social Contract and reads*). The strongest is never strong enough to be always the master, unless he transforms strength into right, and obedience into duty. Hence the right of the strongest, which, though to all seeming meant ironically, is really laid down as a fundamental principle. But are we never to have an explanation of this phrase? Force is a physical power, and I fail to see what moral effect it can have. To yield to force is an act of necessity, not of will—at the most an act of prudence. In what sense can it be a duty?

KUNG (*aside*). They don't make 'em like they used to.

ARDENT. Duty and morals: the royal sceptre and cloak of the most dominant ape, the jabberwocky legitimization of an animal compulsion to rule.

BLUNT (*browsing shelves*). Muckraking. I say, that's what we're doing too, you know. Lincoln Steffens—

ARDENT (*excited*). Yes, yes, look into it, Blunt. Great revolutionary hero, Steffens. Laid bare the natural predatory core of the city. The incomparable urban paleontologist, digging in an Australopithecine underworld of organized crime, organized murder, organized power.

BLUNT (*reads*). I always like to put a story Wundt's assistant,

Külpe, told us after a visit to the neighboring University of Jena to see the aged philosopher Erdmann, whose history of philosophy, in some ten volumes, we had all read and studied. They had a warm, friendly talk, the old scholar and the young scientist, all about the old philosophers and their systems. But when Külpe tried to draw him out on Wundt and the newer school, Erdmann shook his head, declaring that he could not understand the modern men. In my day, he explained, we used to ask the everlasting question: What is man? And you—nowadays you answer it, saying (*voice lowers*), he *was* an ape.

ARDENT. Ach! Nach einmal das Jean-Jacques Rousseau Problem!

FAUCET. Ah, here's a preliminary report from those fellows, Emlen and Schaller, the ones living with mountain gorillas—

ANYONE. No doubt, very happily.

FAUCET. It's buried in this obscure specialist journal, Current Anthropology. (*Takes off glasses and reads.*) It has been possible for Schaller to observe many details of the behavior and social interactions of these animals. He has found a high level of social tolerance prevails among members of a troop—

ANYONE (*quickly interjected*). The primal morality of the in-group, the—

FAUCET. —and even between troops. (*Thoughtfully.*) Several of the troops he has studied include more than one male, and he has never observed signs of aggressiveness among them. Isolated and peripheral males exist, as among other primates; and it is surprising that even these may be accepted into troops without (*voice lowers*) visible displays of antagonism. Neighboring troops have been watched as they peacefully mixed, socialized, and separated. Gorilla troops are apparently nomadic within vaguely defined spatial limits. (*Whispers.*) No traces of territorial behavior have been detected.

ARDENT. Don't let it bother you, old man. Pity the poor gorilla, the harmless Bushman of the higher primates. A dying species, an evolutionary failure. Committed to a forest that has disappeared from under him, he came out of the trees and became a stem eater. His oversized body, his tree-swinger's chest and arms: a mass of architectural incongruities about as meaningful to his present existence as an attic full of memories to a bankrupt nobleman. Doomed by ancient crises beyond control or memory, he knows it, knows it in the balance of instincts which govern his behavior. Vital instincts lose their hold. Primate compulsions fade like color from the skin of the dying. By day he seldom copulates, and by night . . . by night he fouls his own nest! [pp. 112–116]

FAUCET. That's pretty, but is it science?

ARDENT. I detect in you, Faucet, a certain leakiness, a counter-revolutionary romantic tendency, a deviationist drift, a red shift. (*He notices Anyone, who has given up reading and is sitting on the floor.*) What's the matter with *you?*

ANYONE. My lips get tired.

ARDENT. Counter-revolutionary devia— Sh! A noise in the hall! Mary! Mary!

FAUCET (*exasperated*). Not another goddam black-maned lion, not another! Bushman, I told you to stop monkeying around with those paints.

KUNG. But it isn't monkeying.

MARY (*terrified*). Eeek! A mouse (*runs into Faucet's arms. He comforts her. A general hubbub, from which emerges Kung's soothing voice*):

KUNG (*reading*). We walked down the path to the well-house, attracted by the fragrance of the honeysuckle with which it was covered. Someone was drawing water and my teacher placed my hand under the spout. As the cool stream gushed over one hand she spelled into the other the word water, first slowly, then rapidly. I stood still, my whole attention fixed upon the motion of her fingers. Suddenly I felt a misty consciousness as of something forgotten—a thrill of returning thought; and somehow the mystery of language was revealed to me. I knew then that w-a-t-e-r meant that wonderful cool something that was flowing over my hand. The living word awakened my soul, gave it light, hope, joy, set it free! . . . a woman called Keller.

Eve has been absorbed in The Social Contract. She beckons Mary. They sit on the floor, R. Eve speaks sotto voce to her and audience. Ardent engages Blunt in conversation, L., occasionally raising voice enough for all to hear. These outbursts come as counterpoint to Eve's voice.

EVE. This must be *das Problem*. No noble savage here. (*Reads.*) The passage from the state of nature to the civil state produces a very remarkable change in man, by substituting justice for instinct in his conduct, and giving his actions the morality they formerly lacked—

ARDENT. Civilization can never ultimately repress it—

EVE. Then only, when the voice of duty takes the place of physical impulses and the cravings of appetite, does man, who so far had considered only himself, find that he is forced to act on different principles, and to consult his reason before listening to his inclinations—

ARDENT. Conscience as a guiding force in the human drama is one of such small reliability that it assumes very nearly the role of a villain [p. 349]—

EVE. Although, in this state, he deprives himself of some of the advantages which he got from nature—

ARDENT. By nature, a murderer—

EVE. —he gains in return others so great, his faculties are so stimulated and developed, his ideas so extended, his feelings so ennobled, and his whole soul so uplifted, that, did not the abuses of this new condition often degrade him below that which he left—

ARDENT. —the burning flesh of Jews—

EVE. —he would be bound to bless continually the happy moment which took it from him forever, and, instead of a stupid and unimaginative animal, made him an intelligent being and . . . a man. (*She looks at Mary. Mary winks at her.*)

BLUNT (*Sotto voce to Ardent and audience. Interrupted contrapuntally by Eve, still reading to Mary.*) But the Eskimo still baffles me. A complete carnivore he is, and raw meat his dish. The greatest hunter of them all. The bloodthirsty ape in sealskin clothing. Yet look what old Birket-Smith says here. Difficult for the average Eskimo to assert himself against others, he says—

EVE. The social compact substitutes, for such inequalities as nature may have set up between men, an equality that is moral and legitimate. Men, who may be unequal in strength or intelligence, become every one equal by convention and legal right—

BLUNT. And hunting grounds are the property of all and none, res nullius, he says, which not even the tribe can lay claim to. Something else: the Australian Aborigines. Sir Arthur Keith destroyed the Freudian fraud of the primal family by pointing out the Aborigine's larger-than-family society, and we'd go along with that, but you wouldn't want to talk about an Australian band's exclusive territoriality from what I read on these shelves—

EVE. We must clearly distinguish between possession, which is merely the effect of force or the right of the first occupier, from property, which can only be founded on a positive title.

ARDENT (loudly). Dammit, these ethnology shelves are useless. What do the Eskimo and all the other timid, shy, cringing, gentle, gauzy, wistful milquetoasts hiding out from mankind on the ice or in the jungle, what do they mean for pristine man? Precisely nothing, and far less that is than the strutting jackdaw. More harmless people, suffering because of their timid dispositions. Who disputes the Eskimo his blubber, his long night, his home built of ice cubes? No one. By adapting himself to a way of life supremely unattractive to Sioux or Apache, a shy creature has insured his survival in perfect confidence that he will escape the notice of all but romantic anthropologists. All that has been actually demonstrated by this (indicating bookshelves) loosely disciplined but immensely popular raid into the outposts of man's nature has been that timid people tend to live at unfashionable addresses. [pp. 149–150]

ANYONE. Right again, Ardent. And it goes for Sioux blubber too. They cried when they met people, it says here, in order to manifest the lively joy which they felt in meeting them.

KUNG. Crying can have its own vocabulary.

ARDENT (sneers). Now a little child of nature shall lead us.

KUNG. It can happen to people—depends what they call the child. . . . You know, the white shaman comes around and says to me

—me, the magician from way back—I have something new, he says. The latest power, he says, the greatest magic. What, I say. The spell begins like this, he says: in the beginning was the Word. (*Bemused.*) Oh, I tried hard not to laugh, not to his face. Oh, that's great stuff, I said, great stuff. Then he asked me to eat his god . . . and I gave him some of mine. And so I saw the white shaman was far behind the camp of his own people: they had known it all long ago. . . You know, there on the veldt are little white stones on the ground. Now baboons know about these stones, find them lying there. But it's just stones—hard, white, scratchy. To white man they're that too: the same touch, the same color as for the baboon. But then they're something the baboon never will understand—they're diamonds. And not only that—they're wealth: worth getting and giving. And not only that—they're power and they're good, or to some they're power and they're hateful. A whole *world* of name-ideas. More important, more *real* than the touch of it, than the sight of it, than the smell of it. So the white men came to the veldt because of it. And they fought together because of it, and worked together because of it. White men who had been good became bad. Bushmen, who had been bad . . . now they were good: come work for us, nice man, in our holes, they said. The Bushman still smelled as before the stones, as when they drove him out. Now they want us. . . It depends a lot on names.

ARDENT (*exasperated*). Names, names, names. I'm sick of names. The plaintive, inexhaustible primate voice, desperately trying to dupe inexorable vertebrate drives. It's the primeval gene that bursts my spleen, but names will never harm me! (*Flies angrily at shelf, flinging books helter-skelter.*) Oh, just let me get my hands on something we can really use. Some real weapon! I'll forge a knife of prose that will rip those. . . I'll kill the romantic fallacy. I'll murder—(*He finds a small pamphlet. Oakley's, Man the Tool-Maker. Shrieks in triumph. Laughs hysterically.*) Oh, what fools we've been! Taken in by a name—by the same damn device the romantics use to deceive themselves! See this Museum handbook: Man, the *Tool*-Maker. (*Sarcastic laugh.*) *Tool*-Maker. Do you think the British Museum would ever, ever in a million years of orthodox folly,

ever, ever publish a handbook called Man, the *Weapon*-Maker?
[p. 205] Look at these tools. (*Sneer*.) Tools, Ha! Cudgels!
Weapons! (*Dramatically*.) But to suggest that we find in the
competition of weapons the most exhilarating human experience would be blasphemy. Would the Museum dare to provoke in the House of Commons the question period of heroic
proportions? [p. 205] And for a hundred responsible anthropologists gathered in a Rhodesian town to admit—to admit when
Blunt put it to them—that Australopithecus had systematically
used weapons would be to invite a cultural definition of man
as the creature who systematically makes them. Never! Never!
Ha-ha-ha (*waves pamphlet*) but just you wait, Professor Hig-
gins, just you wait. (*Menacingly*.) No matter how eloquently
you say it, no matter what you call it, a weapon by any other
name will kill as neat! (*Leaps to desk, others gather round,
except Kung, who slips out door and runs off*.) Comrades . . .
we have been tried and not found wanting. . . This is our
finest hour. We have tempered the sword of revolution in the
very rose water of the romantic brainwash. (*Exhorts*.) And now
I say to you, surrounded as we are by the pressing weight of
what passes as evidence for those who choose to delude themselves, I say to you. . . Man delights not me—no, nor women
neither!
They exit, chanting, Ardent leading:

CHORUS	ARDENT
Man is evil	Man is evil
Mammalian boll weevil	Mammalian boll weevil
Was arboreal	Was arboreal
Became predatorial	Became predatorial
And carnivorial	And carnivorial
Also territorial	Also territorial
Status seeker	Status seeker
Property keeper	Property keeper
Instinct lies deeper	Instinct lies deeper
Here to stay	Here to stay
Won't go away	Won't go away
No matter what you say	No matter what you say
No matter what you say	No matter what you say

Faucet, lingering, sneaks back, hides a copy of Current Anthropology in his jacket, and hurries out to join the rest.

Curtain

Act III

An apartment in lower Manhattan, late afternoon. One room flat. Door to hallway at rear. Door to bathroom L. Table and chairs R. Other furniture. Ardent, Anyone, Eve, Blunt and the Faucets draped disconsolately about, Ardent sitting on table, feet on chair.

ARDENT. I should have known better than to take that Bushman into the revolutionary movement.

ANYONE. I still say the Bushman couldn't have known. He ran off before we set up the plan to change the labels on the Paleolithic tools—the cudgels, I mean—in the British Museum.

ARDENT. So my gallant band, here we are. Deported victims of the primate British urge to defend a precious isle of ignorance against the shining sea-terrors of truth.

FAUCET. What time is it?

ARDENT. So little time . . . for it is the time of man, the time out of mind, the time of animal slime beyond all present memory, the time of vertebrate-hate-thy-neighbor, the time—

EVE. It's five o'clock.

FAUCET. Tea-time. No wonder I feel so weary.

ARDENT. What really governs the English—and their out-heroding colonials? Is it a protoplasmic urge to ingest? Oh no. A feudal-primate dominance order? Oh no. Big Ben. Ding-dong! Ding-dong! Ding-dong! Ding-dong! Ding-dong! Drink-tea! Drink-tea! Drink-tea! Drink-tea! Drink-tea!

FAUCET. By God, Ardent, I've had enough! It tolls for thee. To impugn mankind is one thing, but to impugn Britons . . . quite another!

BLUNT. Quite!

MARY. Hear, hear!

ARDENT. The territorial poison quite o'ercrows your spirit.

FAUCET. Ardent, I've long had my doubts—and so have Mary and Blunt, I daresay—about your tactics, but now I question the issue, the whole flimsy revolutionary line. Maybe you've just hit the point. Everyone needs to eat. But we eat at five o'clock, you at six; we tea and crumpets, you ravioli and lemon coke. How does the compulsion account for that? What does govern man, not man in the abstract, but man as he presents himself, man as peoples. Perhaps all men fight and all enjoy pointing the gun, but what governs the historic moment, the episode that is war, and who tells man the direction to point the gun?

BLUNT. In-group amity, out-group enmity, you say, as if it were all so obvious—the modern nation the counterpart of the primate horde. Well it isn't obvious. Do explain to me a nation, Ardent. Act out for me the drama of its beginnings after a million years of tribal history. For the nation is a standing miracle, an evolution, a development of human society that went on record as a denial of the tribe, a denial that the tribal tie is stronger than Americanism, that the stranger was not the fellow. Oh, I'll grant that the nation did not abolish strife, only concentrated it. But if men can live peacefully within the nation after a million years of tribal mistrust, who shall say we have reached the limits of the human conception?

MARY. Once, Ardent, the definition of man was a tribal identity. Navaho means people, Eskimos call themselves the men. But who denies today that he is a member of a planetary race? Man has discovered humanity. And our vaunted ultimate weapon, which shall it strengthen in the long run, the fibers of the nation or the fibers of the world, the idea of a chosen people, or the realization that we're all in this bloody thing together?

ARDENT. A troop of howling monkeys, you three. Poor little monketies, lost their crumpe-teas, and they began to cry.

FAUCET. Oh, how tired I am of your secular religion of original sin, without redemption and without morality. What if man's bad? What if he has an urge to possess? Could any human society long survive that didn't define, constrain and satisfy that compulsion on its own terms. What if, as Freud believed, man has a natural propensity to mate with anything in sight? Was ever any human society established on that basis? (*Enter Kung, quietly, unnoticed.*) The urges are repressed, sublimated, twisted this way and that, until in the end man lives in spite of his innermost self. He wars on the playing fields of Eton, dominates by being nicer to others than he is to himself, hunts with paint brush.

KUNG. That's right, you underestimate your player, Ardent.

ARDENT (*and the others*). Bushman! (*Hubbub.*) What are you doing here? (*etc.*)

KUNG. I'm teaching. Primitive religion, at N.Y.U. I just got my Ph.D. at Columbia. In anthropology, of course. Wrote a thesis on the world distribution of theophagy. But I can't say I learned much I didn't know, just a few more names for it. Apparently, you haven't learned much either, Ardent. Bad show, Ardent. The character's still too flat, too stereotyped, the essential villain. And the play, you know nothing about. Like I said, man names things, makes a reality that isn't there, builds it into a system: motherhood, God, fair price, president, twenty dollars or thirty days. And he lives in that reality. It has a name too, I find out . . . culture. I don't believe culture is an inevitable tragedy.

ARDENT. What the hell do those romantics teach in anthropology these days? All the world's a stage? The play's the thing? Well, tell me this: what makes a drama? Do the characters make the play, or the play the characters? Whoever denied that man learns, or that he reasons, or that he can suppress, for a while and in a way, an animal urge? But the frail voice of reason and the timid gesture of the learned response—they are as nothing against the deep command of instinct. And I'll tell you what happens when a basic instinct is held at bay: its energy releases itself through another urge to make its play more terrifying and more irrational. When the Bolsheviks abolished private property, they decreed for themselves a reign of naked power, unleashed a dominance drive that made the English industrial revolution look like a Sunday afternoon picnic on the Thames. The instincts lie deep. They line the human flesh. They are the chemistry of the genes. Cultural instincts, waiting their day. Like a desert river, vanished perhaps season after season, and then, then in a flick of a thunderstorm it comes ripping and raging out of the inscrutable earth. Yes, man builds his own realities. Do you know what it means to believe in the existence of things that don't exist? Self-delusion. All hail, man's unique capacity . . . self-delusion. And against it recollect the ease with which Adolf Hitler brought about in a generation of German youth his education for death. [p. 203] Was this the implanting of a learned response . . . or the release of an instinct? Defend one's own, *Lebensraum,* hate thy— (*Knock at door.*) I'll get it. (*It's Shapiro, carrying a large challah and balancing a plate of gefüllte fish.*) You have the wrong apartment. We didn't order anything. Get out.

SHAPIRO (*politely*). Oh no, you'll excuse me, please, it's the right apartment O.K. Mr. Arbenz? You only today moved in?

ARDENT. Ardent, Ardent—get the name right. Yes, we moved in. We paid our rent. It's our apartment. So beat it!

SHAPIIRO. Vell, you see, ve live down the hall. Shapiro, 2B. And Sarah for the veekend just happened to be making some gefüllte fish. So she says to me, Hymie, why not take some fish to our new neighbors. It's Friday night, maybe they're Catlics? Get acquainted she says, velcome them to the building. Mr. Arbenz, she says, he looks so pale, so bloodless, eat some good . . . Oh, but you'll excuse me. Please, if you're busy, vhy don't you just take the plate and the bread—

EVE (*coming to door*). Please won't you come in, Mr. Shapiro? It's really so nice of you. (*Thank you, thank you, he says, and she and he manage somehow to get the food to the table.*) So thoughtful—

SHAPIRO. Nothing really, absolutely, Mrs. Arbenz. You know, vhen Sarah and I moved in, Mrs. Cassidy, she used to live in this very apartment, she brought us some preserved pig's knuckles that first night. Such good people in this building, so considerate of the others. You know . . . anyhow, taste the gefüllte fish, it's Sarah's best special dish.

EVE (*setting out food*). Here you are, Faucet. Tea-time, old boy C'mon Blunt, Mary, Anyone, Bushman. (*Aside to Ardent.*) Robert, don't sulk. You'll make him feel bad.

Ardent comes to table and starts to cut challah.

SHAPIRO. You'll excuse me, Mr. Arbenz, for taking the liberty. Challah is a kind of bread tastes better it should be torn apart. Here . . . by the nubbles.

BLUNT. How barbarian!

MARY (*sarcastic*).The knife is so much more civilized.

SHAPIRO. Sure, sure, you're right, yes. Then I'll cut it for you. Ve too had problems with the pig's knuckles. Oi! (*cuts finger, sucks blood*) It's nothing, nothing. Eat, eat. Like my mother used to say: eat, Hymie, eat . . . or I'll kill myself. (*Sets plate of fish and bread before Faucet.*)

BLUNT. Faucet, you're pale as a ghost.

FAUCET (*running in screaming anguish to bathroom*). Yeeah! There's blood on the challah!

ANYONE. Did it release his animal instincts?

MARY. His lunch.

SHAPIRO. Vell, you should enjoy yourselves. Sarah said for me I should come right home if they're goyem . . . I mean if they're going to be busy. Come in any time. Shapiro, 2B.

ARDENT (*going to door with him*). Yea, sure, sure . . . and to you the same. I mean, the same to you, you come over here. (*Slams door after Shapiro but then regrets it, so opens it quickly and shuts it again lightly.*)

BLUNT. I wouldn't eat that bloody challah. What's more, I'm fed up with this whole bloody revolution. It's about time, you knew, Ardent. The Faucets and I turned in that fool scheme of changing the museum labels on the Paleolithic tools. It is a science, you know. Just doesn't change like that. Not kosher, you might say.

ARDENT. I was beginning to suspect it. The betrayal, I mean. Incurable romantics. I suspected you all along, all of you. . . Betrayed. Who among us—

BLUNT. Just a second before you produce a new drama, Ardent. Let me tell you just why I'm fed up. It's your mad theory of cultural instincts and compulsions. Vanished like a desert river and then springs up. Shall I grow a long canine soon, or part the hair of my tail behind? But never mind that. It's just too neat, that's the principal part of it. When we're good to our neighbors, it's the in-group amity of a social species, when we're bad, a primeval urge comes out. When there's no war, the instinct's just in hiding, and when there is war, it springs loose. Let a theory violate my beliefs. Let it even violate credulity. It doesn't matter to me. Nor am I afraid to go against the average opinions of geneticists, physiologists, paleontologists, anthropologists, Rousseau, Marx, Jefferson, or Queen Elizabeth. (Faucet: Come, come.) But I must fear to entertain a hypothesis if I can't imagine a situation in which it would fail to stand up. I must be able to conceive its failure. It's not a hypothesis if it can't be tested.

ARDENT (*shouting*). Of course it's not a hypothesis. You know very well what it is, Blunt. Remember well what I put to you the day you first showed me the evidence of man's ancestral depravity. Dare you tell the world, I asked. Dare you tell a world on the brink of international disaster that man is an innate killer? We have tried everything else, you said, why not try the truth for a change. It's no hypothesis, Blunt. (*Screams.*) It's the truth! The Revolutionary Truth!

MARY (*calm*). No wonder it's proved so immune to evidence. The gorilla—

ANYONE (*sneers*). How does that so-called evidence compare? You know very well what the world is like . . . the Bolshevik terror, racism, the Hungarian Revolution, the burning flesh of Jews, the hundred megatons . . . I know it, and you know it.

MARY. Yes, of course you know it, Anyone. Let's go, gentlemen.

(*She takes Faucet by one arm, Kung by the other. They leave, followed by Blunt, who before he goes, says:*)

BLUNT. Good-bye, Eve. You too, Anyone. Ardent, a horde of gibbons guide thee to thy rest. You can forget the fiver you owe me.

(*Exit*)

ARDENT. Betrayed, betrayed . . . the revolution betrayed. How ungrateful! I was doing it for them. What dogs. What worse-than-dogs. Would a dog betray? Never! (*A thought strikes him*) . . . never. You know, a dog couldn't. Only a man. (*Amazed.*) By God! By God! By God!

EVE. Oh, Robert, Robert, oh hast thou slain the Jabberwock? Come to my arms, my beamish boy! Oh frabjous day. Callooh, Callay!

278 MARSHALL D. SAHLINS

ARDENT (*musing. He has seen the light.*) Remarkable animal. . .
Only he betrays . . . and only he is betrayed. (*Grins sheepishly
at Eve. They embrace.*) Ah, Eve. In sickness and in health, in
poverty or wealth, a smash or a flop, till death do us part . . .
the Eve to my Adam, the Damon to my Pythias, the Horatio
to my Hamlet—

EVE. The Sancho to your Quixote.

ARDENT. And Anyone. Dear friend, Anyone. I could always count
on you, couldn't I? You'd always believe in me, Anyone. (*Snaps
out of it.*) C'mon, it's six o'clock. I'm hungry. I'm taking you
both to dinner: a nice, bloody raw steak. On Blunt's fiver. Ha!
And then . . . then to a show. West Side Story! (*Puts on
Anyone's hat and Eve's coat.*)

ANYONE. Ardent, while you're in the mood, you know I would like
to see the United Nations. I've never been in New York before.

ARDENT. No, no, Anyone. Broadway. You'd never understand the
East Side Story without the West Side Story. Never.

EVE. Anyhow, the East Side Story'll have a longer run.

ARDENT. Only because it makes war so well. No, the play's the thing.
(*Takes both by the arm and shepherds them out the door, saying:*) West Side Story. It's got everything. [pp. 330–33] Natural
man. All the instincts right there. The whole damned animal
legacy: the timeless struggle over territory, the gangs of primates, the rigid dominance order, the mutual protection of the
horde, the collective hate of the others, and then. . . then . . .
the unique contribution of man: the supreme dedication to the
switch-blade. Absolutely great. West Side Story. Life follows
Art!

Curtain